Study Guide

Microeconomics

Sixth Edition

Roger A. Arnold

California State University, San Marcos

Australia · Canada · Mexico · Singapore · Spain · United Kingdom · United States

Study Guide for Microeconomics, 6e

by Roger A. Arnold

Editor-in-Chief:
Jack W. Calhoun

Vice President, Team Director:
Michael P. Roche

Publisher of Economics:
Michael B. Mercier

Acquisitions Editor:
Michael W. Worls

Developmental Editor:
Jennifer E. Baker

Executive Marketing Manager:
Lisa L. Lysne

Production Editor:
Starratt E. Alexander

Manufacturing Coordinator:
Sandee Milewksi

Compositor:
Laurel Williams, desktopDIRECT

Printer:
Edwards Brothers - Ann Arbor

Cover Designer:
a small design studio, Cincinnati

Cover Images:
© Paul Hardy/CORBIS and
© Photodisc, Inc.

Printed in the United States of America
2 3 4 5 05 04

For more information contact South-Western, 5191 Natorp Boulevard, Mason, Ohio 45040.
Or you can visit our Internet site at: http://www.swcollege.com

ISBN: 0-324-16361-4

Contents

Chapter 1
What Economics Is About

What This Chapter Is About

This chapter is an introduction to economics. Economics is defined and a few of the important concepts in economics are discussed – such as scarcity, opportunity cost, and more. Also, this chapter introduces you to the economic way of thinking.

Key Concepts in the Chapter

a. scarcity
b. opportunity cost
c. decisions made at the margin
d. theory
e. positive and normative economics
f. equilibrium
g. efficiency

- **Scarcity** is the condition under which people's wants (for goods) are greater than the resources available to satisfy those wants.
- **Opportunity cost** is the most highly valued opportunity or alternative forfeited when a choice is made.
- When we make **decisions at the margin**, we compare the marginal benefits and marginal costs of things.
- A **theory** is an abstract representation of reality.
- **Positive economics** deals with "what is," and **normative economics** deals with what someone thinks "should be."
- **Efficiency** exists when the marginal benefits of doing something equal the marginal costs of doing that something.
- To say that "there is no such thing as a free lunch" is to say that all choices come with opportunity costs.
- **Equilibrium** means "at rest"; it is descriptive of a natural resting place.

Review Questions

1. Is scarcity the condition under which people have infinite wants?

2. What is the difference between a *good* and a *bad*?

3. Give an example of when something is a good one day, and a bad some other day?

4. What is the opportunity cost of your reading this study guide?

5. If the opportunity cost of smoking cigarettes rises, fewer people will smoke. Why?

6. What is a synonym (in economics) for the word *additional*?

7. If Harriet is thinking of studying for one more hour, she considers the marginal benefits and marginal costs of studying for one more hour—not the total benefits and total costs. Why does she consider marginal benefits and costs and not total benefits and costs?

8. In the text the author discussed the unintended effects of wearing seatbelts. Come up with an example of an unintended effect of something.

9. What is the relationship between scarcity and choice? Between scarcity and opportunity cost?

10. What is the relationship between thinking in terms of "what would have been" and opportunity cost?

11. What is a theory?

12. Do people who have never formally built a theory still theorize?

13. What are the seven steps of building and testing a theory?

14. Why is it better to judge a theory by how well it predicts than by whether it sounds right or not?

15. Give an example of an assumption.

16. Give an example of when association is causation. Then give an example of when association is not causation.

17. Is it possible to study too much? Explain your answer.

18. Give an example to illustrate that there is no such thing as a free lunch.

Theory on a Television Show

Read the following account of theorizing on a television show.

Jerry Seinfeld Builds a Theory, George Tests It Out

You may think that building and testing theories is something only economists do. But ordinary people in all walks of life do it every day. Take, for example, George, Jerry Seinfeld's friend, on the hit television show "Seinfeld."

One day George walks into the restaurant where Jerry and Elaine (Jerry and George's best friend) are eating and complains that nothing ever goes right for him. He is a loser, he says. Everything his instincts tell him to do turns out wrong.

A lightbulb goes off over Jerry's head. He tells George that if everything his instincts tell him to do turns out wrong, then he should always do the opposite of what his instincts indicate. If his instincts tell him to turn right, he should turn left; if his instincts tell him to order a chicken sandwich, he should order a ham sandwich instead.

At this point, Jerry is theorizing. To see this explicitly, let's look at the following points of building and testing a theory.

- Point 1 is to *decide on what it is you want to explain or predict.* Jerry wants to explain why everything goes wrong for George.
- Point 2 is to *identify the variables that you believe are important to what you want to explain or predict.* The chief variable (or factor) for Jerry is George's instincts.
- Point 3 is to *state the assumptions of the theory.* Jerry implicitly assumes that George is concerned enough about the dismal state of his life to do whatever is necessary to make things better.
- Point 4 is to *state the hypothesis.* Jerry's hypothesis is that if everything George's instincts tell him to do turns out wrong, then he should do the opposite of his instincts and everything will turn out right.
- Point 5 is to *test the theory by comparing its predictions against real-world events.* In the television show, George puts the theory to the test. He goes against every instinct he has. For instance, he walks up to a woman at the counter in the restaurant. His instincts tell him that to arouse the woman's interest, he should pretend to be something he's not. Instead, he fights his instincts and tells the woman exactly what he is: a balding, middle-aged man, without a job, who lives at home with his parents. The woman immediately takes a liking to him. So far, the evidence supports the theory.

  The storyline continues. George and his date are at a movie when two rowdy young men sitting behind them begin loudly heckling the characters in the movie. George's instincts tell him to slither down into his seat or move but never, under any circumstances, to confront the young men and tell them what he thinks of their rude behavior. George, still testing Jerry's theory, does the opposite of what his instincts tell him to do. He gets up from his seat, tells off the two men, and adds that it they aren't quiet he will take them outside and settle the matter. The two rowdy men shrink back in their seats like shivering puppies. The patrons in the movie theater applaud, and George's date is impressed.
- Point 6 states that *if the evidence supports the theory, then no further action is necessary, although it is a good idea to continue to examine the theory closely.* George continues to test the theory as the show continues, each time the evidence supports it: every time he goes against his instincts, something good happens to him.

The story of Jerry and George is fiction. But this fictional account is representative of what ordinary people do every day. Anyone, in any walk of life, who follows the steps for building a theory is theorizing. The theorizing can be about something as esoteric as the nature of the universe or as ordinary as George's life.

1. Jerry built a theory, George tested it, and the evidence supported the theory. But what might the evidence have been if it had not supported the theory? In other words, what might have happened on the "Seinfeld" show if Jerry's theory had been wrong instead of right?

2. What are some of the things that you think economists theorize about?

Problems

1. Draw a flow chart that shows the relationship between scarcity, choice, and opportunity cost.

2. Jim is considering going to college. He knows there are benefits and costs to attending college. In the table below you will see various factors identified in the first column. Determine whether the factor relates to the cost of going to college or to the benefit of going to college. Next, identify whether the specified change in the factor raises or lowers the cost or benefit of going to college. If it raises the benefit of going to college, place an upward arrow (↑) in the benefits column; if it lowers the benefit of going to college, place a downward arrow (↓) in the benefits column. Do the same for the costs column. Finally, identify whether the change in the factor makes it more likely (Yes or No) Jim will go to college.

Factor	**Benefits of attending college**	**Costs of attending college**	**More likely to go to college? Yes or No**
Jim thought he would earn $20 an hour if he didn't go to college, but learns that he will earn $35 an hour instead.			
His friends are going to college and he likes being around his friends.			
The salary gap between college graduates and high school graduates has widened.			
Jim learns something about himself: he doesn't like to study.			
The college he is thinking about attending just opened a satellite campus near Jim's home.			
The economy has taken a downturn and it looks like there are very few jobs for high school graduates right now.			

3. When people explain or predict something, they usually implicitly make the *ceteris paribus* assumption. For example, Jenny says, "I plan to exercise more in order to lose weight." What Jenny is holding constant, or is assuming does not change, are things such as: (a) how much she eats every day, (b) how much she sleeps every day, (c) how much stress she is under, and so on. In other words, she is saying that if she exercises more, and does everything else the same as she has been doing, she

will lose weight. She is not saying that if she exercises more, and eats more in the process, that she will lose weight.

In the first column in the table, a statement is made by a person. Next to it write something that the person must be assuming is not changing in order for the statement to be true.

Statement	**The person is assuming that this does not change:**
People that don't brush their teeth will get cavities.	
As people get older, they tend to put on weight because their metabolism slows down.	
If he studies more, he will get higher grades.	

4. Identify each of the following questions as related to either a microeconomic or macroeconomic topic.
   a. Why did that firm charge a higher price?
   b. When will the economy slow down?
   c. When will the unemployment rate fall?
   d. Are interest rates rising?
   e. How does that firm decide how many cars it will produce this year?
   f. What is the price of a really fast computer?
   g. Why did that restaurant go out of business?

5. There is an opportunity cost to everything you do. In the first column you will see an activity identified. In the second column, identify what you think the opportunity cost (for you) would be if you undertook that particular activity.

Activity	**Opportunity Cost**
Study one more hour each night	
Take a trip to someplace you have always wanted to visit	
Sit in the back of the room in one of your classes	
Talk up more in class	
Get a regular medical checkup	
Surf the Web more	

What Is Wrong?

In each of the statements below, something is wrong. Identify what is wrong in the space provided.

1. People have finite wants and infinite resources.

2. People prefer more bads to fewer bads.

3. Scarcity is an effect of competition.

4. The lower the opportunity cost of playing tennis, the less likely a person will play tennis.

5. Abstract means to add more variables to the process of theorizing.

6. Microeconomics is the branch of economics that deals with human behavior and choices as they relate to highly aggregate markets or the entire economy.

7. Positive economics is to normative economics as opinion is to truth.

8. Because there are rationing devices, there will always be scarcity.

9. The four factors of production, or resources, are land, labor, capital, and profit.

10. Karen doesn't like to study so no one likes to study. This is an example of the association is not causation issue.

Multiple Choice
Circle the correct answer.

1. Economics is the science of
   a. human relationships in an economic setting.
   b. business and prices.
   c. scarcity.
   d. goods and services.

2. Scarcity exists
   a. in only poor countries of the world.
   b. in all countries of the world
   c. only when society does not employ all its resources in an efficient way.
   d. only when society produces too many frivolous or silly goods.

3. Which of the following statements is true?
   a. Both a millionaire and a poor person must deal with scarcity.
   b. People would have to make choices even if scarcity did not exist.
   c. Scarcity is a relatively new problem in the world's history; it has not always existed.
   d. It is likely that one day scarcity will no longer exist.

4. Which of the following statements is true?
   a. Coca-Cola is a good for everyone, even someone who has an allergy to Coca-Cola.
   b. If you pay someone to take X off your hands, then it is likely that X is a bad.
   c. It is possible, but not likely, that someone can obtain both utility and disutility from a bad.
   d. If there is more of good A than people want at zero price, then good A is an economic good.

5. Kristin Taylor had a safety inspection performed on her car last week and it passed with flying colors. How is this likely to affect her future driving behavior, compared to a situation in which cars did not get safety inspections at all?
   a. She will probably drive faster, and the probability of having an accident is reduced.
   b. She will probably drive slower, and the probability of having an accident is reduced.
   c. She will probably drive faster, and the probability of having an accident is increased.
   d. She will probably drive slower, and the probability of having an accident is increased.

6. Frank is 19 years old and is an actor in a soap opera, "One Life to Ruin." He earns $100,000 a year. Cassandra is also 19 years old and works in a local clothing store. She earns $9 an hour. Which of the two persons is more likely to attend college and for what reason?
   a. Cassandra, because she is smarter.
   b. Frank, because he has higher opportunity costs of attending college than Cassandra.
   c. Cassandra, because she has lower opportunity costs of attending college than Frank.
   d. Frank, because he earns a higher income than Cassandra.

7. A theory
   a. is a simplified abstract representation of the real world.
   b. incorporates critical factors or variables.
   c. is an accurate and complete description of reality.
   d. a and b

8. Which of the following is the best example of a hypothesis?
   a. If a person eats too many fatty foods, then his cholesterol level will rise.
   b. If it is 12 noon in New York City, it is 9 a.m. in Los Angeles.
   c. The daytime temperature is often over 100 degrees in Phoenix in July.
   d. If someone yells "fire" in a crowded theater and everyone runs to the exit, you will be worse off than had everyone walked but you.

9. Evidence can
   a. prove a theory, but never disprove it.
   b. reject (disprove) a theory, but never prove it.
   c. both prove and reject (disprove) a theory (although not at the same time).
   d. change the assumptions of the theory to fit the facts.

10. If an economist tests his or her theory and finds that it predicts accurately, he or she would likely say that the
    a. evidence fails to reject the theory.
    b. theory has been proved correct.
    c. the theory is true.
    d. the theory is better than alternative theories.

11. When an economist says that association is not causation, he or she means that
    a. event X and Y can be related in time (for instance, if one occurs a few minutes before the other) without X causing Y or Y causing X.
    b. if X occurs close in time to Y, it must be that either X is the cause of Y or Y is the cause of X.
    c. what is good for one person is good for all persons.
    d. what is good for one person is usually bad for all persons.

12. *Ceteris paribus* means:
    a. the correct relationship specified
    b. there are too many variables considered in the theory
    c. all other things held constant or nothing else changes
    d. assuming that people are rational human beings

13. Which of the following is an example of a *positive* statement?
    a. If you drop a quarter off the top of the Sears building in Chicago, it will fall to the ground.
    b. The minimum wage should be raised to eight dollars an hour.
    c. There is too much crime in the United States; something should be done about it.
    d. People should learn to get along with each other.

14. Which of the following topics is a microeconomics topic?
    a. the study of what influences the nation's unemployment rate
    b. the study of how changes in the nation's money supply affect the nation's output
    c. the study of prices in the automobile market
    d. the study of what affects the inflation rate

15. "Productive resources" include which of the following?
    a. land, labor, money, management
    b. land, labor, money, entrepreneurship
    c. land, labor, capital, entrepreneurship
    d. land, labor, natural resources, entrepreneurship

16. Efficiency exists if
    a. marginal benefits are greater than marginal costs.
    b. marginal costs are greater than marginal benefits.
    c. marginal costs equal zero.
    d. marginal costs equal marginal benefits.
    e. none of the above

True-False

Write a "T" or "F" after each statement.

17. A good is anything from which individuals receive utility. ____

18. If there is no explicit charge for a good, it is not a scarce good. ____

19. Scarcity implies that choices will be made. ____

20. The higher a person's opportunity cost of time, the more likely a person will stand in a long line to buy a ticket to a concert or some other event, *ceteris paribus*. ____

21. According to Milton Friedman, theories are better judged by their assumptions than by their predictions. ____

22. As economists use the term, a "good" is a tangible item that you can see and touch (rather than an intangible service). ____

Fill in the Blank

Write the correct word in the blank.

23. If one person talks louder than others at a cocktail party, he or she will be better heard. If everyone talks louder at a cocktail party, though, not everyone will be better heard. This is an illustration of the ________________ of ________________.
24. Imo believes that an event that occurs first must be the cause of an event that occurs later. Imo believes that ________________ ________ ________________.
25. If calorie intake causes weight gain and there are numerous things that cause weight loss, then the more cookies you eat, the more weight you will gain, ________________ ________________.
26. ________________ is the branch of economics that deals with highly aggregated markets or the entire economy.
27. If the evidence is consistent with a theory, economists do not say the theory has been proved correct. Instead, they say that the evidence ________________ _______ ________________ the theory.
28. One more unit of something is the ________________ unit.
29. A good that is used to produce other goods, yet is not a natural resource, is called a ________________ good.
30. The person who organizes production in a firm and is responsible for recognizing new business opportunities is an ________________.
31. ________________ ________________ defined economics as the study of mankind in the ordinary business of life.

Chapter 2
Economic Activities: Producing and Trading

What This Chapter Is About

People do it everyday—produce goods and enter into trades. They might produce a desk, computer, or book. They might trade $10 for a book or $2 for a loaf of bread. This chapter is about both producing and trading. It is also about various economic systems.

Key Concepts in the Chapter

a. exchange
b. terms of exchange
c. consumers' surplus
d. producers' (or sellers') surplus
e. transaction costs
f. comparative advantage
g. production possibilities frontier
h. efficiency
i. inefficiency
j. economic system

- **Exchange** is the process of trading one thing for another.
- The **terms of exchange** refer to how much of one thing is traded for how much of something else. For example, the terms of exchange may be $2,000 for one computer.
- **Consumers' surplus** is the difference between the maximum buying price and the price paid (by the consumer). For example, suppose John is willing to pay a maximum price of $40,000 for the car, but instead he pays only $25,000. The consumers' surplus is the difference, or $15,000.
- **Producers' (or sellers') surplus** is the difference between the price received (by the seller) and the minimum selling price. For example, if the minimum price firm X will sell good X for is $40, and the price it sells good X for is $50, then the producers' surplus is the difference, or $10.
- **Transaction costs** are the costs associated with the time and effort needed to search out, negotiate, and consummate an exchange.
- **Comparative advantage** refers to the situation in which someone can produce a good at lower opportunity cost than someone else. For example, if Jones can produce good Z at lower cost than Smith, then Jones has a comparative advantage in the production of good Z.
- A **production possibilities frontier (PPF)** represents the possible combination of two goods that an economy can produce in a certain period of time, under the conditions of a given state of technology, no unemployed resources, and efficient production.
- **Efficiency** implies the impossibility of gains in one area without losses in another.
- **Inefficiency** implies the possibility of gains in one area without losses in another.
- An **economic system** refers to the way in which society decides what goods to produce, how to produce them, and for whom the goods will be produced.

Review Questions

1. José is thinking of buying a house. Is he in the *ex ante* or *ex post* position with respect to exchange?

2. Kenny paid $7 to see a movie at the Cinemaplex at the mall. He would have paid as high as $10 to see the movie. What does his consumers' surplus (CS) equal?

3. How can you use consumers' surplus to know whether a change has made you better off, worse off, or neither?

4. Consumers prefer terms of exchange in their favor. What does this mean?

5. Are the transaction costs of buying a hamburger at a fast food restaurant higher or lower than the transaction costs of selling a house? Explain your answer.

6. Give an example of an exchange with a third-party negative effect.

7. Janet can produce either (a) 10 units of X and 20 units of Y, or (b) 20 units of X and 5 units of Y. What is the cost (to Janet) of producing one unit of X? One unit of Y?

8. Why does specialization and trade benefit people?

9. Why do people trade? What is the necessary condition for trade to take place?

10. Give an example that illustrates the law of increasing costs.

11. What does a straight-line production possibilities frontier (PPF) indicate about costs?

12. What does a bowed-outward (concave downward) PPF indicate about costs?

13. A country can be at either point A or B on its PPF. What does this fact have to do with the economic concept of *tradeoff*?

14. Identify two things that can shift a PPF outward (to the right).

    a.

    b.

15. Give an example of an advance in technology.

16. What are the three economic questions (that deal with production) that every society must answer?

    a.

    b.

    c.

Problems

1. If price paid is $40 and consumers' surplus is $100, then what is the maximum buying price?

2. If price received is $20 and producers' surplus is $5, then what is the minimum selling price?

3. Vernon bought a hat for $40. Identify more favorable terms of exchange for Vernon.

4. Karen's maximum buying price is $400 for good X. Randy's minimum selling price is $350 for good X. Currently, Karen and Randy have to each pay $60 in transaction costs to buy and sell good X. If an entrepreneur charges both the buyer and the seller $5, what is the minimum reduction in transaction costs that that entrepreneur must bring about (for each person) before the trade will be actualized at a price of $370?

5. Can you draw a PPF for grades? Use the data (that follow) to draw a production possibilities frontier for grades.

Hours spent studying Sociology	Grade in Sociology	Hours spent studying Economics	Grade in Economics
6	90	0	60
5	85	1	65
4	80	2	70
3	75	3	75
2	70	4	80
1	65	5	85
0	60	6	90

6. Using the data in the previous question, what is the opportunity cost of earning a 65 instead of a 60 in Economics?

7. Identify the points on the PPF that are efficient.

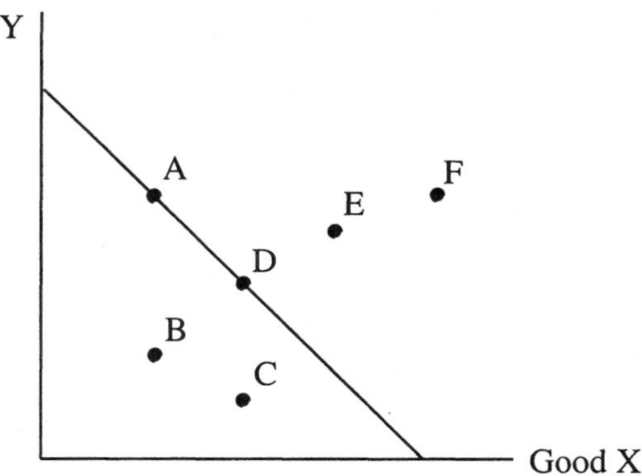

8. Which points on the PPF (in the previous question) are inefficient?

9. Which points on the PPF (in question 7) are unattainable?

10. Suppose that point C, with 100 units of good X and 200 units of good Y, is an efficient point. Could point D, with 75 units of good X and 250 units of good Y, also be an efficient point? Explain your answer.

11. Within a PPF framework, diagrammatically represent the effect of a war that destroys people and property.

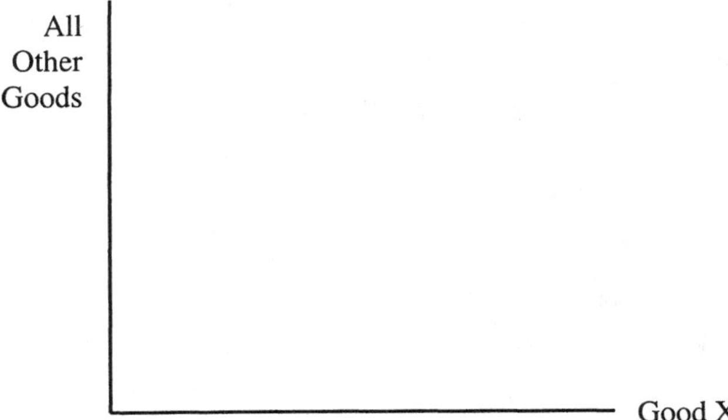

12. Within a PPF framework, diagrammatically represent the effect of an advance in technology.

What Is Wrong?
In each of the statements below, something is wrong. Identify what is wrong in the space provided.

1. If costs are increasing, the PPF is a straight (downward-sloping) line.

2. Mary said that she received $40 consumers' surplus when she paid $50 for the good and only $30 consumers' surplus when she paid $45 for the good.

3. If Jones can produce either (a) 100 units of X and 100 units of Y or (b) 200 units of X and zero units of Y, then he has a comparative advantage in the production of Y.

4. The following PPF represents a two-for-one opportunity cost of apples.

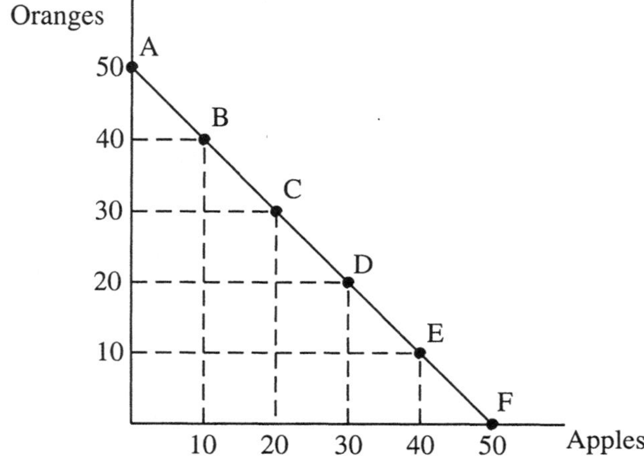

5. There are probably more unemployed resources at point A than at point D.

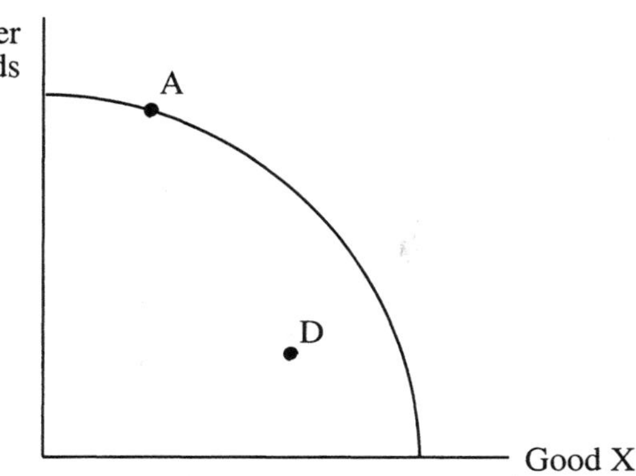

6. Efficiency implies the possibility of gains in one area without losses in another area.

7. If Georgina reads one more book, she will have to give up doing something else. This shows that Georgina is inefficient.

8. For a given quantity of output, a rise in price reduces producers' surplus and increases consumers' surplus.

9. If Bobby can produce either (a) 100 units of good X and 50 units of good Y, or (b) 25 units of good X and 80 units of good Y, then the cost of 1 unit of good X is 1.5 units of good Y.

10. John says, "I bought this sweater yesterday and I think I got a bad deal." It follows that in the *ex ante* position John thought he would be better off with the sweater than with the money he paid for it, but in the *ex post* position he prefers the money to the sweater.

Multiple Choice

Circle the correct answer.

1. Which of the following statements is true?
   a. The production possibilities frontier is always bowed outward.
   b. The production possibilities frontier is usually bowed outward.
   c. The production possibilities frontier is never bowed outward.
   d. The production possibilities frontier is usually a straight line.

2. Which of the following statements is false?
   a. A straight-line production possibilities frontier represents increasing costs.
   b. A bowed outward production possibilities frontier represents constant costs.
   c. An efficient point is located on the production possibilities frontier.
   d. a and b

3. If there is always a constant tradeoff between goods A and B, the production possibilities frontier between A and B is
   a. circular.
   b. a downward-sloping curve bowed toward the origin.
   c. a downward-sloping straight line.
   d. a downward-sloping straight line that is broken at one point.

4. Consider two points on the production possibilities frontier: point X, at which there are 100 cars and 78 trucks, and point Y, at which there are 90 cars and 70 trucks. If the economy is currently at point X, the opportunity cost of moving to point Y is
   a. 12 cars.
   b. 1 truck.
   c. 10 cars.
   d. 79 trucks.
   e. none of the above

5. If it is possible to increase production of one good without getting less of another, then currently the economy is
   a. operating efficiently.
   b. sluggish.
   c. operating inefficiently.
   d. operating at technological inferiority.

6. The production possibilities frontier represents the possible combinations of two goods that an economy can produce
   a. in a certain time.
   b. in a certain time, under the condition of a given state of resources.
   c. given that there are not unemployed resources.
   d. under the condition of efficient production.
   e. None of the answers is complete enough.

7. When the economy exhibits inefficiency, it is not producing the
   a. maximum output with the available resources and technology.
   b. minimum output with minimum resources and technology.
   c. the goods and services consumers wish to buy.
   d. b and c

8. The three economic questions that must be answered by every society are
   a. How will the goods be produced? What goods will be produced? What services will be produced?
   b. For whom will the goods be produced? What goods will be produced? How will the goods be produced?
   c. What goods will be produced? How will the goods be produced? For what purpose will the goods be produced?
   d. What goods will be produced? Who will produce the goods? Why are the goods produced?

9. When Beverly trades $60 for good X, economists assume that she is trading something
   a. of less value to her for something of more value to her.
   b. of more value to her for something of less value to her.
   c. that gives her less utility for something that gives her more utility.
   d. a and c
   e. none of the above

10. The ________ refer(s) to how much of one thing is traded for how much of something else.
    a. exchange process
    b. terms of exchange
    c. duality prices
    d. consumers' surplus
    e. producers' surplus

11. As the terms of exchange move in a buyer's favor, ________ rises and ________ falls.
    a. consumers' surplus; producers' surplus
    b. producers' surplus; consumers' surplus
    c. *ex ante* surplus; *ex post* surplus
    d. *ex post* surplus; *ex ante* surplus
    e. a and c

12. Transaction costs are
    a. the costs associated with the time and effort needed to search out, negotiate, and consummate an exchange.
    b. the costs a consumer pays in the *ex ante* position.
    c. the costs a seller pays in the *ex post* position.
    d. identical to the terms of exchange.
    e. always higher for buyers than sellers.

13. If Mark and Bob are not currently trading $10 for a book, it may be because
    a. transaction costs are too high.
    b. transaction costs are too low.
    c. at least one of the two individuals does not think he would be made better off by the trade.
    d. both individuals think they will be made worse off by the trade.
    e. a, c, and d

14. If Sean can bake bread at a lower cost than Jason, and Jason can produce paintings at a lower cost then Sean, it follows that
    a. Sean has a comparative advantage in paintings and Jason has a comparative advantage in baking bread.
    b. Both Sean and Jason have a comparative advantage in baking bread.
    c. Both Sean and Jason have a comparative advantage in producing paintings.
    c. Sean has a comparative advantage in baking bread and Jason has a comparative advantage in producing paintings.
    d. There is not enough information to answer the question.

15. Vernon can produce the following combinations of X and Y: 100X and 20Y, 50X and 30Y, or 0X or 40Y. The opportunity cost of one unit of Y for Vernon is
    a. five units of Y.
    b. two units of Y.
    c. three units of Y.
    d. one-half unit of Y.
    e. none of the above

True-False
Write a "T" or "F" after each statement.

16. Because scarcity exists, individuals and societies must make choices. ____

17. If the production of good X comes in terms of increasing costs of good Y, then the production possibilities frontier between the two goods is a downward-sloping straight line. ____

18. Economic growth shifts the production possibilities frontier inward. ____

19. It is possible for a legal institutional arrangement to be inefficient, and for an illegal institutional arrangement to be efficient. ____

20. Without scarcity, there would be no production possibilities frontier. ____

Fill in the Blank
Write the correct word in the blank.

21. The three questions (economists say) that all societies must answer are:
    a) ____
    b) ____
    c) ____

22. ______________ implies it is possible to obtain gains in one area without losses in another.

23. ______________ implies it is impossible to obtain gains in one area without losses in another.

24. At point A on a production possibilities frontier there are 50 apples and 60 oranges. At point B there are 49 apples and 68 oranges. If the economy is currently at point B, the opportunity cost of moving to point A is ______oranges.

Chapter 3
Supply and Demand: Theory

What This Chapter Is About

This chapter is about markets. A market has two sides—a demand side and a supply side. The chapter first discusses demand, then supply, then it puts both sides of the market together and discusses the price and quantity of goods.

Key Concepts in the Chapter

a. demand
b. law of demand
c. supply
d. law of supply
e. equilibrium price
f. shortage
g. surplus
h. consumers' surplus
i. producers' surplus

- **Demand** is the willingness and ability to buy different quantities of a good at different prices over some period of time. Keep in mind that if a person doesn't have both the willingness and ability to buy a good, then there is no demand.
- The **law of demand** states that price and quantity demanded are inversely related, *ceteris paribus*. This means that as price rises, quantity demanded falls, and as price falls, quantity demanded rises, *ceteris paribus*.
- **Supply** is the willingness and ability to produce and offer to sell different quantities of a good at different prices over some period of time.
- The **law of supply** states that price and quantity supplied are directly related, *ceteris paribus*. This means that as price rises, quantity supplied rises, and as price falls, quantity supplied falls, *ceteris paribus*.
- **Equilibrium price** is the price at which the quantity demanded of a good equals the quantity supplied. For example, if, at $40, the quantity supplied of good X is 100 units, and quantity demanded of good X is also 100 units, then $40 is the equilibrium price.
- **Equilibrium quantity** is the quantity that corresponds to equilibrium price. At equilibrium, quantity demanded = quantity supplied = equilibrium quantity.
- A **shortage** exists in a market if quantity demanded is greater than quantity supplied. If buyers want to buy 100 units of good X, and sellers only want to sell 30 units, then there is a shortage.
- A **surplus** exists in a market if quantity supplied is greater than quantity demanded. If buyers want to buy 100 units of good X, and sellers want to sell 300 units, then there is a surplus.
- **Consumers' surplus** is the difference between the maximum buying price and price paid. For example, if Smith is willing to pay a maximum of $40 for good X, and he only has to pay $10, then the difference, or $30, is consumers' surplus.
- **Producers' surplus** is the difference between the price paid and the minimum selling price. For example, if Jones is willing to sell good X for $10, but is paid $50, then the difference, or $40, is producers' surplus.

Review Questions

1. What does the law of demand state?

2. What does it mean to say that price and quantity demanded are inversely related?

3. What is quantity demanded?

4. How does quantity demanded differ from demand?

5. Demand is a function of five factors. Stated differently, if there is a change in any of these five factors, demand will either increase or decrease. What are these five factors?

   a.

   b.

   c.

   d.

   e.

6. If demand for a good increases, will the demand curve (that represents the good) shift to the right or to the left?

7. If demand for a good decreases, will the demand curve (that represents the good) shift to the right or to the left?

8. What is quantity supplied?

9. If a supply curve is vertical, what does this mean?

10. If a supply curve is upward-sloping, what does this mean?

11. Supply is a function of six factors. Stated differently, if there is a change in any of these six factors, supply will either increase or decrease. What are these six factors?

    a.

    b.

    c.

    d.

    e.

    f.

12. If the supply of a good increases, will the supply curve (that represents the good) shift to the right or to the left?

13. If the supply of a good decreases, will the supply curve (that represents the good) shift to the right or to the left?

14. Consider the standard supply and demand diagram. The demand curve is downward-sloping and the supply curve is upward-sloping.

    What is on the horizontal axis?

    What is on the vertical axis?

15. What is the difference between the relative price of a good and the absolute price of a good?

16. Demand rises and supply is constant. What happens to equilibrium price and quantity?

17. Supply rises and demand is constant. What happens to equilibrium price and quantity?

18. Demand rises by more than supply rises. What happens to equilibrium price and quantity?

19. Supply falls by more than demand rises. What happens to equilibrium price and quantity?

20. If price rises, what happens to consumers' surplus?

Problems

1. There are many factors that can directly affect supply and demand and indirectly affect price and quantity. In the first column we identify a change in a given factor. How does the change in the factor affect supply or demand? How does it affect price and quantity? Draw an upward arrow (↑) in the demand column if demand rises and a downward arrow (↓) if demand falls. The same holds for supply, equilibrium price, and equilibrium quantity.

Factor	**Demand**	**Supply**	**Equilibrium Price**	**Equilibrium Quantity**
Price of a substitute rises				
Price of a complement falls				
Income rises (normal good)				
Income falls (inferior good)				
Price of relevant resource rises				
Technology advances				
Quota				
Number of buyers rises				
Number of sellers rises				
Buyers expect higher price				
Sellers expect higher price				
Tax on production				
Preferences become more favorable with respect to the good				

2. Draw a rise in demand that is greater than a rise in supply.

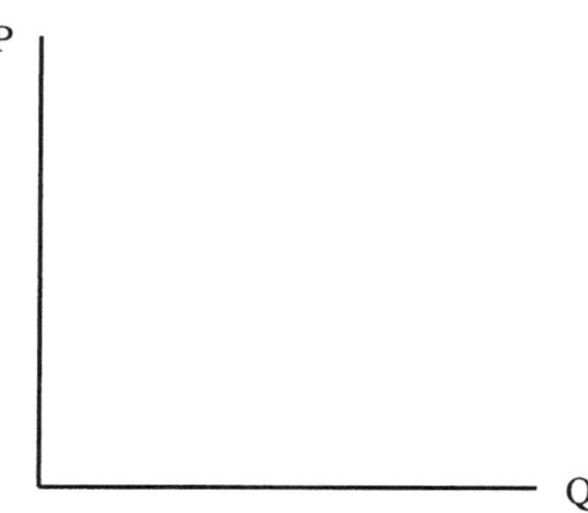

3. Draw a fall in supply that is greater than an increase in demand.

4. What area(s) does consumers' surplus equal at 100 units?

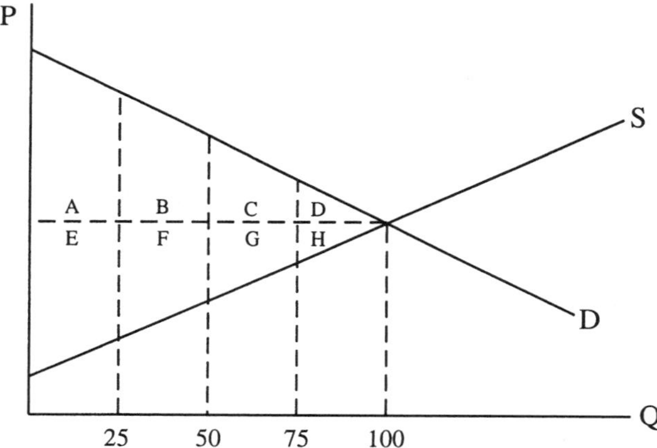

5. What area(s) does producers' surplus equal at equilibrium quantity?

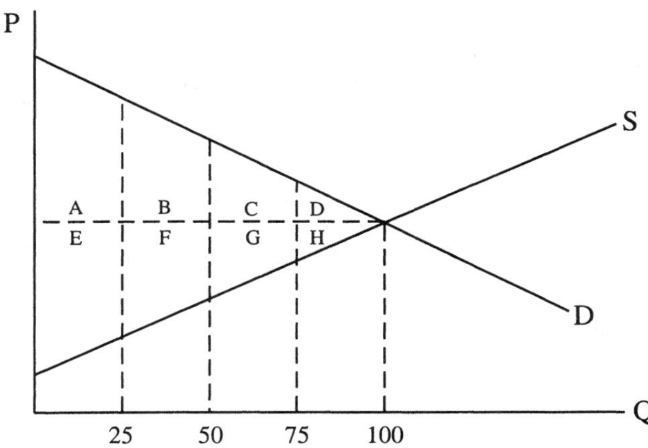

6. What is the shortage equal to at a price ceiling of $6?

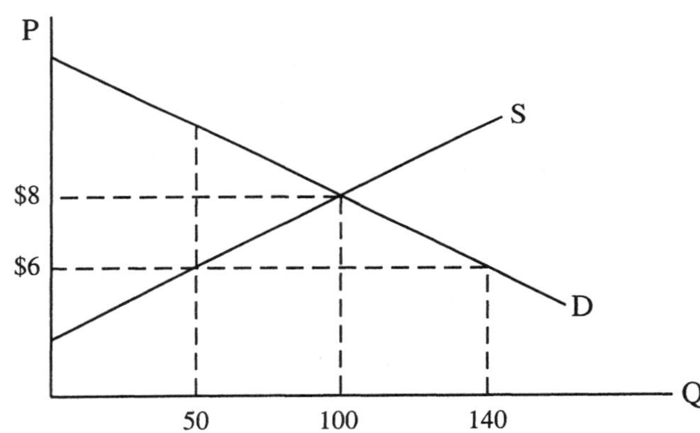

7. What is the surplus equal to at a price floor of $10?

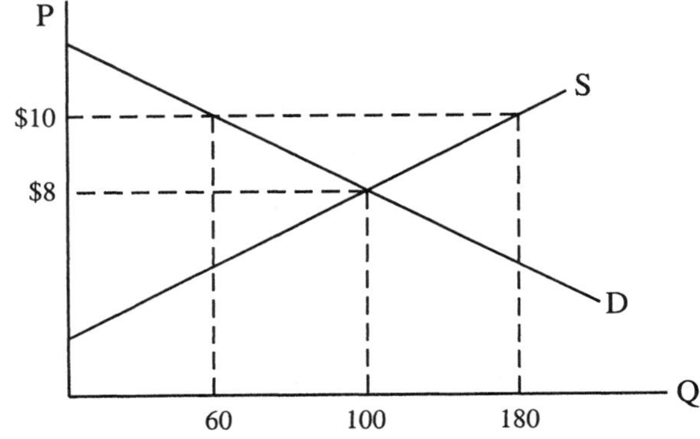

8. There are two buyers in a market, John and Mary. Below you see the quantity demanded for each at various prices. What is the quantity demanded (on the market demand curve) at each price specified? Write in the various quantities demanded in the spaces provided in the table.

Price	Quantity demanded by John	Quantity demanded by Mary	Quantity demanded (market demand)
$10	100	130	
$12	80	120	
$14	50	100	

9. If the price ceiling for good X is $4, and the maximum buying price for good X is $10, what is the highest price for a good that is "tied" to good X (as in a tie-in sale)?

10. Give an example that illustrates the law of diminishing marginal utility.

What Is Wrong?

In each of the statements below, something is wrong. Identify what is wrong in the space provided.

1. If the price of a good rises, the demand for the good will fall.

2. Consumers' surplus is equal to the minimum selling price minus the price paid.

3. As income rises, demand for a normal good rises; as income falls, demand for an inferior good falls.

4. The supply curve for Picasso paintings is upward-sloping.

5. As price rises, supply rises; as price falls, supply falls.

6. Quantity demanded is greater than supply when there is a shortage.

7. If supply rises, and demand is constant, equilibrium price rises and equilibrium quantity rises.

8. The law of diminishing marginal utility states that as a consumer consumes additional units of a good, each successive unit gives him or her more utility than the previous unit.

9. According to the law of demand, as the price of a good rises, the quantity demanded of the good rises, *ceteris paribus*.

Multiple Choice

Circle the correct answer.

1. The law of demand states that
   a. price and demand are inversely related, *ceteris paribus*.
   b. price and demand are directly related, *ceteris paribus*.
   c. price and quantity demanded are directly related, *ceteris paribus*.
   d. price and quantity demanded are inversely related, *ceteris paribus*.

2. Which of the following persons would be most likely to prefer first-come-first-served (FCFS) as a rationing device?
   a. A person who has just returned from visiting a busy city.
   b. A person who has just returned from visiting a small town.
   c. A person with low opportunity cost of time.
   d. A person with high opportunity cost of time.

3. At a price ceiling (below equilibrium price),
   a. there is a surplus.
   b. quantity supplied is greater than quantity demanded.
   c. quantity demanded equals quantity supplied.
   d. supply equals demand.
   e. quantity demanded is greater than quantity supplied.

4. Which of the following statements is true?
   a. A demand schedule is the same thing as a demand curve.
   b. A downward-sloping demand curve is the graphical representation of the law of demand.
   c. Quantity demanded is a relationship between price and demand.
   d. Quantity demanded is the same as demand.

5. Because of a price ceiling on light bulbs, the quantity demanded of light bulbs exceeds the quantity supplied. The owner of the light bulbs decided to sell them on a first-come-first-served basis. This is an example of a
   a. surplus.
   b. tie-in sale.
   c. nonprice rationing device.
   d. black market.
   e. none of the above.

6. A neutral good is a good
   a. the demand for which does not change as income falls.
   b. the demand for which does not change as income rises.
   c. the demand for which rises as income falls.
   d. the demand for which falls as income rises.
   e. a and b.

7. If the absolute price of good X is $600 and the absolute price of good Y is $400, then the relative price of good Y is
   a. 2 units of X.
   b. 2/3 unit of X.
   c. 1-1/3 unit of X.
   d. 1-1/2 unit of X.
   e. none of the above.

8. If an increase in income leads to an increase in the demand for sausage, then sausage is
   a. an essential good.
   b. a normal good.
   c. a luxury good.
   d. a discretionary good.

9. Which of the following can shift the demand curve rightward?
   a. an increase in income
   b. an increase in the price of a substitute good
   c. an increase in the price of a complementary good
   d. all of the above
   e. a and b

10. Which of the following cannot increase the demand for good X?
   a. an increase in income
   b. a decrease in the price of good X
   c. an increase in the price of a substitute good
   d. more buyers
   e. a change in preferences in favor of good X

11. The law of supply states that price and quantity supplied are
   a. directly related.
   b. inversely related.
   c. inversely related, *ceteris paribus*.
   d. directly related, *ceteris paribus*.

12. A change in the quantity supplied of a good is directly brought about by a
   a. change in the good's own price.
   b. decrease in income.
   c. technological advance.
   d. fall in the price of resources needed to produce the good.
   e. none of the above.

13. Five dollars is the equilibrium price for good Z. At a price of $2, there is
    a. a shortage.
    b. surplus.
    c. excess supply.
    d. aggregate demand.

14. If supply rises by a greater amount than demand rises,
    a. equilibrium price rises and equilibrium quantity falls.
    b. equilibrium price falls and equilibrium quantity falls.
    c. equilibrium price rises and equilibrium quantity rises.
    d. equilibrium price falls and equilibrium quantity rises.

15. If supply rises and demand is constant,
    a. equilibrium price rises and equilibrium quantity falls.
    b. equilibrium price falls and equilibrium quantity falls.
    c. equilibrium price rises and equilibrium quantity rises.
    d. equilibrium price falls and equilibrium quantity rises.

True-False
Write a "T" or "F" after each statement.

16. One of the effects of a price ceiling is that quantity supplied is greater than quantity demanded. ____

17. Demand is more important to the determination of market price than supply. ____

18. At the equilibrium price for good X, good X is scarce. ____

19. "Supply" is a specific amount of a good, such as 50 units of good Y. ____

20. There is a tendency for price to rise when the quantity demanded of a good is greater than the quantity supplied. ____

Fill in the Blank
Write the correct word in the blank.

21. As price rises, quantity demanded ________________ and quantity supplied ________________.

22. A ________________ is any arrangement by which people exchange goods and services.

23. If Matt's demand for motorcycles rises as his income falls, then motorcycles are a(n) ________________ good for Matt.

24. If demand rises more than supply falls, then equilibrium quantity ________________.

25. At equilibrium, the quantity demanded of a good ________________ the quantity supplied of the good.

26. Suppose you live in New York City and are required to rent the furniture in an apartment before you can rent the apartment. This is called a ___________ - ___________ sale.

Chapter 4
Supply and Demand: Practice

What This Chapter Is About

In the last chapter you learned the basic theory of supply and demand. You learned what a demand curve is, what factors will shift it right and left, what a supply curve is, what factors will shift it right and left, and so on. The theory of supply and demand is worth little unless you can apply it. That is what we do in this chapter. We present a series of applications of supply and demand.

Key Concepts in the Chapter

a. law of demand
b. law of supply
c. nonprice rationing device
d. minimum wage
e. price floor
f. price ceiling

- The **law of demand** states that price and quantity demanded are inversely related, *ceteris paribus*.
- The **law of supply** states that price and quantity supplied are directly related, *ceteris paribus*.
- Just as price can serve as a rationing device, so can other things. These other things we call **nonprice rationing devices**. First-come-first-served (FCFS) is a nonprice rationing device.
- The **minimum wage** is the lowest wage a worker can be paid. The minimum wage is an example of a price floor.
- The **price floor** is a government-mandated minimum price below which legal trades cannot be made.
- A **price ceiling** is a government-mandated maximum price above which legal trades cannot be made.

Review Questions

1. The tuition students pay at University X (T_1) is lower than the equilibrium tuition (T_E). If the tuition students pay remains constant, and demand to attend University X rises, what do you predict will happen to the requirements for admission? Explain your answer.

2. "If marijuana is legalized, the price of marijuana will fall." What does this statement assume about the supply of and demand for marijuana after legalization?

3. How would kidneys (for transplants) be rationed in a free market?

4. In the discussion of the used car market (in the text) we saw that the demand for new cars was higher with a used car market than without a used car market. Do you think this same phenomenon (higher demand if the good can be resold than if it cannot be resold) holds for any other goods? If so, which goods?

5. How can the pricing scheme that a college chooses to allocate student parking spots have anything to do with whether or not a student is late to class?

6. There is freeway congestion on Interstate 5 at 8 a.m. on Monday morning. What are three solutions to the problem of freeway congestion at this time?

7. Why are gold prices the same everywhere?

8. Will patients pay more for health care if they have the right to sue their provider than if they don't have the right to sue? Explain your answer.

9. In the text it was argued that people pay for good weather. How do they pay for good weather?

10. Why do people pay a tip to be seated at many shows in Las Vegas, but do not pay a tip to be seated at a major league baseball game?

Problems

1. Use the law of demand to explain why Yvonne loses her temper with her mother but not with her father.

2. Older people tend to drive more slowly than younger people. For example, a 68-year-old retired person may drive more slowly than a working 32-year-old person. Some people say this is because as people age, their reflexes slow down, their eyesight becomes less clear, and so on. All this may be true. Still, might there be an explanation that has to do with the price of driving? If so, what is this explanation?

3. Suppose the equilibrium tuition at college X is $2,000 a semester, but students only pay $800 a semester. The state taxpayers pay the $1,200 difference. Do you think professors will teach differently knowing their students paid a below-equilibrium tuition instead of the equilibrium tuition? Why or why not?

4. Richard Posner states, "The law of demand doesn't operate just on goods with explicit prices. Unpopular teachers sometimes try to increase enrollment by raising the average grade of the students in their courses, thereby reducing the price of the course to the student." In other words, unpopular teachers give away grades, thus becoming more popular. Do you think the same holds, with necessary changes, for unpopular people? Do unpopular people try to change the price of being around them? Or are they unpopular because the price they charge to be around them is too high?

5. Under what condition will the decriminalization of marijuana lead to an unchanged price for marijuana?

6. Some people argue that an increase in the minimum wage will lead to a large cutback in the number of unskilled workers employed, while others argue that it will lead to only a small cutback in the number of unskilled workers employed. Are the two groups of people arguing over a change in direction or a change in magnitude?

7. "The same number of kidneys will be forthcoming for transplants no matter what the price paid for a kidney." For this statement to be true, what must the supply curve of kidneys look like?

8. Why does a candy bar sell for the same price (or nearly the same price) everywhere in the country, but houses do not?

9. Jones has tried to sell his car for six months. No buyers. Does Jones have a really bad car that no one wants to buy?

10. "Professors in economics, sociology, and biology all lecture, grade papers, meet with students, and so on. It follows, then, that economists and sociologists should be paid the same dollar salary." What does the person who makes this statement forget, overlook, or ignore?

What May Have Been Overlooked?

In each of the statements below, something may have been overlooked or ignored. Identify what may have been overlooked or ignored.

1. The higher the demand for something, the greater the quantity demanded.

2. I think how I behave is independent of the setting that I am in. I act the same way no matter what the setting.

3. If there were no flea markets or garage sales (where people can buy old furniture), new furniture companies would sell more (new) furniture.

4. The rock band has the best interest of its fans in mind. It knows it can charge $80 a ticket, but it charges only $20 a ticket so that its fans won't have to pay so much.

5. If my university doesn't charge for student parking, then I am definitely better off than I would be if it did charge for student parking.

6. The tuition at Harvard is very high, so Harvard must be charging the equilibrium tuition to students. Still, Harvard uses such things as GPA, SAT and ACT scores for admission purposes. It must be wrong that these nonprice rationing devices (GPA, etc.) are only used by colleges and universities that charge below-equilibrium tuition.

7. If a good doesn't have a money price, it has no price at all.

Multiple Choice

Circle the correct answer.

1. There is no toll charge to drive on freeway A. If there is freeway congestion at 9 a.m., there will be greater freeway congestion at 11 a.m. if
   a. the demand to drive on the freeway is the same at both times.
   b. the demand to drive on the freeway at 11 a.m. is less than the demand to drive on the freeway at 9 a.m.
   c. the demand to drive on the freeway at 9 a.m. is greater than the demand to drive on the freeway at 11 a.m.
   d. fewer people carpool at 11 a.m. than at 9 a.m.
   e. none of the above

2. If goods are not rationed according to price, it follows that
   a. they won't get rationed at all.
   b. something will ration the goods.
   c. first-come-first-served will necessarily be the rationing device.
   d. there will be surpluses in the market.
   e. none of the above

3. Market X can be divided into two submarkets, A and B. The supply in each submarket is the same, but the demand in A is greater than the demand in B. If submarket B is in equilibrium, it follows that
   a. A is in equilibrium.
   b. there is a shortage in A.
   c. there is a surplus in A.
   d. there is a shortage in B only if there is a surplus in A.
   e. none of the above

4. The demand to attend a certain college is represented by a downward-sloping demand curve. The supply of spots at the college is represented by a vertical supply curve. At the tuition that students are charged, there is a shortage of spots at the college. If the demand to attend the college falls, but the tuition stays constant, if follow that the
   a. GPA required to attend the college will probably rise.
   b. GPA required to attend the college will probably fall.
   c. SAT score required to attend the college will probably not change.
   d. a and c
   e. There is not enough information to answer the question.

5. There are two groups of workers, A and B, who are equally productive. Currently, employers discriminate against workers in group B. It follows that
   a. the demand for workers in group B is higher than the demand for workers in group A.
   b. the demand for workers in groups A and B is the same.
   c. the demand for workers in group A is higher than the demand for workers in group B.
   d. There is not enough information to answer the question.

6. If the minimum wage is the same as the equilibrium wage, then
   a. there will be a shortage of labor.
   b. there will be a surplus of labor.
   c. quantity demanded of labor will equal quantity supplied of labor.
   d. fewer people will be working than if the minimum wage were lower than the equilibrium wage.
   e. none of the above

7. If there is a price ceiling in the kidney (available for transplant) market , and the price ceiling is lower than the equilibrium price, it follows that
   a. the supply of kidneys will be vertical.
   b. the quantity demanded of kidneys will be greater than it would be at equilibrium price.
   c. the quantity demanded of kidneys will be smaller than it would be at equilibrium price.
   d. a and b
   e. a and c

8. A state law is passed that places a price ceiling on retail electricity, but not on wholesale electricity. It follows that there
   a. will *not* be a shortage of electricity in the wholesale market.
   b. will be a shortage of electricity in the retail market.
   c. will be a surplus of electricity in the wholesale market.
   d. a and c
   e. a and b

9. A seller's minimum price for providing a good rises. It follows that
   a. the supply curve does not change.
   b. the supply curve shifts upward and to the left.
   c. the supply curve shifts downward and to the right.
   d. equilibrium price will end up falling.
   e. b and d

10. The supply for sociologists and economists is the same, but the demand for sociologists is higher. If both sociologists and economists are paid the same salary, it follows that
    a. there is a shortage of sociologists.
    b. there is a surplus of economists.
    c. there is neither a shortage of, nor surplus of, sociologists or economists.
    d. a and b
    e. There is not enough information to answer the question.

11. If there is freeway congestion at 8 a.m., we can reduce (or eliminate) the congestion by
    a. building more freeways.
    b. raising the price to drive on the freeway at 8 a.m.
    c. giving people an incentive to carpool
    d. a and b
    e. a, b, and c

12. If parking spots on campus were auctioned to the highest bidder,
    a. the closest spots to buildings would probably fetch the highest prices.
    b. the people with the lowest time costs would park the closest to the buildings.
    c. there would always be shortages.
    d. a and b
    e. a, b, and c

13. The university offers "free" seat cushions to any football fan that will arrive at least an hour before the game starts. It is correct to say that these cushions are offered at
    a. zero price.
    b. zero money price.
    c. zero nominal price.
    d. either a or b.
    e. none of the above

14. Aisle seats on commercial airplanes are priced the same as window seats. If the demand for aisle seats is greater than the demand for window seats, the supply of each kind of seat is the same, and the window-seat market is in equilibrium, it follows that
    a. the aisle-seat market is in equilibrium, too.
    b. there is a shortage of aisle seats.
    c. there is a surplus of aisle seats.
    d. There is not enough information to answer the question.

15. The price of speeding (on a highway) is equal to the price of a speeding ticket times the probability of being caught speeding. If the demand curve for speeding is downward-sloping, it follows that
    a. a higher probability of getting caught speeding will reduce speeding.
    b. a higher ticket price will reduce speeding
    c. a lower ticket price combined with a higher probability of getting caught speeding will reduce speeding.
    d. a and b.
    e. a, b, and c

True–False

Write a "T" or "F" after each statement.

16. The higher the demand to attend a given college or university, the higher its equilibrium tuition, *ceteris paribus*. ____

17. If there is a price ceiling in the kidney market, and the price ceiling is below the equilibrium price for a kidney, there will be a shortage of kidneys available for transplant. ____

18. Economist Robert Solow said, "I am a supply-and-demand economist. When I come across something, I ask myself, 'What is being transferred here and where does the supply come from and where does the demand come from?" ____

19. Law 1 gives tenants three months to vacate an apartment, and Law 2 gives tenants six months. Apartment rent is likely to be higher under Law 1. ____

20. The price of pencils is more likely to be the same everywhere than the price of houses. ____

Fill in the Blank

Write the correct word in the blank.

21. At a given price, the greater demand is, the greater ____________ ____________ is.
22. If there is good weather in City X and bad weather in City Y, and everything is the same about the two cities except the weather, the demand to live in City X will be ____________ than the demand to live in City Y.
23. First-come-first-served is a ____________ ____________ device.
24. The tip for a good seat in a Las Vegas showroom will equal the difference between the ____________ price of a good seat and the ____________ price to the show.
25. John earns $100 an hour and Bill earns $20 an hour. If it takes time to make friends, then the ____________ price of friendship is higher and, *ceteris paribus*, ____________ will make more friends.

Chapter 5
Elasticity

What This Chapter Is About

Elasticity is one of the most important topics in economics. There are different types of elasticity—price elasticity of demand, cross elasticity of demand, income elasticity of demand, and price elasticity of supply. All four of these concepts are discussed in this chapter.

Key Concepts in the Chapter

a. price elasticity of demand
b. cross elasticity of demand
c. income elasticity of demand
d. price elasticity of supply

- **Price elasticity of demand** measures the responsiveness in quantity demanded to a change in price.
- **Cross elasticity of demand** measures the responsiveness in quantity demanded of one good to a change in price of another good.
- **Income elasticity of demand** measures the responsiveness in quantity demanded to a change in income.
- **Price elasticity of supply** measures the responsiveness in quantity supplied to a change in price.

Review Questions

1. What is price elasticity of demand?

2. What is the relationship between price elasticity of demand and the number of substitutes for a good?

3. If a good has many substitutes, does it follow that demand for the good is elastic?

4. What is the relationship between time (since a change in price) and price elasticity of demand?

5. What is the relationship between the percentage of one's budget spent on a good and price elasticity of demand?

6. What does cross elasticity of demand measure?

7. What does it mean if a good is income inelastic?

8. What is price elasticity of supply?

Problems

1. Fill in the blanks in the table.

Price and quantity demanded at point A		Price and quantity demanded at point B		Price elasticity of demand is equal to	Is demand (elastic, unit elastic, or inelastic)?
$10	100	$8	140		
$8	200	$15	120		
$7	40	$10	33		

2. Fill in the blanks in the table.

Price elasticity of demand is	Change	Price elasticity of demand (rises, falls, remains unchanged)
0.34	more substitutes for the good	
1.99	more time passes since change in price	
2.20	smaller percentage of one's budget spent on the good	

3. Fill in the blanks in the table.

Demand is	Price (rises, falls)	Total revenue (rises, falls, remains unchanged)
elastic	falls	
inelastic	rises	
unit elastic	rises	
inelastic	falls	
elastic	rises	

4. Fill in the blanks in the table.

Price of good X (rises, falls)	Quantity demanded of good Y (rises, falls)	Cross elasticity of demand is	The two goods, X and Y, are (substitutes, complements)
rises by 10 percent	falls by 5 percent		
falls by 20 percent	rises by 4 percent		
rises by 8 percent	rises by 5 percent		

5. Fill in the blanks in the table.

Income (rises, falls)	Quantity demanded (rises, falls)	Income elasticity of demand is
rises by 20 percent	rises by 10 percent	
falls by 10 percent	falls by 15 percent	
rises by 5 percent	rises by 20 percent	

6. Fill in the blanks in the table.

Price (rises, falls)	Quantity supplied (rises, falls)	Is supply (elastic, inelastic, unit elastic)?
rises 3 percent	rises 4 percent	
rises 1 percent	rises 6 percent	
falls 20 percent	falls 10 percent	

7. Fill in the blanks in the table.

Initial equilibrium price and quantity		New equilibrium price and quantity (after $1 tax has been placed on supplier)		Percentage of the tax paid by the seller in terms of a higher price	Percentage of the tax paid by the seller in terms of a lower price kept
$40	100	$40.44	90		
$9	87	$9.57	80		
$10	200	$10.76	150		

8. Diagrammatically prove that the more inelastic the demand curve, the larger the percentage of a tax (placed on a the seller) that is paid for by the buyer.

Price

Quantity

What Is the Question?

Identify the question for each of the answers that follow.

1. Measures the responsiveness of quantity demanded given a change in price.

2. Price and total revenue are directly related.

3. Quantity demanded changes by 20 percent if price changes by 10 percent.

4. There is no change in quantity demanded as price changes.

5. The number of substitutes, the percentage of one's budget spent on the good, time (since the change in price), and luxury vs. necessity.

6. Price of one good rises and quantity demanded for another good rises.

7. In either of these cases, the tax placed on the seller is fully paid by the buyer.

What Is Wrong?

In each of the statements that follow, something is wrong. Identify what is wrong in the space provided.

1. If price rises, and total revenue falls, then demand is inelastic.

2. The elasticity coefficient is greater than 1 for a good that is income inelastic.

3. Cars have more substitutes than Ford cars.

4. As we move down a demand curve, price elasticity of demand rises.

5. For inelastic demand, quantity demanded changes proportionately more than price changes.

6. A perfectly inelastic demand curve can be downward-sloping.

7. The elasticity coefficient is greater than zero for goods that are complements.

8. If demand is inelastic, buyers pay the full tax that is placed on sellers.

9. If income elasticity of demand is 1.24, it means that for every 1 percent change in income there is a 1.24 percent change in price.

10. Price elasticity of supply measures the responsiveness of quantity supplied to changes in income.

Multiple Choice

Circle the correct answer.

1. In general, elasticity deals with
   a. the responsiveness in one variable to a change in another variable.
   b. price and quantity demanded.
   c. income and quantity demanded.
   d. supply and demand.
   e. b and c

2. Price elasticity of demand is a measure of the responsiveness of quantity demanded to changes in
   a. interest rates.
   b. supply.
   c. price.
   d. demand.

3. If quantity demanded rises by 27 percent as price falls by 30 percent, price elasticity of demand equals
   a. 2.4.
   b. 0.9.
   c. 1.1.
   d. 1.7.
   e. none of the above.

4. Price rises from $12 to $14 and the quantity demanded falls from 80 units to 60 units. What is the price elasticity of demand between the two prices?
   a. approximately 1.86
   b. approximately 0.80
   c. approximately 0.53
   d. 1.00
   e. none of the above

5. If the percentage change in quantity demanded is greater than the percentage change in price, demand is
   a. inelastic.
   b. unit elastic.
   c. elastic.
   d. perfectly elastic.
   e. perfectly inelastic.

6. If quantity demanded is completely unresponsive to changes in price, demand is
   a. inelastic.
   b. unit elastic.
   c. elastic.
   d. perfectly inelastic.
   e. perfectly elastic.

7. If the price of good X falls and the demand for good X is elastic, then
   a. the percentage rise in quantity demanded is greater than the percentage fall in price and total revenue rises.
   b. the percentage rise in quantity demanded is less than the percentage fall in price and total revenue falls.
   c. the percentage rise in quantity demanded is greater than the percentage fall in price and total revenue falls.
   d. the percentage fall in quantity demanded is greater than the percentage fall in price and total revenue rises.
   e. the percentage rise in quantity demanded is equal to the percentage fall in price and total revenue remains constant

8. The more substitutes a good has, *ceteris paribus*,
   a. the higher its price elasticity of demand.
   b. the lower its price elasticity of demand.
   c. the less elastic the demand for the good.
   d. the more inelastic the demand for the good.

9. *Ceteris paribus*, the price elasticity of demand is lowest for which of the following goods?
   a. McDonald's hamburgers
   b. hamburgers
   c. Wendy's hamburgers
   d. Burger King hamburgers
   e. it is between a, c, and d

10. _________ measures the responsiveness of changes in the quantity demanded of one good to changes in the price of another good.
    a. Price elasticity of demand
    b. Income elasticity of demand
    c. Price elasticity of supply
    d. Cross elasticity of demand

11. _________ measures the responsiveness of changes in the quantity demanded of a good to changes in income.
    a. Price elasticity of demand
    b. Price elasticity of supply
    c. Income elasticity of demand
    d. Cross elasticity of demand

12. Income elasticity of demand for an inferior good is
    a. less than zero.
    b. greater than zero.
    c. equal to zero.
    d. none of the above.

13. Suppose someone says that because of the per-unit tax being placed on the producers of good Y, the producers of good Y will end up paying the full tax. This person assumes that the demand curve for good Y is
    a. elastic.
    b. perfectly inelastic.
    c. inelastic.
    d. perfectly elastic.
    e. unit elastic.

14. If price and total revenue move in the opposite direction, then
    a. demand is elastic.
    b. demand is inelastic.
    c. demand is unit elastic.
    d. supply is elastic.
    e. supply is inelastic.

15. If price and total revenue move in the same direction, then
    a. demand is elastic.
    b. demand is inelastic.
    c. demand is unit elastic.
    d. supply is elastic.
    e. supply is inelastic.

True-False
Write "T" of "F" after each statement.

16. The greater the percentage of one's budget spend on a good, the higher the price elasticity of demand. ____

17. The less time that passes (after a change in price), the lower the price elasticity of demand. ____

18. A normal good can be income inelastic but not income elastic. ____

19. Supply is elastic if price changes by a greater percent than quantity supplied.

20. Total revenue always rises when price rises. ____

Fill in the Blank
Write the correct word in the blank.

21. If the percentage in quantity demanded is greater than the percentage change in price, the ________________ ________________ is greater than 1, and demand is ________________.

22. If price rises and total revenue rises, too, demand is ________________.

23. As we move up a straight-line downward-sloping demand curve from lower to higher prices, price elasticity of demand ________________.

24. The short-run price elasticity of demand for gasoline is likely to be ________________ than the long-run price elasticity of demand for gasoline.

25. If price falls and total revenue rises, then demand is ________________.

Chapter 6
Consumer Choice: Maximizing Utility and Behavioral Economics

What This Chapter Is About

How do consumers make decisions? How do they decide how many units of a good to buy? This chapter answers these questions and more. In a way, this chapter gives you a deeper understanding of demand, discussed in an earlier chapter. It also introduces you to the marginal benefits-marginal costs framework of analysis, which is used extensively in economics.

Key Concepts in the Chapter

a. utility
b. total utility
c. marginal utility
d. law of diminishing marginal utility
e. consumer equilibrium
f. substitution effect
g. income effect

- **Utility** is a measure of satisfaction, happiness, or benefit that results from the consumption of a good.
- **Total utility** is the total satisfaction a person receives from consuming a particular quantity of a good.
- **Marginal utility** is the additional utility a person receives from consuming an additional unit of a particular good.
- The **law of diminishing marginal utility** states that the marginal utility gained by consuming equal successive units of a good will decline as the amount consumed increases.
- **Consumer equilibrium** exists when the consumer has spent all income and the marginal utility-price ratios (MU-P ratios) are the same.
- The **substitution effect** refers to that portion of the change in the quantity demanded of a good that is attributable to a change in its relative price.
- The **income effect** refers to that portion of the change in the quantity demanded of a good that is attributable to a change in real income (brought about by a change in absolute price).

Review Questions

1. Give an example to illustrate the difference between total utility and marginal utility.

2. Give an example to illustrate the law of diminishing marginal utility.

3. Give an example of a person making an interpersonal utility comparison. Define what it means to make an interpersonal utility comparison.

4. What is the diamond-water paradox?

5. What is the solution to the diamond-water paradox?

6. What does this say: $MU_a/P_a > MU_b/P_b$? Of what significance is this condition to a buyer?

7. Explain how consumers achieve consumer equilibrium.

8. Give an example to illustrate what the substitution effect is.

9. Give an example to illustrate what the income effect is.

10. What is marginal cost?

11. Describe the experiments of the economists Zizzo and Oswald.

12. What does it mean if a person compartmentalizes?

Problems

1. Fill in the blank spaces in the table.

Unit	Total utility (utils)	Marginal utility (utils)
1st	100	
2nd	146	
3rd		28

2. At what quantity of X and Y is the consumer in equilibrium if the price of X is $2, the price of Y is $1, and the consumer has $7?

Good X (units)	Total utility (utils)	Good Y (units)	Total utility (utils)
1	60	1	80
2	110	2	100
3	150	3	110

3. Fill in the blank spaces in the table.

Price falls by	Change in quantity demanded	Additional units consumer would buy due to higher real income	Additional units purchased due to the substitution effect
$2	133	60	
$4	187	85	
$3	222	125	

4. Fill in the blank spaces in the table.

Units of good X	Total cost	Marginal cost
1	$40	
2	$89	
3	$149	

5. Fill in the blank spaces in the table.

Number of hours playing baseball	Total benefits (in utils)	Marginal benefits (in utils)
1	100	
2	178	
3	210	

What Is the Question?

Identify the question for each of the answers that follow.

1. The additional utility gained from consuming an additional unit of good X.

2. Marginal utility turns negative.

3. The consumer will buy more of good X and less of good Y.

4. That portion of the change in the quantity demanded of a good that is attributable to a change in its relative price.

5. The change in total cost divided by the change in quantity of output.

6. It slopes downward (left to right) because of the law of diminishing marginal utility.

7. Ownership makes things more valuable.

What Is Wrong?

In each of the statements that follow, something is wrong. Identify what is wrong in the space provided.

1. If total utility is falling, then marginal utility is greater than zero.

2. A millionaire gets less utility from an additional $100 than a poor person receives from an additional $100.

3. The income effect refers to that portion of the change in the quantity demanded of a good that is attributable to a change in its relative price.

4. If total cost rises, marginal cost must rise, too.

5. If total benefits rise, then marginal benefits must rise, too.

6. If the marginal utility-price ratio for good A is greater than the marginal utility-price ratio for good B, then a consumer will buy more of both good A and B.

Multiple Choice
Circle the correct answer.

1. If Fiona says that drinking soda gives her utility, what specifically does she mean?
   a. That there are things worse than drinking soda.
   b. That drinking soda is tasty.
   c. That drinking soda is something that gives her satisfaction or pleasure.
   d. That there is nothing better than drinking soda.
   e. b and d

2. Suppose Will consumes 5 units of good X and receives 20 utils from the first unit, 18 from the second, 12 from the third, 7 from the fourth, and 1 from the fifth. The total utility Will receives from consuming 5 units is
   a. 50 utils.
   b. 58 utils.
   c. 40 utils.
   d. 45 utils.
   e. none of the above

3. Suppose Bob received 123 utils from consuming one banana and 159 utils from consuming two bananas. What is the marginal utility of the second banana?
   a. 282 utils.
   b. 30 utils.
   c. 0 utils.
   d. 36 utils.
   e. none of the above.

4. The law of diminishing marginal utility says that the marginal utility gained by consuming equal ________ units of a good will ________ as the amount consumed ________.
   a. successive; decline; decreases
   b. successive; decline; increases
   c. large; decline; decreases
   d. small; decline; increases
   e. none of the above

5. Which of the following is false?
   a. It is impossible for total utility to rise as marginal utility falls.
   b. Marginal utility is the same as average utility.
   c. Marginal utility is greater than total utility for the first unit of a good consumed.
   d. a and c
   e. a, b, and c

6. In which of the following settings is an interpersonal utility comparison not being made?
   a. Brady says to Armand, "I get a lot more satisfaction from eating hamburgers than you do."
   b. Francis says, "I don't know what he is feeling or thinking; I can't read a person's heart or mind."
   c. Ida ways to Lucy, "I know you like this course a lot more than I do."
   d. a and b
   e. a, b, and c

7. Suppose for a consumer the marginal utility of pickles is 50 utils and the MU of milk is 30 utils; the price of pickles is $1.00 and the price of milk is $1.25. Given this,
   a. the same amount of utility per penny is gained from consuming milk as pickles.
   b. more utility per penny is gained from consuming milk than pickles.
   c. more utility penny is gained from consuming pickles than milk.
   d. the consumer is in consumer equilibrium.

8. The price of good Y, a normal good, falls from $10 to $8. As a result, the quantity demanded of good Y rises from 125 units to 155 units. Holding real income constant, the quantity demanded of good Y rises 20 units. Which of the following is true?
   a. The consumer consumes 20 more units of Y because it has become relatively cheaper; therefore this is the income effect.
   b. The consumer consumes 10 more units of Y because he or she has more real income; therefore this is the income effect.
   c. The consumer consumes 20 more units of Y because it has become relatively cheaper; therefore this is the substitution effect.
   d. The consumer consumes 10 more units of Y because it has become relatively more expensive; therefore this is the income effect.

9. In the study of the "buying" behavior of two white rats, as the "relative price" of one beverage was raised,
   a. one white rat began to consume more of the higher priced beverage and the other began to consume less.
   b. both white rats began to consume less of the higher priced beverage.
   c. both white rats began to consume more of the higher priced beverage.
   d. both white rats continued consuming the same amount of the beverage as before its price was raised.

10. Which of the following statements is false?
    a. If Tracy receives 30 utils from consuming one hamburger and 55 utils from consuming two hamburgers, the marginal utility of the second hamburger is 25 utils.
    b. The law of diminishing marginal utility says that the more of a particular good one consumes, the more utility one receives from the consumption of that good.
    c. The consumption of gold probably takes place at relative high marginal utility, since there is little gold in the world.
    d. b and c
    e. none of the above

11. We would expect the total utility of diamonds to be _________ than the total utility of water, and the marginal utility of diamonds to be _________ than the marginal utility of water.
    a. higher; higher
    b. lower; lower
    c. higher; lower
    d. lower; higher

12. In order for an individual to achieve consumer equilibrium through the consumption of two goods, A and B, that individual must fulfill the condition
    a. $TU_A = TU_B$
    b. $TU_A/P_A = TU_B/P_B$
    c. $MU_A = MU_B$
    d. $MU_A/P_A = MU_B/P_B$
    e. $MU_B/P_A = MU_A/P_B$

13. If the marginal utility of a good is negative, then consumers
    a. should buy less of it.
    b. will only consume it if it is free.
    c. should buy more of it to make its marginal utility rise.
    d. either b or c
    e. none of the above

14. If total utility of a good is high while the price of the good is low, it is likely that the good
    a. is plentiful.
    b. is inferior.
    c. is rare.
    d. has high marginal utility.

15. Real income is
    a. income adjusted for price changes.
    b. the amount of money a person earns in a year.
    c. income after taxes.
    d. the amount of money a person spends in a year.
    e. none of the above

True-False

Write "T" or "F" after each statement.

16. One makes an interpersonal utility comparison if he or she compares the utility one person receives from a good with the utility another person receives from the same good. ____

17. That portion of the change in quantity demanded of a good that is attributable to a change in its relative price is called the substitution effect. ____

18. A consumer is in disequilibrium if she receives different marginal utility per dollar for different goods she purchases. ____

19. Total utility may increase as marginal utility decreases. ____

20. The law of diminishing marginal utility can be used to make interpersonal utility comparisons. ____

Fill in the Blank

Write the correct word in the blank.

21. The ________________ – ________________ ________________ states that that which sometimes has great value in use has little value in exchange, and that which has little value in use sometimes has great value in exchange.

22. When the consumer has spent all his income, and the marginal utilities per dollar spent on each good purchased are equal, the consumer is said to be in ________________.

23. That portion of the change in the quantity demanded of a good that is attributable to a change in real income (brought about by a change in absolute price) is called the ________________ ________________.

24. Prices reflect ________________ ________________.

25. If total utility for two units of a good is more than double what it is for one unit, then the marginal utility of the second unit is ________________ than the marginal utility of the first unit.

Chapter 7
The Firm

What This Chapter Is About

This chapter is about the firm—why the firm exists, different types of firms, how firms finance their activities, and more.

Key Concepts in the Chapter

a. market coordination
b. managerial coordination
c. shirking
d. separation of ownership from control

- **Market coordination** is the process by which individuals perform tasks, such as producing certain quantities of goods, based on changes in market forces.
- **Managerial coordination** is the process by which managers direct employees to perform certain tasks.
- **Shirking** refers to the behavior of a worker who is putting forth less than the agreed-effort.
- **Separation of ownership from control** refers to the division of interests between owners and managers that may occur in large business firms.

Review Questions

1. Give an example of market coordination.

2. Give an example of managerial coordination.

3. According to Alchian and Demsetz, what condition is necessary before teams (firms) are formed?

4. What affects how much a person shirks?

5. What is a residual claimant?

6. How might above-market wages influence shirking?

7. There are markets inside and outside the firm. Explain.

8. What is the difference between satisficing behavior and trying to maximize profits?

9. What does it mean to say a sole proprietor has unlimited liability?

10. What are the disadvantages of a partnership?

11. What are the disadvantages of a corporation?

12. What is the difference between limited liability and unlimited liability?

13. What does the net worth of a firm equal?

14. What is the difference between a person that buys a bond issued by Corporation X and a person who buys shares of stock in Corporation X?

15. What is the difference between a nonprofit firm and a business firm?

Problems

1. Fill in the blank spaces in the table.

Type of firm	Example
Proprietorship	
Partnership	
Corporation	

2. Fill in the blank spaces in the table.

Advantages of proprietorships	Disadvantages of proprietorships
1.	1.
2.	2.
3.	3.

3. Fill in the blank spaces in the table.

Assets ($ millions)	Liabilities ($ millions)	Net worth ($ millions)
10	7	
100	65	
198	77	

4. Fill in the blank spaces in the table.

Face value of bond	Coupon rate	Annual coupon payments
$10,000	5.0 percent	
$20,000	7.5 percent	
$10,000	6.5 percent	

What Is the Question?
Identify the question for each of the answers that follow.

1. These economists suggest that firms are formed when benefits can be obtained from individuals working as a team.

2. The process in which managers direct employees to perform certain tasks.

3. This rises as the cost of shirking falls.

4. This is the person in a business firm who coordinates team production and reduces shirking.

5. Persons who share in the profits of a business firm.

6. Richard Cyert, James March, and Herbert Simon.

7. This type of business firm generated the largest percentage of total business receipts.

8. One advantage is that they are easy to form and to dissolve.

9. One disadvantage is that profits are taxed twice.

10. It is also known as equity.

11. Assets minus liabilities.

What Is Wrong ?

In each of the statements that follow, something is wrong. Identify what is wrong in the space provided.

1. Alchian and Demsetz argue that firms are formed when there are benefits to forming firms.

2. Five people form a firm and decide to equally split the proceeds of what they produce and sell. The individual costs of shirking are lower in this setting than in a setting where ten people form a firm and decide to equally split the proceeds of what they produce and sell.

3. Economists who advance the efficiency wage theory argue that paying employees above-market wage rates will cause them to shirk more than if they were simply paid market wage rates.

4. Partnerships are the most common form of business organization in the United States.

5. Assets plus liabilities equal net worth.

6. Total liabilities plus net worth equal accounts payable.

7. When a person buys a share of stock issued by a firm, the person effectively grants a loan to the firm.

8. There are fewer residual claimants in a business firm than in a nonprofit firm.

9. In private and public nonprofit firms, taxpayers pay the costs of the firm.

Multiple Choice

Circle the correct answer.

1. "The market guides and coordinates individuals' actions." Which of the following is an example of this happening?
   a. An employer tells an employee to come to work on Saturday instead of Friday.
   b. The manager of a plant issues a directive that there will be no more smoking inside or outside the plant.
   c. The price of computers rises, the profit from producing computers rises, and more firms end up producing computers.
   d. a and c
   e. a, b, and c

2. Economists Alchian and Demsetz suggest that firms are formed when
   a. people demand goods.
   b. the sum of what individuals can produce alone is greater than what they can produce as a team.
   c. capital gains taxes are lowered.
   d. the sum of what individuals can produce as a team is greater than what they can produce alone.
   e. c and d

3. In which setting is there likely to be the least amount of shirking?
   a. Fifty individuals decide to work together to produce shoes; they decide to split the proceeds equally.
   b. Harrison works for himself producing watches.
   c. Nineteen individuals decide to work together to produce book covers; they decide to split the proceeds equally.
   d. a and c, since the costs of shirking are equally low in these two settings.

4. Some persons argue that the monitor-employee relationship is one of the monitor exploiting the employee. The "theory of the firm" proposed in the text, however, comes closer to being one where the monitor-employee relationship is one of
   a. shared residual claimant status.
   b. mutual trust.
   c. mutual benefit.
   d. shared decision-making.

5. Economist ________ has argued that firms seek to maximize sales.
   a. Richard Cyert
   b. William Baumol
   c. James March
   d. Herbert Simon

6. As a percentage of U.S. firms, which type of business firm is least common?
   a. proprietorships
   b. partnerships
   c. corporations
   d. nonprofit corporations

7. Which of the following is not an advantage of the partnership form of organization?
   a. ease of organization
   b. benefits of specialization
   c. unlimited life
   d. absence of double taxation of profits

8. Limited liability is one of the advantages of a
   a. proprietorship.
   b. partnership.
   c. corporation.
   d. b and c
   e. none of the above

9. What does "separation of ownership from control" refer to?
   a. It refers to the unlimited liability provision of proprietorships.
   b. It refers to some persons in a firm having more decision-making authority than others; for example, the president has more decision-making authority than the vice president of finance.
   c. It refers to the owners of the corporation being different persons from the managers who control it on a day-to-day basis.
   d. It refers to the fact that many firms are physically so large that they are impossible to control on a day-to-day basis.

10. Which of the following statements is true?
    a. A person who buys a bond always pays more than the face value for the bond.
    b. If a corporation issues a bond and you purchase it, you become one of the owners of the corporation.
    c. A stockholder of Firm X does not have an ownership right in Firm X.
    d. If the coupon rate on a bond is 11 percent, this means the owner of the bond receives periodic payments equal to the coupon rate times the price he paid for the bond (whether or not the price he paid for the bond equals the face value of the bond).
    e. none of the above.

11. Which of the following is true?
    a. There are residual claimants in nonprofit firms.
    b. A police force that receives state-appropriated funds is a private nonprofit firm.
    c. A charitable organization is considered a profit firm.
    d. a and b
    e. none of the above.

12. A partnership is a form of business that is owned by
    a. two or more co-owners, who share any profits the business earns and who are legally responsible for any debts incurred by the firm.
    b. a single owner, who keeps all the profits and incurs all the losses.
    c. five or more equal shareholders who have unlimited responsibility.
    d. a group of proprietors who act in their mutual best interest before worker union groups.
    e. none of the above.

13. Assets minus liabilities equals net
    a. worth.
    b. margin.
    c. product.
    d. profit.

14. A thing of value to which a firm has a legal claim is called
    a. an estate.
    b. a factor.
    c. a resource.
    d. an asset.

15. The major disadvantage of a corporation is
    a. the double taxation of corporate income or profits.
    b. its large size.
    c. the social pressures placed upon it.
    d. the government regulations it must submit to.

True-False
Write "T" or "F" at the end of each statement.

16. The invisible hand of the marketplace refers to market coordination and not managerial coordination. ____

17. The lower the cost of shirking, the more shirking, *ceteris paribus*. ____

18. A residual claimant receives the excess of revenues over costs as his or her income. ____

19. Herbert Simon has argued that firms do not try to maximize profits, but instead try to achieve some satisfactory target profit level. ____

20. One of the disadvantages of corporations is that their profits are taxed twice. ____

Fill in the Blank
Write the correct word in the blank.

21. ________________ ________________ is a legal term that signifies that the personal assets of the owners(s) of a firm may be used to pay off the debts of the firm.

22. A ________________ is a legal entity that can conduct business in its own name the way an individual does.

23. Nonprofit firms are firms in which there are no ________________ ________________.

24. In a ________________ ________________ there are usually general partners and limited partners.

25. ________________ ________________ assures the owners that if the corporation should incur debts that it cannot pay, creditors do not have recourse to the owners' personal property for payment.

Chapter 8
Production and Costs

What This Chapter Is About

This chapter deals with the production and cost side of the firm. In later chapters, the revenue side of the firm will be discussed.

Key Concepts in the Chapter

a. explicit cost
b. implicit cost
c. normal profit
d. sunk cost
e. fixed costs
f. variable costs
g. marginal cost
h. law of diminishing marginal returns
i. average-marginal rule

- An **explicit cost** is a cost that is incurred when an actual monetary payment is made.
- An **implicit cost** is a cost that represents the value of resources used in production for which no actual monetary payment is made.
- **Normal profit** is zero economic profit. A firm that earns normal profit is earning revenues equal to its total opportunity costs (explicit plus implicit costs).
- **Sunk cost** is a cost incurred in the past that cannot be changed by current decisions and therefore cannot be recovered.
- **Fixed costs** are costs that do not vary with output.
- **Variable costs** are costs that vary with output.
- **Marginal cost** is the change in total cost that results from a change in output. It is the additional cost of producing additional output.
- The **law of diminishing marginal returns** states that as ever larger amounts of a variable input are combined with fixed inputs, eventually the marginal physical product of the variable input will decline.
- The **average-marginal rule** states that if the marginal magnitude is below the average magnitude, the average magnitude is declining; if the marginal magnitude is above the average magnitude, the average magnitude is rising.

Review Questions

1. Give an example of an explicit cost.

2. Give an example of an implicit cost.

3. Why is economic profit smaller than accounting profit?

4. A firm that earns zero economic profit is likely to stay in business. Why?

5. Give an example of sunk cost.

6. When making decisions, economists say it is better to ignore sunk cost. Give an example that illustrates why it would be better to ignore sunk cost than not to ignore it.

7. Give an example of a fixed input.

8. Give an example of a variable input.

9. What is the difference between average total cost and marginal cost?

10. Give an example that illustrates the law of diminishing marginal returns.

11. How are diminishing marginal returns related to rising marginal cost?

12. What is the difference between marginal productivity and average productivity?

13. What do diminishing marginal returns (in production) have to do with rising average total costs?

14. Give an example that illustrates the average-marginal rule.

15. What is the long-run average total cost (LRATC) curve?

16. What does it mean if a firm experiences economies of scale?

17. Explain how a change in taxes can affect a firm's cost curves.

18. Why does the AFC curve continually decline over output?

Problems

1. Fill in the blanks in the table.

Explicit costs	Implicit costs	Total revenue	Economic profit	Accounting profit
$40,000		$100,000	$20,000	$60,000
	$30,000	$230,000	$50,000	
$30,000	$40,000	$300,000		

2. Fill in the blank spaces in the table.

Variable cost	Fixed cost	Units of output produced	Average variable cost	Average fixed cost
$500	$1,000	100		
$400	$500	200		
$1,000	$200	400		

3. Fill in the blank spaces in the table.

Variable cost	Fixed cost	Units of output produced	Average total cost
$500	$200	100	
$300	$400	50	
$400	$1,000	75	

4. Fill in the blank spaces in the table.

Average total cost is	Marginal cost is	Average total cost is (rising, fall, remaining unchanged)
$40	$45	
$30	$20	
$20	$37	

5. Fill in the blank spaces in the table.

Variable input (units)	Fixed input (units)	Quantity of output	Marginal physical product of variable input
0	1	0	0
1	1	20	
2	1	45	

6. Fill in the blank spaces in the table.

Marginal physical product (units)	Variable cost	Marginal cost
20	$400	
18	$360	
33	$660	

7. Diagrammatically represent a TFC curve. Explain why you drew the curve the way you did.

$

Q

8. Diagrammatically represent an AFC curve. Explain why you drew the curve the way you did.

9. In the following diagram the ATC curve is drawn. Draw the MC curve in relation to the ATC curve. Why did you draw the MC curve the way you did?

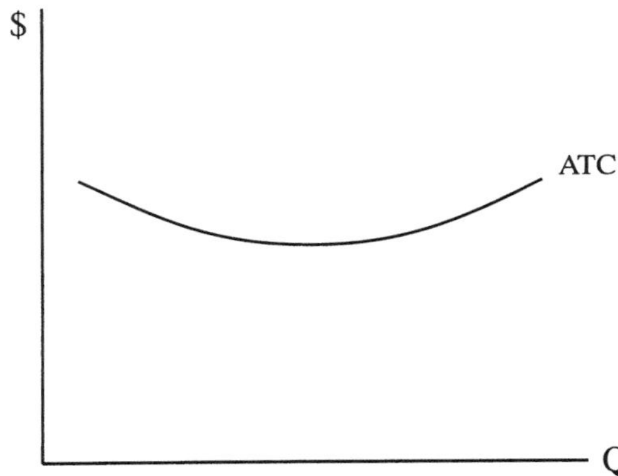

10. A firm initially faces increasing marginal returns, then constant marginal returns, and finally diminishing marginal returns. Draw the marginal cost curve that would reflect these changes in production. Explain why you drew the MC curve the way you did.

What Is the Question?
Identify the question for each of the answers that follow.

1. A cost that is incurred when an actual monetary payment is made.

2. It is a cost that cannot be recovered.

3. When marginal physical product is rising, this cost is declining.

4. These costs do not vary with output.

5. Total cost divided by output.

6. When this cost is above average total cost, average total cost is rising.

7. As output increases, the difference between average variable cost and this cost becomes smaller.

8. The lowest output level at which average total costs are minimized.

9. This exists when inputs are increased by some percentage and output increases by a smaller percentage, causing unit costs to rise.

What Is Wrong?

In each of the statements or diagrams that follow, something is wrong. Identify what is wrong in the space provided.

1. Economic profit is the difference between total revenue and explicit costs.

2. When a firm earns zero economic profit it has not covered its total opportunity costs.

3. The difference between the ATC curve and the AVC curve gets larger as output rises.

4. Marginal physical product is equal to output divided by units of the variable input.

5. When marginal physical product falls, marginal cost falls, too.

6.

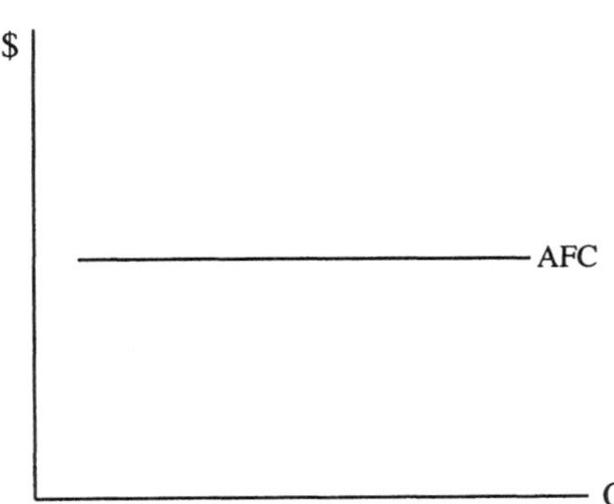

7.

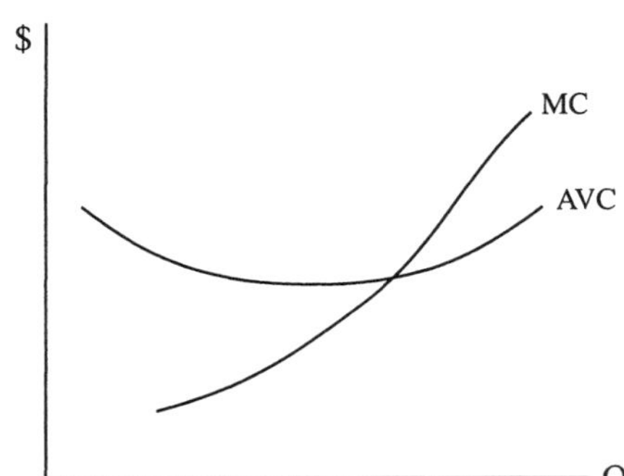

8.

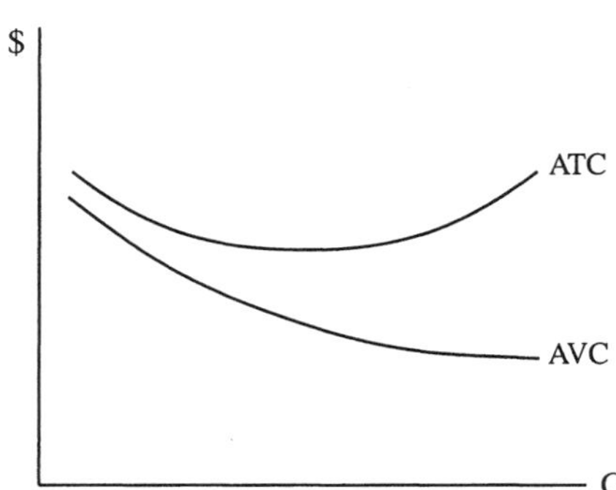

9.

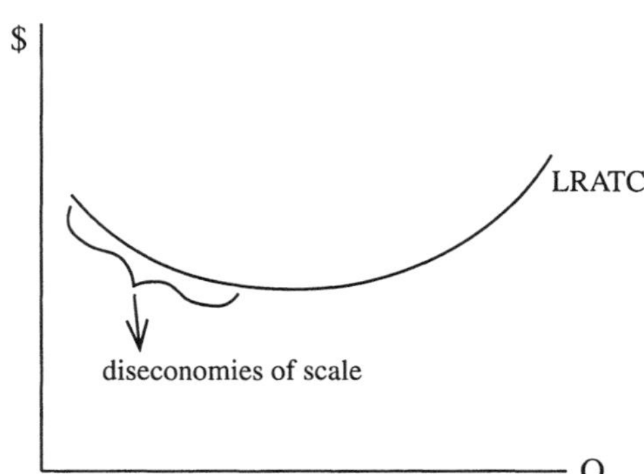

Multiple Choice
Circle the correct answer.

1. Which of the following statements is true?
   a. Implicit costs are necessarily higher than explicit costs.
   b. Explicit costs are necessarily higher than implicit costs.
   c. Tammy owns a restaurant; she paid Jack $15,000 for the curtains he installed in the restaurant. The $15,000 for curtains is an explicit cost.
   d. An implicit cost is a cost that represents actual monetary payment.
   e. none of the above

2. Which of the following is false?
   a. Economic profit is always higher than accounting profit.
   b. Accounting profit is the difference between total revenue and explicit costs.
   c. Economic profit is the difference between total revenue and implicit costs.
   d. a and c
   e. a, b, and c

3. Here is some information that relates to a business Max opened last year (all data relate to a year): price = $5; quantity sold = 15,000; implicit cost = $4,500; explicit cost = $8,500. What did economic profits equal for the year?
   a. $66,500
   b. $62,000
   c. $52,000
   d. $70,500

4. You purchased a lamb chop from the grocery store yesterday for $5. The store has a no-return policy. The $5 purchase of the lamb chop is best described as
   a. an average cost.
   b. a normal cost.
   c. a sunk cost.
   d. a low fixed cost.

5. Evie recently went into the business of producing and selling greeting cards. For this business, which of the following is likely to be a fixed cost?
   a. paper costs
   b. labor costs
   c. the six-month lease for the factory
   d. long distance telephone costs
   e. a, b, and d

6. Which of the following statements is true?
   a. Since fixed costs are constant as output changes in the short run, it follows that average fixed cost is constant in the short run, too.
   b. Marginal cost is the additional cost of producing an additional unit of output.
   c. Changes in variable costs are reflected dollar-for-dollar in total cost.
   d. b and c
   e. a and b

7. The law of diminishing marginal returns states that
   a. as ever larger amounts of a variable input are combined with fixed inputs, eventually the marginal physical product of the variable input will increase.
   b. as ever smaller amounts of a variable input are combined with fixed inputs, eventually the marginal physical product of the variable input will increase.
   c. as ever larger amounts of a fixed input are combined with a variable input, eventually the marginal physical product of the fixed input will decline.
   d. as ever larger amounts of a variable input are combined with a fixed input, eventually the marginal physical product of the variable input will decline

8. The production of a good usually requires two types of inputs,
   a. variable and fixed.
   b. long-run and short-run.
   c. total and unit.
   d. sunk and fixed.
   e. none of the above

Exhibit A

(1) Variable input	(2) Fixed input	(3) Quantity of output	(4) MPP of variable input
0	1	0	
1	1	40	A
2	1	62	B
3	1	80	C
4	1	96	D
5	1	106	E
6	1	114	F

Note: MPP = marginal physical product

9. In Exhibit A above, the numbers that go in blanks A and B are, respectively,
   a. 40; 22
   b. 0; 22
   c. 20; 20
   d. 1; 2
   e. 20; 22

10. In Exhibit A above, the numbers that go in blanks C and D are, respectively,
    a. 18; 16
    b. 20; 16
    c. 40; 184
    d. 20; 22
    e. none of the above

11. If the average variable cost curve is falling,
    a. the marginal cost (MC) curve must be above it.
    b. MC must be less than AVC.
    c. the MC curve is necessarily rising.
    d. the MC curve is horizontal (neither rising nor falling).

Exhibit B

(1) Variable input	(2) Price per variable input	(3) Fixed cost	(4) Output	(5) Marginal cost
1	$15	$100	30	
2	$15	$100	31	A
3	$15	$100	33	B
4	$15	$100	36	C
5	$15	$100	38	D

12. In Exhibit B above, the dollar amounts that go in blanks A and B are, respectively,
    a. $10.00; $7.50
    b. $10.00; $5.00
    c. $15.00; $7.50
    d. $5.00; $5.00
    e. $2.00; $12.00

13. In Exhibit B above, the dollar amounts that go in blanks C and D are, respectively,
    a. $5.00; $7.50
    b. $10.00; $3.33
    c. $5.00; $10.00
    d. $10.00; $10.00
    e. $9.33; $10.00

14. If, in the production process, inputs are increased by 18 percent and output increases by more than 18 percent, ____________ are said to exist.
    a. economies of scale
    b. diminishing marginal returns
    c. diseconomies of scale
    d. constant returns to scale
    e. none of the above

15. If, in the production process, inputs are increased by 10 percent and output increases by less than 10 percent, ____________ are said to exist.
    a. economies of scale
    b. diminishing marginal returns
    c. diseconomies of scale
    d. constant returns to scale
    e. none of the above

True-False
Write "T" or "F" at the end of each statement.

16. Accounting profit equals economic profit if there are no implicit costs. ____

17. Accounting profit is the difference between total revenue and explicit costs. ____

18. A firm that earns zero economic profit is earning a normal profit. ____

19. In the long run, there are only fixed costs. ____

20. The average-marginal rule states that if the marginal magnitude is below the average magnitude, the average magnitude rises. ____

Fill in the Blank
Write the correct word in the blank.

21. The ____________ – ____________ ______________ ______________ ______________ curve shows the lowest unit cost at which the firm can produce any given level of output.

22. The ______________ ______________ ______________ is the lowest output level at which average total costs are minimized.

23. If inputs are increased by some percentage and output increases by a smaller percentage, unit costs ____________, and ______________ ________ ______________ are said to exist.

24. Assume labor and some fixed input are used to produce good X. As the marginal physical product of labor increases, marginal cost ____________.

25. The ______________ ______________ ______________ of the variable input is equal to the change in output that results from changing the variable input by one unit, holding all other inputs fixed.

Chapter 9
Perfect Competition

What This Chapter Is About

Beginning in this chapter, and continuing for the next two chapters, market structures are discussed. Think of a market structure as the setting in which a firm finds itself. That setting relates to the number of buyers and sellers in the market, the good being produced, whether or not there is easy entry into the market, and more.

Key Concepts in the Chapter

a. price taker
b. marginal revenue
c. profit-maximization rule
d. resource allocative efficiency

- A **price taker** is a seller that does not have the ability to control the price of the product it sells; it takes the price determined in the market.
- **Marginal revenue** is the change in total revenue that results from selling one additional unit of output.
- The **profit-maximization rule** states that profit is maximized by producing the quantity at which MR = MC.
- **Resource allocative efficiency** exists when the firm produces the quantity of output at which price equals marginal cost, P = MC.

Review Questions

1. What are the four assumptions in the theory of perfect competition?

2. Firm A is a price taker when it comes to selling its good. What does this mean?

3. Why are the demand curve and marginal revenue curve the same curve for the perfectly competitive firm?

4. Explain why a perfectly competitive firm is resource-allocative efficient.

5. The MR curve is downward sloping and the MC curve is upward sloping. Why will a profit-maximizing firm produce the quantity of output at which MR = MC instead of producing the quantity of output at which there is the greatest difference between MR and MC?

6. What does a firm consider when deciding whether or not to shut down (its operation) in the short run?

7. If a firm produces the quantity of output at which MR = MC, is it guaranteed to earn profit? Explain your answer.

8. The firm's supply curve is that portion of its MC curve that is above its AVC curve. Why isn't the entire MC curve the firm's supply curve instead of only a portion of it?

9. How is the market supply curve derived?

10. What is the link between the market supply curve and the law of diminishing marginal returns?

11. What conditions does a perfectly competitive firm satisfy when it is in long-run equilibrium?

12. If price is above short-run average total cost, the perfectly competitive firm is not in long-run equilibrium. Why?

13. If SRATC is greater than LRATC, the perfectly competitive firm is not in long-run equilibrium. Why?

14. What is a constant cost industry?

15. There are positive economic profits in a perfectly competitive market. Explain what happens as a result.

16. Will a perfectly competitive firm advertise its product? Why or why not?

17. Firm X is not productive efficient. What does this mean?

Problems

1. Fill in the blank spaces in the table.

Price	Quantity	Total revenue	Marginal revenue
$10	1		
$10	2		
$10	3		

2. Assuming the firm is a perfectly competitive firm, fill in the blank spaces in the table.

Price	Quantity	Total revenue
$40		$4,000
	50	
	80	

3. Assuming the firm is a perfectly competitive firm, fill in the blank spaces in the table.

Price	Quantity	Marginal revenue
$15	1	
	2	
	3	

4. Fill in the blank spaces in the table.

Price	Quantity	Average variable cost	Average total cost	Total variable cost	Will the firm (continue to produce, shut down)
$10	100	$7	$9		
$15	50	$13	$16		
$23	1,000	$24	$26		

5. Fill in the blank spaces in the table.

Price	Quantity	Average variable cost	Average total cost	Average fixed cost	Total cost
$10	100	$4	$6		
$40	2,000	$45	$46		
$25	198	$21	$23		

6. Fill in the blank spaces in the table.

Price	Marginal cost	ATC	Is the perfectly competitive firm earning profits? (yes, no)	Is the perfectly competitive firm in long-run equilibrium? (yes, no)
$40	$40	$30		
$30	$30	$35		
$25	$25	$23		

7. Fill in the blank spaces in the table.

Price	Quantity	ATC	AVC	Profit (+) or Loss (–)
$33	1,234	$31	$30	
$55	2,436	$25	$20	
$100	1,000	$110	$99	

What Is the Question?

1. A seller that does not have the ability to control the price of the product it sells.

2. The firm sells its good at market equilibrium price.

3. When price is below average variable cost.

4. That portion of its MC curve above its AVC curve.

5. The horizontal summation of the individual firms' supply curves.

6. There is no incentive for firms to enter or exit the industry, there is no incentive for firms to produce more or less output, and there is no incentive for firms to change plant size.

7. P = SRATC, P = MC, and SRATC = LRATC.

8. The long-run supply curve is upward sloping.

9. The long-run supply curve is downward-sloping.

10. P = MC.

11. The firm produces its output at the lowest possible per-unit cost.

What Is Wrong?

In each of the statements that follow, something is wrong. Identify what is wrong in the space provided.

1. Firms in a perfectly competitive market have easy entry into the market and costly exit from the market.

2. In long-run competitive equilibrium, the average or representative firm may earn positive economic profit.

3. Price is greater than marginal revenue for a perfectly competitive firm.

4. A perfectly competitive firm will shut down in the short run if its price is below average total cost.

5. If a firm produces the quantity of output at which MR = MC, it is guaranteed to earn profits.

6. The market supply curve is the vertical summation of the individual firms' supply curves.

7. If SRATC = LRATC for a firm, there is no incentive for the firm to enter or exit the industry.

8. The long-run supply curve is downward-sloping for an increasing cost industry.

9. When average fixed cost is positive, average total cost is usually, but not always, greater than average variable cost.

10. A firm that produces its output at the lowest possible per unit cost is said to exhibit resource allocative efficiency.

Multiple Choice
Circle the correct answer.

1. Which of the following is one of the assumptions upon which the theory of perfect competition is built?
   a. there are few buyers and few sellers
   b. there are many buyers and few sellers
   c. there are few buyers and many sellers
   d. there are many buyers and many sellers

2. Which of the following markets comes closest to being a perfectly competitive market?
   a. the corn market
   b. the cigarette market
   c. the insurance market
   d. the soft drink market

3. In a perfectly competitive market there are
   a. neither barriers to entry nor to exit.
   b. barriers to entry, but not to exit.
   c. barriers to exit, but not to entry.
   d. barriers to both entry and exit.

4. A firm that is a price taker is a firm that
   a. has the ability to control the price of the product it sells.
   b. has the ability, albeit limited, to control the price of the product it sells.
   c. can raise the price of the product it sells and still sell some units of its product.
   d. sells a high-quality product.
   e. none of the above

5. Which of the following statements is true?
   a. In the theory of perfect competition, the single firm's demand curve is downward-sloping.
   b. In the theory of perfect competition, the market demand curve is downward-sloping.
   c. In the theory of perfect competition, the single firm's demand curve is horizontal.
   d. In the theory of perfect competition, the market demand curve is horizontal.
   e. b and c

6. If the firm produces the quantity of output at which marginal revenue (MR) equals marginal cost (MC), is it guaranteed of maximizing profit?
   a. Yes, when MR=MC, it follows that total revenue (TR) is greater than total cost (TC), and thus the firm maximizes profit.
   b. Yes, since it is always the case that if the MC curve is rising, the average variable total cost curve lies below it and thus profit is earned.
   c. No, when the firm produces the quantity at which MR = MC, it could be the case that average total cost is greater than price. If this is the case, the firm will take a loss, not earn a profit.
   d. No, at the quantity of output at which MR = MC, it could be the case that average total cost is greater than price. If this is the case, the firm will take a loss, not earn a profit.

7. Consider the following data: equilibrium price = $12, quantity of output produced = 100 units, average total cost = $9, and average variable cost = $6. Given this, total revenue is _________, total cost is _________ and fixed cost is _________.
   a. $1,200; $900; $300
   b. $1,200; $700; $100
   c. $1,200; $900; $600
   d. $1,000; $800; $200
   e. none of the above

8. Consider the following data: equilibrium price = $12, quantity of output produced = 50 units, average total cost = $9, and average variable cost = $8. What will the firm do, and why?
   a. Shut down in the short run, since it is taking a loss of $150.
   b. Continue to produce in the short run, since firms are always stuck with having to produce in the short run.
   c. Shut down in the short run, since average total cost is greater than average variable cost.
   d. Continue to produce in the short run, since price is greater than average variable cost.

9. The perfectly competitive firm's short-run supply curve is that portion of its
   a. average variable cost curve above its marginal revenue curve.
   b. marginal cost curve above its average total cost curve.
   c. marginal cost curve above its average variable cost curve.
   d. average total cost curve above price.
   e. none of the above

10. Which of the following conditions does not characterize long-run competitive equilibrium?
    a. Economic profit is positive.
    b. Firms are producing the quantity of output at which price is greater than marginal cost.
    c. No firm has an incentive to change its plant size.
    d. a and b
    e. a, b and c

11. The following holds: (1) there is no incentive for firms to enter or exit the industry; (2) for some firms in the industry short-run average total cost is greater than long-run average total cost at the level of output where marginal revenue equals marginal cost; (3) all firms in the industry are currently producing the quantity of output at which marginal revenue equals marginal cost; (4) all firms in the industry are producing a homogeneous product. Is the industry in long-run competitive equilibrium?
    a. Yes.
    b. No, because of numbers 1 and 2.
    c. No, because of numbers 2 and 3.
    d. No, because of number 2.
    e. No, because of numbers 1, 2, 3 and 4.

12. An increasing-cost industry has a long-run (industry) supply curve that is
    a. upward-sloping
    b. downward-sloping
    c. horizontal
    d. vertical

13. Demand increases in a decreasing-cost industry that is initially in long-run competitive equilibrium. After full adjustment, price will be
    a. equal to its original level.
    b. below its original level.
    c. above its original level.
    d. There is not enough information to answer the question.

14. The change in total revenue which results from selling one additional unit of output is called
    a. average revenue.
    b. median revenue.
    c. marginal revenue.
    d. standard revenue.

15. Which of the following conditions about a firm in long-run competitive equilibrium is false?
    a. P = AVC
    b. P = MC
    c. P = SRATC
    d. P = LRATC

True-False

Write "T" or "F" after each statement.

16. A real-world market has to meet all the assumptions of the theory of perfect competition before the theory predicts well. ____

17. In the theory of perfect competition, price is greater than marginal revenue. ____

18. A perfectly competitive firm is a price searcher. ____

19. A decreasing-cost industry is an industry in which average total costs decrease as industry output increases. ____

20. If price is above average total costs, the firm earns profits and will continue to operate in the short run. ____

Fill in the Blank

Write the correct word in the blank.

21. A firm that produces the quantity of output at which price equals marginal cost is said to exhibit ______________ ______________ ______________.

22. In the long run in perfect competition, profits are ______________.

23. Firms attempt to produce that quantity of output at which (the condition) __________ = __________ holds.

24. The firm's ______________ – ____________ ______________ curve is that portion of its marginal cost curve that lies above the average variable cost curve.

25. The greater the fixed cost-total cost ratio, the ______________ likely the firm will operate in the short run.

Chapter 10
Monopoly

What This Chapter Is About
This chapter discusses the theory of monopoly.

Key Concepts in the Chapter

a. price searcher
b. deadweight loss of monopoly
c. rent seeking

- A **price searcher** is a seller that has the ability to control to some degree the price of the product it sells.
- **Deadweight loss of monopoly** refers to the net value of the difference between the monopoly quantity of output and the competitive quantity of output.
- **Rent seeking** refers to the actions of individuals and groups who spend resources to influence public policy in the hope of redistributing (transferring) income to themselves from others.

Review Questions

1. What are the three assumptions of the theory of monopoly?

2. What is a natural monopoly?

3. Why is a monopoly a price searcher?

4. How does the monopoly seller decide what quantity of output to produce?

5. Compared with a perfectly competitive seller, a monopoly seller produces too little output and charges too high a price. Explain.

6. Economist Gordon Tullock has argued that rent-seeking behavior is individually rational but socially wasteful. What does this mean?

7. Identify and define the three types of price discrimination.

8. What are the necessary conditions for price discrimination?

9. Is the perfectly price-discriminating monopolist resource allocative efficient? Explain your answer.

Problems

1. Fill in the blank spaces in the table.

Price	Quantity	Total revenue	Marginal revenue
$10	1		
$9	2		
$8	3		

2. Using the diagram that follows, identify the consumers' surplus under perfect competition and monopoly.

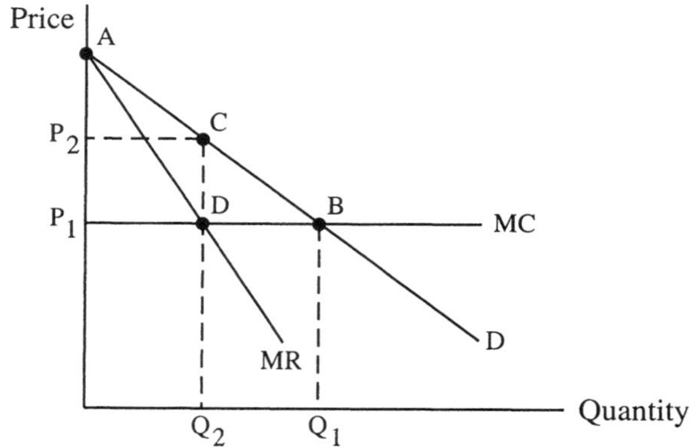

Consumers' surplus under perfect competition = ________________

Consumers' surplus under monopoly = ________________

3. Using the diagram that follows, identify the deadweight loss triangle of monopoly.

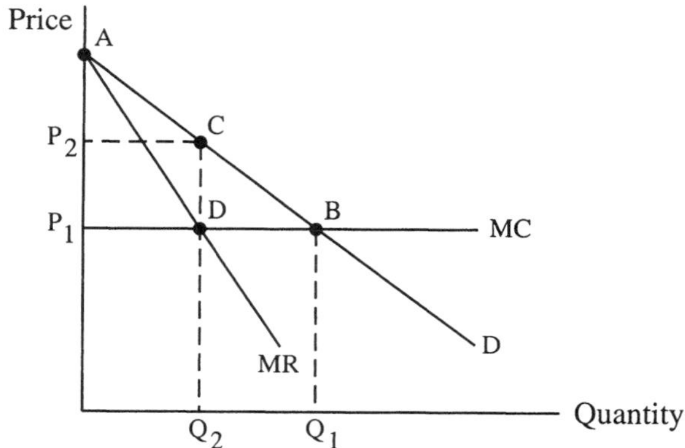

4. Diagrammatically represent the quantity of output the monopolist produces and the price it charges.

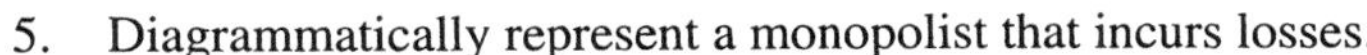

5. Diagrammatically represent a monopolist that incurs losses.

What Is the Question?
Identify the question for each of the answers that follow.

1. A right granted to a firm by government that permits the firm to provide a particular good or service and excludes all others from doing the same.

2. An exclusive right to sell something.

3. Price is greater than marginal revenue.

4. Actions of individuals and groups who spend resources to influence public policy in the hope of redistributing (transferring) income to themselves from others.

5. This occurs when the seller charges a uniform price per unit for one specific quantity, a lower price for an additional quantity, and so on.

6. The increase in costs and organizational slack in a monopoly resulting from the lack of competitive pressure to push costs down to their lowest possible level.

7. Total revenue is greater if the monopolist can do this.

8. If it does this, the monopolist will be resource allocative efficient.

What Is Wrong?

In each of the statements that follow, something is wrong. Identify what is wrong in the space provided.

1. The single-price monopolist exhibits resource allocative efficiency.

2. One of the assumptions in the theory of monopoly is that the single seller sells a product for which there are no perfect substitutes.

3. For the monopolist, price is equal to marginal revenue.

4. If fixed costs exist, then a firm that maximizes revenue automatically maximizes profit, too.

5. The monopoly seller produces the quantity of output at which MR = P and charges the highest price per unit for this quantity.

6. A monopoly seller cannot incur losses, since it is the single seller of a good.

7. Perfect price discrimination occurs when the seller charges a uniform price per unit for one specific quantity, a lower price for an additional quantity, and so on.

8. A monopoly seller can charge any price it wants for the good it produces and sells.

Multiple Choice
Circle the correct answer.

1. Which of the following is *not* an assumption of the theory of monopoly?
   a. There is only one seller in the industry.
   b. The seller sells a product for which there are no close substitutes.
   c. The seller has high variable costs.
   d. There are high barriers to entry into the industry.

2. Which of the following is the best example of a barrier to entry into a monopolistic industry?
   a. diminishing returns
   b. economies of scale
   c. comparative advantage
   d. high elasticity of demand

3. In the United States, patents are granted to inventors of a product or process for a period of
   a. 2 years.
   b. 12 years.
   c. 20 years.
   d. 22 years.
   e. none of the above.

4. A price searcher
   a. faces a horizontal demand curve.
   b. is a seller that searches for good employees and pays them a low wage.
   c. is a seller that searches for the best price at which to buy its nonlabor inputs.
   d. is a seller that has the ability to control, to some degree, the price of the product it sells.
   e. a and c

5. Which of the following statements is true?
   a. A price searcher must raise price to sell an additional unit of its product.
   b. For a price searcher, price equals marginal revenue for all units except the first.
   c. For a price searcher, price is less than marginal revenue for all units except the first.
   d. A price searcher, like a price taker, produces that quantity of output for which marginal revenue equals marginal cost.
   e. c and d

6. The marginal revenue curve lies above the demand curve for a
   a. monopoly firm.
   b. price taker.
   c. price searcher.
   d. a and c
   e. none of the above

7. Economic or monopoly rent is a payment in excess of
   a. price.
   b. average variable cost.
   c. opportunity cost.
   d. explicit cost, but not necessarily a payment in excess of implicit cost.
   e. none of the above

8. When a seller charges different prices for the product he sells and the price differences do not reflect cost differences, the seller is engaging in
   a. rent seeking.
   b. arbitrage.
   c. the capitalization of profits.
   d. price discrimination.

9. A seller who charges the highest price each consumer would be willing to pay for the product rather than go without that product is practicing
   a. perfect price discrimination.
   b. disciplined price discrimination.
   c. ideal price discrimination.
   d. competitive price discrimination.

10. For a firm that perfectly price discriminates,
    a. price equals marginal revenue.
    b. price is less than marginal cost.
    c. price is greater than average total cost.
    d. There is not enough information to answer the question.

11. Which of the following is a rent-seeking activity?
    a. Carol produces shoes that will be purchased by the Army.
    b. Mick produces blankets that are sold in Egypt.
    c. Jackie produces suntan lotion that is sold exclusively in Hawaii.
    d. a and b
    e. none of the above

12. According to Gordon Tullock,
    a. monopoly profits or rents are subject to rent seeking.
    b. the welfare cost triangle is subject to rent seeking.
    c. X-inefficiency is something that differentiates government monopolies from private monopolies.
    d. the theory of monopoly is superior to the theory of perfect competition.

13. (Single-price) monopoly firms produce
    a. the resource allocative efficient output.
    b. more than the resource allocative efficient output.
    c. less that the resource allocative efficient output.
    d. where P = MC.

14. The monopolist will maximize profits at a level of output at which marginal revenue equals
    a. average fixed cost.
    b. average variable cost.
    c. average total cost.
    d. marginal cost.

15. Perfect price discrimination is sometimes called discrimination among
    a. buyers.
    b. sellers
    c. quantities.
    d. units.

True-False
Write "T" or "F" after each statement.

16. If a firm is a price searcher, it necessarily cannot price discriminate. ____

17. The revenue-maximizing price is the profit-maximizing price when there are no variable costs. ____

18. A monopoly firm charges a higher price and produces more output than a perfectly competitive firm with the same cost conditions. ____

19. Monopoly profits can turn out to be zero in the long run through the capitalization of profits. ____

20. In perfect competition, P = MC; in monopoly, P < MC. ____

Fill in the Blank
Write the correct word in the blank.

21. ________________ ________________ is the condition where economies of scale are so pronounced in an industry that only one firm can survive.

22. ________________ ________________ is a seller that has the ability to control to some degree the price of the product it sells.

23. Buying a good in a market where its price is low, and selling the good in another where its price is higher, is called ________________.

24. _____ – ________________ is the increase in costs and organization slack in a monopoly resulting from the lack of competitive pressure to push costs down to their lowest possible level.

25. The major developer of the theory or rent seeking is ________________ ________________.

Chapter 11
Monopolistic Competition, Oligopoly, and Game Theory

What This Chapter Is About
We have discussed two market structures so far—perfect competition and monopoly. In this chapter we discuss two more market structures—monopolistic competition and oligopoly. We also discuss game theory.

Key Concepts in the Chapter
a. monopolistic competition
b. oligopoly
c. game theory

- The theory of **monopolistic competition** is based on three assumptions: (1) many sellers and buyers, (2) firms produce and sell slightly differentiated products, (3) easy entry and exit.
- The theory of **oligopoly** is based on three assumptions: (1) few sellers and many buyers, (2) firms produce either homogeneous of differentiated products, (3) significant barriers to entry.
- **Game theory** is a mathematical technique used to analyze the behavior of decision makers who try to reach an optimal position for themselves through game playing or the use of strategic behavior, are fully aware of the interactive nature of the process at hand, and anticipate the moves of other decision makers.

Review Questions

1. What are the three assumptions of the theory of monopolistic competition?

2. How is a monopolistic competitor like a perfectly competitive firm?

3. How is a monopolistic competitor like a monopoly firm?

4. What quantity of output will the monopolistic competitor produce?

5. Is a monopolistic competitor resource allocative efficient? Explain your answer.

6. Why does a monopolistic competitor have excess capacity?

7. What are the three assumptions of the theory of oligopoly?

8. What is a four-firm concentration ratio?

9. What is the essence of the prisoner's dilemma game? Stated differently, how do we know something is a prisoner's dilemma game?

10. What is the objective of a cartel?

11. Why might cartel members try to cheat on each other (break their agreement not to compete)?

12. What conditions does a contestable market satisfy?

13. Explain the arms race between the U.S. and the (former) Soviet Union in game theoretic terms.

Problems

1. Diagrammatically represent a monopolistic competitive firm incurring losses.

Price

Quantity

2. Diagrammatically represent the excess capacity for a monopolistic competitive firm.

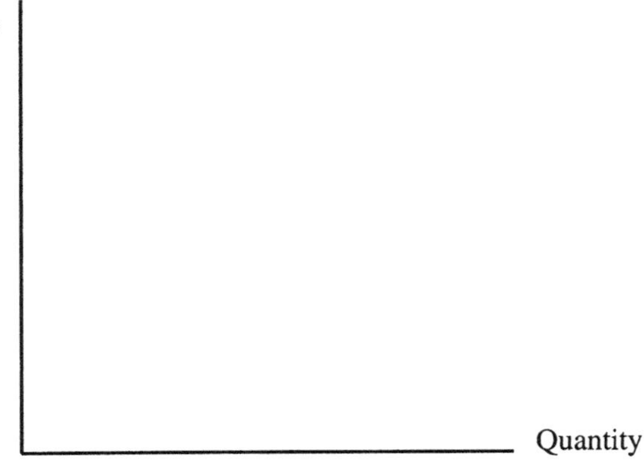

3. Several firms form a cartel. Before the cartel, each firm earns normal profit. As a part of the cartel, each firm charges P_1 in the diagram that follows. What are profits equal to for the firm that holds to the cartel? What are profits equal to for the firm if it cheats on the cartel agreement while no other firms cheat on the cartel agreement.

Profits if the firm holds to the cartel agreement =

____

Profits if the firm cheats on the cartel agreement while no other firms cheat on the agreement =

____

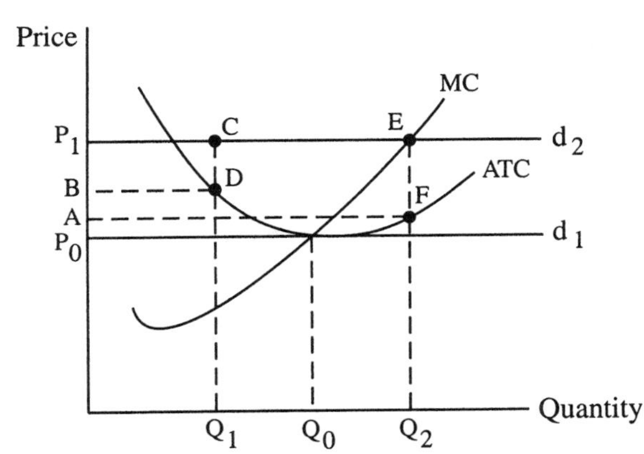

4. Give an example that illustrates how to compute the four-firm concentration ratio.

5. What are the four problems associated with a cartel?

What Is the Question?
Identify the question for each of the answers that follow.

1. States that a monopolistic competitor in equilibrium produces an output smaller than the one that would minimize its costs of production.

2. It does not produce at the lowest point on its ATC curve because the demand curve it faces is downward-sloping.

3. There are significant barriers to entry in this market structure.

4. Individually rational behavior leads to a jointly inefficient outcome.

5. The key behavioral assumption is that oligopolists in an industry act as if there is only one firm in the industry.

6. This is a way out of the prisoner's dilemma for two firms trying to form a cartel.

7. If a single firm lowers price, other firms will do likewise, but if a single firm raises price, other firms will not follow suit.

8. The theory fails to explain how the original price comes about.

9. One firm determines price and the all other firms take this price as given.

10. There is easy entry into the market and costless exit from the market, new firms entering the market can produce the product at the same cost as current firms, and firms exiting the market can easily dispose of their fixed assets by selling them elsewhere.

What Is Wrong?

In each of the statements that follow, something is wrong. Identify what is wrong in the space provided.

1. The monopolistic competitor is a price taker and the oligopolist is a price searcher.

2. For the monopolistic competitor, price lies below marginal revenue.

3. When profits are normal, the monopolistic competitor exhibits resource allocative efficiency.

4. The cartel theory assumes that firms in an oligopolistic industry act in a manner consistent with there being only a few firms in the industry.

5. The kinked demand curve theory assumes that if a single firm raises price, other firms will do likewise, but if a single firm lowers price, other firms will not follow.

6. The price leadership theory assumes that the dominant firm in the industry determines price and all other firms sell below this price.

7. Both monopolistic competitive firms and oligopolistic firms produce the quantity of output at which price equals marginal revenue.

8. A contestable market is one in which there is easy entry into the market and costless exit from the market, new firms entering the market can produce the product at the same costs as current firms, and firms exiting the market only have to suffer the loss of their fixed assets.

Multiple Choice

Circle the correct answer.

1. Which of the following is *not* an assumption of the theory of monopolistic competition?
   a. There are high barriers to entry.
   b. There are many sellers and many buyers.
   c. Each firm in the industry produces and sells a highly differentiated product.
   d. a and c
   e. all of the above

2. The monopolistic competitor
   a. is a price searcher.
   b. is a price taker.
   c. is a mix between a price taker and a price searcher (it has elements of competition and monopoly).
   d. produces that quantity of output at which MR > MC.

3. Total industry sales for Year 1 are $10 million. The top four firms, A, B, C, and D, account for sales of $2 million, $2.5 million, $3.1 million, and $0.5 million, respectively. What is the four-firm concentration ratio?
   a. 0.91
   b. 0.55
   c. 0.69
   d. 0.81
   e. none of the above

4. Concentration ratios are not perfect guides to industry concentration because they do not
   a. take into account foreign competition and competition from substitute goods.
   b. adjust for inflation.
   c. adjust for quality of products.
   d. adjust for price.

5. If a single firm lowers price, other firms will do likewise, but it a single firm raises price, other firms will not necessarily follow suit. This is the behavioral assumption in the
   a. cartel theory.
   b. price leadership theory.
   c. kinked demand curve theory.
   d. price discrimination theory.
   e. none of the above

6. Which of the following statements is true?
   a. According to the kinked demand curve theory, the marginal cost (MC) curve can shift within a certain region and the firm will continue to produce the same quantity but charge a different price.
   b. According to the kinked demand curve theory, the marginal cost (MC) curve can shift within a certain region and the firm will continue to produce the same quantity and charge the same price.
   c. According to the kinked demand curve theory, the demand curve can shift within a certain region and the firm will continue to produce the same quantity and charge the same price.
   c. According to the kinked demand curve theory, the demand curve can shift within a certain region and the firm will continue to produce the same quantity but charge a different price.

7. The top firm in the industry determines price and all other firms take this price as given. This is the behavioral assumption of the
   a. kinked demand curve theory.
   b. price leadership theory.
   c. both the cartel and price leadership theories.
   d. monopolistic competitive theory.

8. In the price leadership theory, at a price of $5 per unit, the fringe firms supply the entire market. At a price of $4, the (market) quantity demanded is 900 units and the quantity supplied by fringe firms is 430. Given this, which of the following quantity-price combinations is represented by a point on the dominant firm's demand curve?
   a. 1,330 units at $5
   b. 230 units at $4
   c. 470 units at $4
   d. 470 units at $5
   e. 1 unit at $5

9. The key behavioral assumption of the cartel theory is that oligopolists in an industry
   a. try to maximize revenue instead of profits.
   b. act as if they are perfect monopolistic competitors.
   c. act in a manner consistent with there being only one firm in the industry.
   d. try to manipulate government into subsidizing their activities.
   e. b and d

10. Which of the following is an example of an oligopoly?
    a. a law partnership
    b. a local gas company
    c. a dental firm
    d. General Motors Company
    e. none of the above

11. Product differentiation is most likely a form of
    a. advertising.
    b. nonprice competition.
    c. lowering variable costs.
    d. lowering the fixed costs to total cost ratio.
    e. none of the above

12. *Ceteris paribus*, the free rider problem is more serious
    a. the smaller the number of potential cartel members.
    b. the larger the number of potential cartel members.
    c. the higher total costs.
    d. the lower total costs.
    e. b and c

13. Which of the following statements is true?
    a. One of the developers of contestable markets theory is William Baldwin.
    b. Orthodox market structure theory places much greater weight than contestable markets theory on the number of firms in an industry as a major factor in determining a firm's behavior.
    c. Contestable markets theory emphasizes product differentiation; orthodox market structure theory does not.
    d. Contestable markets theory emphasizes nonprice competition; orthodox market structure theory does not.
    e. a and b

14. The prisoner's dilemma game illustrates that
    a. what is good for you and me individually may be bad for us collectively.
    b. what is good for me is good for you.
    c. cartels are likely to be stable in the long run.
    d. what is high is low and what is low is high.
    e. none of the above.

15. A monopolistic competitor has a demand curve that is
    a. more elastic than a perfectly competitive firm.
    b. less elastic than a perfectly competitive firm.
    c. less elastic than a monopoly firm.
    d. b and c

True-False

Write "T" or "F" after each statement.

16. There is easy entry but costly exit in monopolistic competition. ____

17. In monopolistic competition, the marginal revenue curve lies below the demand curve. ____

18. In equilibrium a monopolistic competitor produces an output smaller than the one that would minimize its costs of production.

19. Third-degree price discrimination is sometimes seen in the form of cents-off coupons. ____

20. There are few sellers and few buyers in oligopoly. ____

Fill in the Blank

Write the correct word in the blank.

21. The economist ________________ ________________ found no evidence that the oligopolists he examined were more reluctant to match price increases than price cuts.

22. A ______________ is an organization of firms that reduces output and increases price in an effort to increase joint profits.

23. Once a cartel agreement is made, there is an incentive for cartel members to ______________ on the agreement.

24. The ________________ ________________ ________________ states that a monopolistic competitor will, in equilibrium, produce an output smaller than the one at which average total costs (unit costs) are minimized.

25. The tactic of ___________ – ___________ – ___________ is possible in a contestable market.

Chapter 12
Government and Product Markets:
Antitrust and Regulation

What This Chapter Is About
This chapter deals with government involvement in product markets. Essentially, it looks at government's attempts to apply the antitrust laws and to regulate.

Key Concepts in the Chapter
a. antitrust law
b. network good
c. lock-in effect

- **Antitrust law** is legislation passed for the stated purpose of controlling monopoly power and preserving and promoting competition.
- A **network good** is a good whose value increases as the expected number of units sold increases.
- The **lock-in effect** is descriptive of the situation where a particular product or technology becomes settled upon as the standard and is difficult or impossible to dislodge as the standard.

Review Questions

1. What is exclusive dealing?

2. Of what relevance to antitrust policy is how broadly or narrowly a market is defined?

3. Give an example to illustrate how the Herfindahl index is computed.

4. What is the difference between a vertical merger and a horizontal merger?

5. What antitrust issue was relevant to the Utah pie case?

6. What is the relevance of switching costs to a network monopoly?

7. On May 18, 1998, the U.S. Justice Department issued a civil action complaint against Microsoft, Inc. What did the complaint charge?

8. Outline the details of the capture theory of regulation.

9. What is a criticism of profit regulation (with respect to a natural monopolist)?

10. How do economists view regulation? Are they pro-regulation, anti-regulation, or neither pro- nor anti-regulation? Explain your answer.

Problems

1. Fill in the blank spaces in the table.

Provision of the antitrust act	Name of the Act
Every person who shall monopolize, or attempt to monopolize, or combine or conspire with any other person or persons to monopolize any part of the trade or commerce…shall be guilty of a misdemeanor.	
Prohibits suppliers from offering special discounts to large chain stores unless they also offer the discounts to everyone else.	
Empowers the Federal Trade Commission to deal with false and deceptive acts or practices.	
Declares illegal unfair methods of competition in commerce.	
Declares illegal exclusive dealing and tying contracts.	

2. Fill in the blank spaces in the table.

Number of firms in the industry	Market shares of the firms, in order from top to bottom	Herfindahl index
6	20, 20, 20, 20, 10, 10	
10	20, 10, 10, 10, 10, 10, 10, 10, 5, 5	
10	10, 10, 10, 10, 10, 10, 10, 10, 10, 10	

3. Fill in the blank spaces in the table.

Proposed merger	What type of merger? (horizontal, vertical, conglomerate)
Between two firms, each of which produces and sells tires.	
Between two firms, one of which produces and sells houses and the other which produces and sells wood.	
Between two firms, one of which produces and sells books and one of which produces and sells bottled water.	

4. Using the diagram that follows, what price will the natural monopoly charge if it is resource allocative efficient?

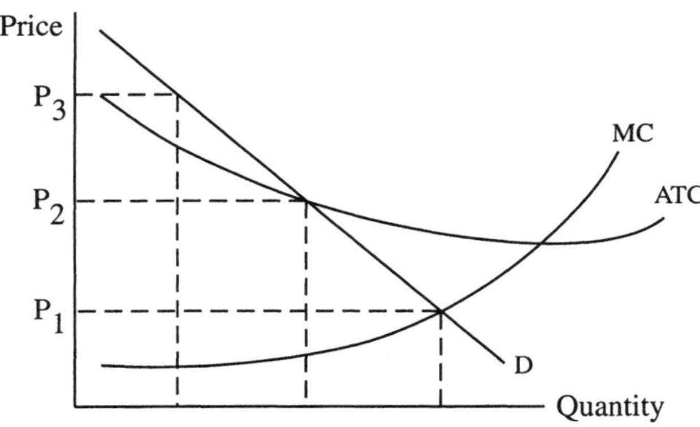

5. Using the diagram in question 4, what price will the natural monopoly charge under profit regulation?

6. Diagrammatically show that price regulation can lead to a natural monopoly incurring losses.

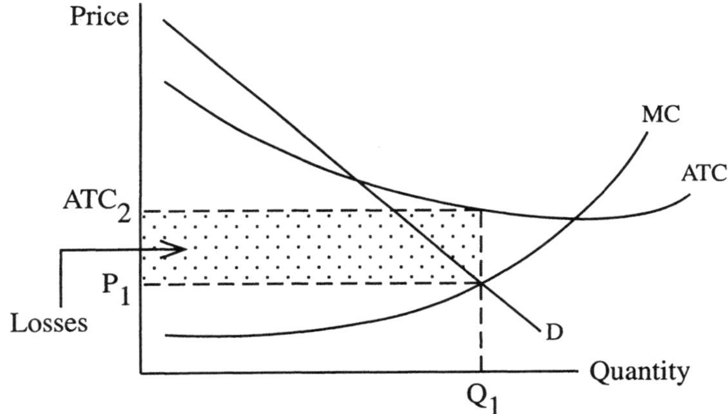

What Is the Question?
Identify the question for each of the answers that follow.

1. This antitrust act made interlocking directorates illegal.

2. One advantage is that it provides information about the dispersion of firm size in an industry.

3. This is descriptive of the situation where a particular product or technology becomes settled upon as the standard and is difficult or impossible to dislodge as the standard.

4. This is the time period between when a natural monopoly's costs change and when the regulatory agency adjusts prices of the natural monopoly.

5. Holds that regulators are seeking to do, and will do through regulation, what is in their best interest.

6. One criticism is that it does not explain which specific acts constitute "restraint of trade."

7. This theory holds that regulators are seeking to do, and will do through regulation, what is in the best interest of the public or society at larger.

What Is Wrong?

In each of the statements that follow, something is wrong. Identify what is wrong in the space provided.

1. The size of the market is irrelevant to whether a firm is a monopolist or not.

2. A conglomerate merger is a merger between companies in the same market.

3. For a network good, its value increases as the expected number of units bought decreases.

4. The lock-in effect reduces switching costs.

5. The more broadly a market is defined, the more likely a firm will be considered a monopolist.

6. George Stigler and Claire Friedland studied both unregulated and regulated electric utilities and found a small difference in the rates charged by them.

7. The federal government looks more closely at proposed vertical mergers than horizontal mergers.

8. A profit-maximizing natural monopoly will produce the quantity of output at which MR = MC and charge the price that equals its ATC.

9. The capture theory of regulation holds that no matter what the motive for the initial regulation and the establishment of the regulatory agency, eventually the bureaucrats that run the agency will control the industry.

Multiple Choice
Circle the correct answer.

1. The Clayton Act made
   a. price discrimination illegal.
   b. price discrimination legal.
   c. mergers between companies in the same industry illegal.
   d. union strikes illegal in certain states.

2. Selling to a retailer on the condition that the seller not carry any rival products is called ________, and it was made illegal by the ________ Act.
   a. exclusive dealing; Robinson-Patman
   b. exclusive dealing; Clayton
   c. a tying contract; Wheeler-Lea
   d. price discrimination; Clayton

3. The piece of antitrust legislation which declares illegal "unfair methods of competition in commerce" is the ________ Act.
   a. Sherman
   b. Federal Trade Commission
   c. Clayton
   d. Robinson-Patman
   e. none of the above

4. Which of the following statements is true?
   a. In the Dupont case in 1956, the market relevant to Dupont was ruled to be the cellophane market, rather than the broader flexible wrapping materials market.
   b. In 1975, a court ruled that Alcoa was a monopoly.
   c. The way a market is defined can have much to say as to whether a firm is viewed as a monopoly or not.
   d. a and c
   e. a, b, and c

5. The advantage of the Herfindahl index over the four-firm and eight-firm concentration ratios is that it provides information about
   a. the dispersion of firm size in an industry.
   b. the price effects of industry concentration.
   c. merger acquisitions.
   d. b and c
   e. none of the above

6. Consider a merger between Firm A, with a market share of 19 percent, and Firm B, with a market share of 16 percent. Will the Antitrust Division of the Justice Department file suit against these two firms if they enter into a merger?
   a. No, because together they have 35 percent of the market.
   b. Yes, because the Herfindahl index is 617 (which is more than 200).
   c. No, because the difference between the Herfindahl index when the two firms are not merged and the Herfindahl index when they are merged is more than 200.
   d. No, because neither firm has a market share under 10 percent.
   e. No, because the Herfindahl index is 139 (which is more than 100).

7. When one firm can supply the entire output demanded at lower cost than two or more firms can, we have a(an)
   a. natural market.
   b. natural monopoly.
   c. regulated firm.
   d. efficient firm.
   e. none of the above

Exhibit 12

(1) Firm	(2) Quantity	(3) Average total cost
A	200 units	$5
B	400 units	$4
	600 units	$7

8. In Exhibit 12 above, the resource-allocative efficient output is 600 units. Currently, Firm B is the only firm supplying the good; it is supplying 400 units. Based on the data presented in Exhibit 12, is Firm B a natural monopoly? If so, why?
   a. No, because Firm A can supply 200 units at a lower average total cost than Firm B can supply 400 units.
   b. No, because it is not the only firm that can supply the good.
   c. Yes, because it can supply the entire output.
   d. No, because it cannot supply the entire output (600 units) at lower cost ($4,200) than the two firms together (where Firm A produces 200 units at $5 per unit and Firm B produces 400 units at $4 per unit).

9. In marginal-cost price regulation of the natural monopoly firm, the objective is to set a price
   a. that will guarantee zero economic profit.
   b. equal to average total cost.
   c. consistent with the maximization of profits.
   d. equal to the quantity of output at which demand intersects marginal cost.
   e. none of the above

10. One of the criticisms of average-cost pricing regulation of the natural monopoly firm is:
    a. if the natural monopoly firm knows it is guaranteed a price equal to average total cost, it will cut costs and decrease quality.
    b. the natural monopoly firm is forced into taking a loss.
    c. the natural monopoly is guaranteed a positive economic profit.
    d. none of the above

11. Which of the following is usually noted as a natural monopoly?
    a. a firm that builds houses
    b. a company that sells electricity
    c. a bank
    d. a cruise ship company
    e. none of the above

12. Under Civil Aeronautics Board (CAB) chairman ________, the airline industry began to be deregulated in 1978.
    a. Alfred Kahn
    b. R. T. McClow
    c. Everett George
    d. Michael Kennedy
    e. none of the above

13. George Stigler is closely associated with the ________, which says ________.
    a. public interest theory of regulation; regulators work hard to benefit the public interest
    b. capture hypothesis; regulatory agencies are "captured" by the special interests of the industry that are being regulated
    c. capture hypothesis; eventually the public "captures" the benefits of regulation through lower prices
    d. public interest theory or regulation; the public is dissatisfied with the efforts of the regulatory agencies but can do little about this situation.

14. One of the major criticisms of the antitrust laws is that
    a. certain antitrust acts hinder, rather than promote, competition.
    b. they are too short in length.
    c. they do not all employ the Herfindahl index.
    d. they do not all employ the four-firm concentration ratio.

15. Which of the following is a way of regulating a natural monopoly firm?
    a. output regulation
    b. average-cost regulation
    c. marginal-cost price regulation
    d. a, b, and c
    e. none of the above

True-False
Write "T" or "F" after each statement.

16. A criticism of profit regulation is that firms have no incentive to hold costs down. ____

17. The Herfindahl index is equal to the sum of the squares of the market shares of each firm in the industry divided by two. ____

18. Antitrust law is legislation passed for the stated purpose of increasing monopoly power and reducing competition. ____

19. The Wheeler-Lea Act empowered the Federal Trade Commission to deal with false and deceptive acts or practices. ____

20. The Clayton Act made tying contracts illegal. ____

Fill in the Blank
Write the correct word in the blank.

21. The ______________ ________________ ______________ _____ _________________ holds that regulators are seeking to do and will do through regulation what is in the best interest of the public or society at large.

22. The ________________ ______________ ________________ ________ declared illegal "unfair methods of competition in commerce."

23. The local gas company is usually cited as an example of a ________________ ________________.

24. The way a ________________ is defined will help determine whether a particular firm is considered a monopoly or not.

25. The Herfindahl index and the four- and eight-firm concentration ratios have been criticized from implicitly arguing from ______________ to ______________ ________________.

Chapter 13
Factor Markets:
With Emphasis on the Labor Market

What This Chapter Is About

There are many markets in an economy. This chapter is about a market that most people are particularly interested in—the labor market.

Key Concepts in the Chapter

a. derived demand
b. marginal revenue product
c. factor price taker
d. least-cost rule
e. marginal productivity theory

- **Derived demand** is demand that is the result of some other demand. For example, factor demand is the result of the demand for the products that factors go to produce.
- **Marginal revenue product** is the additional revenue generated by employing an additional factor unit.
- A **factor price taker** is a firm that can buy all of a factor it wants at the equilibrium price.
- The **least-cost rule** specifies the combination of factors that minimizes costs. It requires that the MPP/P ratio for each factor be the same.
- **Marginal productivity theory** states that firms in competitive or perfect product and factor markets pay factors their marginal revenue products.

Review Questions

1. Give an example that illustrates what derived demand is.

2. When is the factor demand curve downward sloping?

3. When is value marginal product the same as marginal revenue product?

4. How many units of a factor should a firm buy? Explain your answer.

5. How are costs minimized if the least-cost rule is observed?

6. What are three main determinants of elasticity of demand for labor?

7. As the wage rate rises, the quantity supplied of labor rises. Does it follow that the income effect does not occur? Explain your answer.

8. What affects the demand for labor?

9. What affects the supply of labor?

10. Explain how what appears to be employer discrimination may be an information problem instead.

Problems

1. Fill in the blank spaces in the table.

Quantity of factor Z	Quantity of output	Product price	Total revenue	Marginal revenue product
1	30	$40		
2	50	$40		
3	60	$40		

2. Fill in the blank spaces in the table.

Quantity of factor Z	Price of factor Z	Total cost	Marginal factor cost
1	$10		
2	$10		
3	$10		

3. Fill in the blank spaces in the table.

MPP of factor X (units)	Price of factor X	MPP of factor Y (units)	Price of factor Y	Should the firm buy more of factor X or factor Y?
30	$2	40	$1.25	
50	$4	100	$5	
100	$30	100	$40	

4. Fill in the blank spaces in the table.

Change	Does this affect the demand for labor (yes, no)?	Does this affect the supply of labor (yes, no)?	Effect on wage (up, down, no change)
product supply falls			
product demand rises			
training costs rise			
positive change in the nonpecuniary aspects of the job			

5. Diagrammatically represent the VMP and MRP curves for a monopolist, monopolistic competitor, and oligopolist.

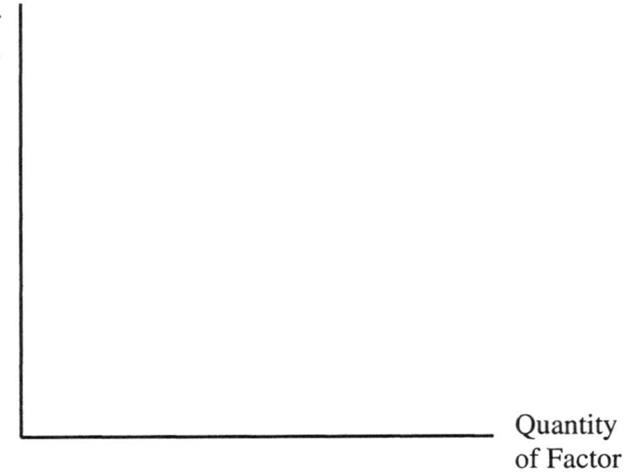

6. Diagrammatically represent the factor supply curve for a factor price taker.

What Is the Question?
Identify the question for each of the answers that follow.

1. The additional revenue generated by employing an additional factor unit.

2. It is also the factor demand curve.

3. It slopes downward because the MPP of the factor eventually declines.

4. It will buy the number of factor units for which MRP = MFC.

5. The firm will buy more of factor X and less of factor Y.

6. It is equal to the MPP of the factor divided by the cost of the factor.

7. The percentage change in the quantity demanded of labor divided by the percentage change in the wage rate.

8. It is upward sloping because the substitution effect outweighs the income effect.

9. One of the reasons is that jobs have different nonpecuniary qualities.

10. States that firms in competitive or perfect product and factor markets pay factors their marginal revenue products.

What Is Wrong?

In each of statements that follow, something is wrong. Identify what is wrong in the space that is provided.

1. If price equals marginal revenue, then VMP is greater than MRP.

2. The factor demand curve usually lies above the MRP curve.

3. The firm will purchase the quantity of a factor at which the difference between the MRP and MFC of the factor are maximized.

4. An increase in MPP will shift the factor demand curve to the left.

5. If the demand for the product that labor produces is highly elastic, a small percentage increase in price will decrease quantity demanded of the product by a relatively small percentage.

6. The more substitutes for labor, the lower the elasticity of demand for labor; the fewer substitutes for labor, the higher the elasticity of demand for labor.

7. Screening is the process used by employers to increase the probability of choosing good employees (to promote) from within the firm.

8. A firm minimizes costs by buying factors in the combination at which the MPP-to-price ratio for the expensive factors is greater than the MPP-to-price ratio for the less expensive factors.

9. The supply curve is upward-sloping for a factor price taker.

10. The higher the labor cost-total cost ratio, the lower the elasticity of demand for labor.

Multiple Choice

Circle the correct answer.

1. A factor price taker is a firm that
   a. can buy all of a factor it wants at the equilibrium price.
   b. can sell all of a product it wants at the equilibrium price.
   c. must pay a higher price to buy an additional unit of a factor.
   d. must lower price to sell an additional unit of the good it produces.

2. A firm that is a price taker in a factor market faces
   a. an upward-sloping supply curve of factors.
   b. a vertical supply curve of factors.
   c. a downward-sloping supply curve of factors.
   d. a horizontal supply curve of factors.

3. The demand for factors is
   a. a derived demand.
   b. an extra demand.
   c. an indirect demand.
   d. a distinct demand.
   e. none of the above

Exhibit 14

(1) Units of Factor X	(2) Quantity of output	(3) Product price	(4) Marginal revenue product
0	10	$12	
1	20	$12	A
2	29	$12	B
3	36	$12	C
4	41	$12	D

4. In Exhibit 14, the collar amounts that go in blanks A, B, C, and D are, respectively,
   a. $120; $108; $84; $60
   b. $100; $204; $30; $40
   c. $190; $180; $70; $40
   d. $105; $140; $40; $30

5. Suppose a factor price searcher purchases one unit of factor X for $15. What would it purchase the second unit of factor X for, and what would marginal factor cost (MFC) equal?
   a. It would purchase the second unit for $15, and MFC equals $15.
   b. There is not enough information to know what it would purchase the second unit for, and thus we do not know what MFC equals.
   c. It would purchase the second unit for $15, but there is not enough information to know what MFC equals.
   d. There is not enough information to know what it would purchase the second unit for, but MFC equals $15.
   e. none of the above

6. The marginal factor cost (MFC) curve is
   a. vertical for a factor price taker.
   b. horizontal for a factor price taker.
   c. horizontal for a factor price searcher.
   d. upward-sloping for a factor price searcher.
   e. b and d

7. For a product price searcher,
   a. VMP = MRP.
   b. VMP < MRP.
   c. VMP > MRP.
   d. There is not enough information to answer the question.

8. For a price taker in both the product and factor markets, at the profit-maximizing factor quantity,
   a. VMP = MRP > MFC = factor price
   b. VMP < MRP = MFC = factor price
   c. VMP > MRP = MFC = factor price
   d. VMP = MRP = MFC = factor price

9. The wage rate increases 30 percent and the quanitity demanded of labor falls by 90 percent. The elasticity of demand for labor is ______.
   a. 1.33
   b. 2.40
   c. 1.50
   d. 3.00
   e. none of the above

10. The lower the elasticity of demand for a product,
    a. the higher the ratio of labor costs to total costs.
    b. the lower the ratio of labor costs to total costs.
    c. the lower the elasticity of demand for the labor that produces the product.
    d. the higher the elasticity of demand for the labor that produces the product.
    e. none of the above

11. A rise in the wage rate
    a. shifts the supply curve of labor rightward.
    b. increases the quantity supplied of labor.
    c. shifts the supply curve of labor leftward.
    d. decreases the quantity supplied of labor.

12. The supply of labor curve will slope upward if the
    a. substitution effect outweighs the income effect.
    b. income effect outweighs the substitution effect.
    c. wage rises.
    d. wage falls.

13. Marginal factor cost is
    a. the additional cost incurred by employing an additional factor unit.
    b. the additional revenue generated by employing an additional factor unit.
    c. always equal to marginal revenue product.
    d. constant in the long run.
    e. a and d

14. The marginal revenue product (MRP) curve is the firm's
    a. marginal output curve.
    b. factor supply curve.
    c. average revenue curve.
    d. factor demand curve.

15. The more substitutes there are for labor,
    a. the more sensitive buyers of labor will be to a change in the price of labor.
    b. the less sensitive buyers of labor will be to a change in the price of labor.
    c. the higher costs will rise in the short run.
    d. the greater marginal revenue will be in the long run.
    e. none of the above

True-False

Write "T" or "F" after each statement.

16. The firm minimizes costs by buying factors in the combination at which the MPP-price ratio for each is the same. ____

17. Marginal productivity theory states that firms in competitive or perfect product and factor markets pay factors their marginal revenue products. ____

18. A factor price taker faces a horizontal supply curve of factors. ____

19. A firm can be a product price taker and a factor price searcher, but it cannot be a product price searcher and a factor price taker. ____

20. If the demand curve for the product that labor produces shifts rightward, the demand curve for labor shifts leftward. ____

Fill in the Blank

Write the correct word in the blank.

21. ________________ ________________ ________________ = P x MPP.

22. The process used by employers to increase the probability of choosing "good" employees based on certain criteria is called ________________.

23. The elasticity of demand for labor is defined as the percentage change in the ________________ ________________ ______ ________________ divided by the percentage change in the ______________ ______________.

24. The firm buys and employs the factor quantity at which (the condition) __________ = __________ holds.

25. The demand for labor is ________________.

Chapter 14
Wages, Unions, and Labor

What This Chapter Is About
This chapter discusses the labor union, its practices, and its effects.

Key Concepts in the Chapter
a. collective bargaining
b. monopsony

- **Collective bargaining** is the process whereby wage rates and other issues are determined by a union bargaining with management on behalf of all union members.
- A **monopsony** is a single buyer in a factor market.

Review Questions

1. What are three possible labor union objectives when it comes to the labor union employment?

2. The labor union faces a wage-employment tradeoff. Explain.

3. How might a labor union try to lower the elasticity of demand for its labor?

4. How might a labor union try to increase the demand for its labor?

5. What is the difference between a union shop and a closed shop?

6. Why is a monopsony sometimes called a buyer's monopoly?

7. What is the relationship between marginal factor cost and the wage rate for a monopsonist?

8. Explain how changes in supply conditions and wage rates in the unionized sector can cause changes in supply and wage rates in the nonunionized sector.

9. What is the traditional (or orthodox) view of labor unions?

10. What quantity of a factor does a monopsonist purchase?

Problems

1. Fill in the blank spaces in the table.

Description	Type of union
A union whose membership is made up of individuals who practice the same craft or trade.	
A union whose membership is made up of individuals who work for the local, state, or federal government.	
A union whose membership is made up of individuals who work in the same firm or industry but do not all practice the same craft or trade.	

2. Fill in the blank spaces in the table.

Action	Effect on elasticity of demand for union labor (rises, falls, remains unchanged)
reduced availability of substitute products	
reduced availability of substitute factors	

3. Fill in the blank spaces in the table.

Action	Effect on demand for union labor (rises, falls, remains unchanged)
MPP of union labor falls	
product demand rises	
substitute factor prices fall	

4. Fill in the blank spaces in the table.

Action	Does it affect the demand for union labor, or the supply of union labor?
MPP of union labor rises	
substitute factor prices rise	
introduction of union shop	

5. Diagrammatically show that a labor union can change the supply of labor through collective bargaining and a strike.

6. Fill in the blank spaces in the table.

Number of workers	Wage rate	Total labor cost	Marginal factor cost
1	$10.00		
2	$10.10		
3	$10.20		
4	$10.30		
5	$10.40		

What Is the Question?
Identify the question for each of the answers that follow.

1. An organization whose members belong to a particular profession.

2. The labor union will want this wage rate to prevail if its objective is to maximize the total wage bill.

3. The wage-employment tradeoff decreases.

4. The purpose is to convince management that the supply curve is what the union says it is.

5. MFC is greater than the wage rate.

6. An organization in which an employee must belong to the union before he or she can be hired.

7. Increasing product demand, increasing substitute factor prices, and increasing marginal physical product.

8. The change in total labor cost divided by the change in the number of workers.

What Is Wrong?

In each of the statements that follow, something is wrong. Identify what is wrong in the space provided.

1. If the objective of the labor union is to maximize the total wage bill, it will want the wage rate that corresponds to the inelastic portion of the labor demand curve.

2. The more substitutes for union labor, the lower the elasticity of demand for union labor.

3. The National Working Rights Act allowed states to pass right-to-work laws.

4. The MFC curve lies below the supply of labor curve for a monopsonist.

5. The percentage of the national income that goes to labor has been rising over the past 30 years.

6. If labor is homogeneous and mobile, an increase in the wage rate in the union sector will bring about an increase in the wage rate in the nonunion sector.

7. An industrial union is a union whose membership is made up of individuals who practice the same craft or trade.

Multiple Choice
Circle the correct answer.

1. Labor Union A faces an inelastic demand curve for its labor. Labor Union B faces an elastic demand curve for its labor. Which of the two labor unions is less likely to push for higher wages, *ceteris paribus*, and why?
   a. Labor Union A, because for A it is more costly (in terms of union members losing jobs) than it is for B to push for higher wages.
   b. Labor Union B, because for B it is more costly (in terms of union members losing jobs) than it is for A to push for higher wages.
   c. Labor Union A, because the members of it work in the manufacturing sector of the economy and not the service sector.
   d. Labor Union B, because the members of it work in the service sector of the economy and not the manufacturing sector.

2. ________, the lower the elasticity of demand for the product, which in turn means the lower the elasticity of demand for union labor, which means the union will have a smaller cutback in employment for higher wages (the wage-employment tradeoff is less pronounced).
   a. The fewer substitutes that exist for the product the labor union produces
   b. The more substitutes that exist for the product the labor union produces
   c. The more workers in the labor union
   d. The higher the profits of the firm the labor union works for

3. Unions may be interested in increasing the productivity of their members because as their productivity rises, ________, and their wages rise.
   a. the demand for their labor falls
   b. the supply of their labor falls
   c. the supply of their labor rises
   d. the demand for their labor rises

4. The ________ Act prohibited the closed shop.
   a. Norris-LaGuardia
   b. Taft-Hartley
   c. Wagner
   d. Bush
   e. none of the above

5. Which of the following comes closest to being a monopsony?
   a. a computer company in California
   b. a Burger King in a big city
   c. a farmer who hires labor
   d. a firm in a small town and there are no other firms for miles around
   e. a and b are equally monopsonistic

6. Which of the following statements is false?
   a. A monopsony cannot buy additional units of a factor without increasing the price it pays for the factor.
   b. A monopsony can buy additional units of a factor without increasing the price it pays for the factor.
   c. The supply curve a monopsony faces is the industry supply of a factor.
   d. a and c.

7. During the time labor unions have been in existence,
   a. there has been almost no change in the fraction of national income that goes to labor.
   b. the fraction of national income that goes to labor has decreased.
   c. the fraction of national income that goes to labor has increased.
   d. the fraction of national income that goes to rent has increased.

8. In a perfectly competitive industry, do higher wages for labor union members diminish profits?
   a. No, higher wage costs can only affect profits if they affect labor morale, and this doesn't happen.
   b. Yes, in the long run, but no in the short run, since in the short run profits are (close to being) fixed.
   c. Yes, in the short run, but not in the long run, since in the long run some firms will exit the industry because of higher costs and losses and price will rise, reestablishing zero economic profit.
   d. No, because higher labor costs usually bring more firms into the industry and this effect dampens price hikes.

9. The traditional or orthodox view of the effects of labor unions is that they
   a. positively impact productivity and efficiency.
   b. negatively impact productivity and efficiency.
   c. do not drive an artificial wedge between the wages of comparable labor in the union and nonunion sectors of the labor market.
   d. a and c
   e. b and c

10. Which of the following is consistent with the view of labor unions as a collective voice?
   a. Job exiting is increased.
   b. Workers feel less secure in their jobs.
   c. The turnover rate is increased.
   d. Labor productivity declines.
   e. none of the above

11. Which of the following is an example of an employee association?
   a. the American Medical Association
   b. the International Brotherhood of the Teamsters
   c. the Letter Carriers Union
   d. a and b
   e. none of the above

12. The act that says "every person who shall monopolize, or attempt to monopolize, or combine or conspire with any other person or persons, to monopolize any part of the trade or commerce among the several States, or with foreign nations, shall be deemed guilty of a midemeanor," is the
    a. McCormick Harvester Act.
    b. Wagner Act.
    c. Sherman Antitrust Act.
    d. Norris-LaGuardia Act.
    e. none of the above

13. Which of the following does not affect the demand for or quantity demanded of labor?
    a. increasing the marginal physical product of labor
    b. rising factor prices for labor
    c. increasing demand for the product that labor produces
    d. a strike

14. Over the past two decades one of the fast growing subsets of the union movement has been
    a. teamster union membership
    b. public employee union membership.
    c. garment workers membership.
    d. postal worker membership.

15. In 2001, approximately _____ percent of the labor force in the United States belonged to labor unions.
    a. 13.5
    b. 12.3
    c. 10.2
    d. 7.5

True-False
Write "T" or "F" at the end of each statement.

16. Less than one out of every five workers in the United States in 1990 was a union member. ____

17. The American Federation of Labor was formed in 1886 under the leadership of Taft Hartley. ____

18. The Landrum-Griffin Act was passed with the expressed intent of policing the internal affairs of labor unions. ____

19. There is evidence that labor unions generally have the effect of increasing their members' wages and lowering the wage rates of nonunion labor. ____

20. Some economists contend that employee associations are a type of labor union. ____

Fill in the Blank
Write the correct word in the blank.

21. Laws that make it illegal to require union membership for purposes of employment are called ________________ – ________ – _______________ laws.

22. A single buyer in a factor market is called a __________________.

23. The total wage bill is maximized at that point where the demand for labor is ________________ ___________________.

24. A ________________ occurs when unionized employees refuse to work at a certain wage or under certain conditions.

25. The monopsonist buys the factor quantity at which (the condition) __________ = __________ holds.

Chapter 15
The Distribution of Income and Poverty

What This Chapter Is About

In an earlier chapter we discussed the factors that determine income. In this chapter we discuss the income distribution—specifically, how the income that is earned in society is distributed. We also discuss the issue of poverty. What are its causes? Why are some people poor and other people rich? What are the policies used to deal with poverty?

Key Concepts in the Chapter

a. *ex ante* distribution of income
b. *ex post* distribution of income
c. Lorenz curve
d. Gini coefficient
e. human capital
f. wage discrimination
g. poverty income threshold

- The ***ex ante*** **distribution of income** is the before-tax-and-transfer payment distribution of income.
- The ***ex post*** **distribution of income** is the after-tax-and-transfer payment distribution of income.
- The **Lorenz curve** is a graph of the income distribution. It expresses the relationship between cumulative percentage of households and cumulative percentage of income.
- The **Gini coefficient** is a measurement of the degree of inequality in the income distribution.
- **Human capital** refers to education, the development of skills, and anything else that is particular to the individual and increases his or her productivity.
- **Wage discrimination** is the situation that exists when individuals of equal ability and productivity are paid different wage rates.
- The **poverty income threshold** is the income level below which people are considered to be living in poverty.

Review Questions

1. What is the difference between the *ex ante* distribution of income and the *ex post* distribution of income?

2. What are the four components of individual income?

3. Explain how a Lorenz curve is constructed.

4. What is a limitation of the Gini coefficient?

5. Identify the factors that contribute to income inequality.

6. What is the Rawlsian normative standard of the income distribution?

7. What is absolute poverty? What is relative poverty?

8. How does age affect the income distribution?

9. What is the marginal productivity normative standard of income distribution?

10. What is the public good-free rider argument for taxing persons to pay for the welfare assistance of some?

Problems

1. Fill in the blank spaces in the table.

Quintile	**Percentage of total income, 2000**
Lowest fifth	
Second fifth	
Third fifth	
Fourth fifth	
Highest fifth	

2. Fill in the blank spaces in the table.

Quintile	**Income share (percent)**	**Cumulative percentage of income**	**Cumulative percentage of households**
Lowest fifth	10		
Second fifth	12		
Third fifth	22		
Fourth fifth	25		
Highest fifth	31		

3. Fill in the blank spaces in the table.

Group	Percent of group in poverty, 2000
Total population	
White	
African-American	
Hispanic	
Under 18 years of age	
18-24 years old	
65 years old and older	

4. Diagrammatically represent the Lorenz curve if there is a perfectly equal income distribution.

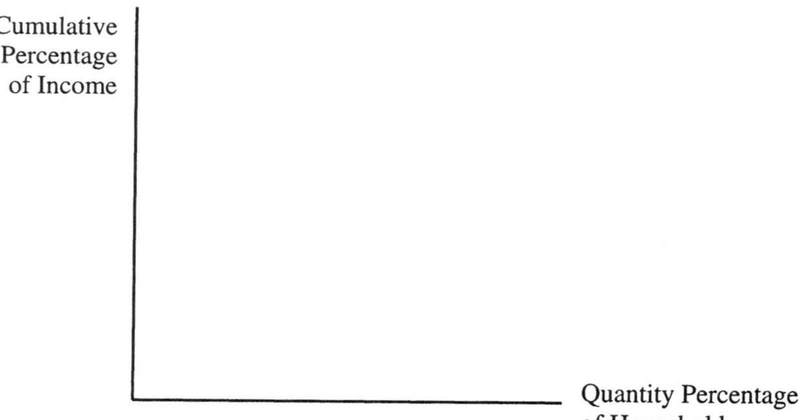

5. Use the first table to fill in the blank spaces in the second table.

Cumulative percentage of households	Cumulative percentage of income
20	10
40	30
60	51
80	73
100	100

Quintile	Income share
Lowest fifth	
Second fifth	
Third fifth	
Fourth fifth	
Highest fifth	

What Is the Question?

Identify the question for each of the answers that follow.

1. Payments to persons that are not made in return for goods and services currently supplied.

2. Labor income plus asset income plus transfer payments minus taxes.

3. This exists when individuals of equal ability and productivity are paid different wage rates.

4. It is determined in factor markets.

5. The Gini coefficient is 1.

6. The income level below which people are considered to be living in poverty.

7. An example is that everyone who earns less than $5,000 is living in poverty.

8. An example is that the bottom one-tenth of income earners are living in poverty.

9. It holds that individuals currently not receiving welfare think they might one day need welfare assistance and thus are willing to take out a form of insurance for themselves by supporting welfare programs.

What Is Wrong?

In each of the statements that follow, something is wrong. Identify what is wrong in the space provided.

1. The income distribution in the United States in 2000 was more nearly equal than it was in 1967.

2. The government can change the distribution of income through taxes, but not through transfer payments.

3. The Lorenz curve is a measurement of the degree of inequality in the distribution of income.

4. The Rawlsian normative standard of the income distribution holds that there should be complete income equality.

5. Asset income is equal to the wage rate an individual receives multiplied by the number of hours he or she works.

6. In general, human capital refers to the increases in productivity brought about by humans when they use physical capital goods.

7. The Gini coefficient is zero (0) if there is an unequal income distribution.

Multiple Choice
Circle the correct answer.

1. Which of the following statements is true?
   a. Between 1967 and 2000, the income distribution in the United States has become less equal.
   b. In 1967, the lowest 20% of all income earners earned over 10% of the total money income.
   c. The people that make up the highest fifth of all income earners are millionaires.
   d. a and c
   e. a, b, and c

2. The *ex post* income distribution is
   a. less equal then the *ex ante* income distribution.
   b. more equal then the *ex ante* income distribution.
   c. as equal as the *ex ante* income distribution.
   d. not adjusted for taxes and transfer payments.
   e. b and d

3. The smaller the Gini coefficient, the
   a. greater the degree of income inequality.
   b. greater the degree of income equality.
   c. higher the birth rate.
   d. larger the population.
   e. none of the above

4. Which of the following statements is false?
   a. Economists agree that it is better for a country to have a lower Gini coefficient than a higher one.
   b. Economists agree that it is better for a country to have a higher Gini coefficient than a lower one.
   c. There is greater income equality in the United States than Sweden.
   d. Because the Gini coefficient is lower in Country A than Country B, the lowest income group in Country A has a greater percentage of total income than the lowest income group in Country B.
   e. all of the above

5. One way to increase the degree of income inequality is to
   a. decrease transfer payments going to people with low labor and asset incomes and decrease taxes on people with high labor and asset incomes.
   b. increase transfer payments going to people with low labor and asset incomes and decrease taxes on people with high labor and asset incomes.
   c. increase transfer payments going to people with low labor and asset incomes by more than you increase taxes on the same people.
   d. increase transfer payments going to people with high labor and asset incomes by less than you increase taxes on the same people.
   e. a and d

6. Which of the following statements is true?
   a. If people were alike in terms of their marketable innate abilities and attributes, there would be less income inequality.
   b. Some degree of income inequality can be attributed to the fact that some people consume more leisure than others.
   c. Schooling is referred to as human capital.
   d. a and c
   e. a, b, and c

7. Human capital refers to
   a. equal pay.
   b. education and development of skills.
   c. factories and computers.
   d. a and c
   e. none of the above

8. The proponents of absolute income equality sometimes argue that an equal income distribution of income will maximize total utility. Their argument goes like this:
   a. Individuals are alike when it comes to how much satisfaction they receive from an increase in income; receiving additional income is subject to the law of diminishing marginal utility, redistributing income from the rich to the poor helps the poor less than it hurts the rich, so total utility rises.
   b. Individuals are alike when it comes to how much satisfaction they receive from an increase in income; receiving additional income is subject to the law of constant marginal costs, redistributing income from the rich to the poor helps the poor more than it hurts the rich, so total utility rises.
   c. Individuals are not alike when it comes to how much satisfaction they receive from an increase in income; receiving additional income is subject to the law of diminishing marginal utility, redistributing income from the rich to the poor helps the poor less than it hurts the rich, so total utility rises.
   d. Individuals are alike when it comes to how much satisfaction they receive from an increase in income; receiving additional income is subject to the law of diminishing marginal utility, redistributing income from the rich to the poor helps the poor more than it hurts the rich, so total utility rises.

9. Which of the following is a definition of poverty in relative terms?
   a. A family is in poverty if it receives less than $10,000 a year.
   b. A family is in poverty if it receives an income that places it in the lowest 5 percent of family income recipients.
   c. A family is in poverty if the majority of families receive more income than it receives.
   d. b and c
   e. a, b, and c

10. Which of the following leads to an underestimate of the number of persons in poverty?
   a. illegal income
   b. unreported income
   c. some poor persons can't be found, therefore they can't be counted
   d. a and b
   c. a, b, and c

True-False

Write "T" or "F" at the end of each statement.

11. The *ex ante* distribution of income is the before-tax and before-transfer distribution of income. ____

12. The Lorenz curve is a graphical representation of the distribution of income. ____

13. The *ex post* distribution of income (in the U.S.) is more equal than the *ex ante* distribution of income. ____

14. John Rawls wrote *A Theory of Justice*. ____

15. The acceptance of the public good-free rider argument leads individuals to conclude that government is justified in taxing all persons to pay for welfare assistance for some. ____

Fill in the Blank

Write the correct word in the blank.

16. ____________________ ____________________ are payments to persons that are not made in return for goods and services currently supplied.

17. The ________________ ____________________ is a measurement of the degree of inequality in the income distribution.

18. ______________ ____________________ exists when individuals of equal ability and productivity, as measured by their marginal revenue products, are paid different wage rates.

19. The closer the Gini coefficient is to __________, the greater the degree of income inequality.

20. The _______ ___________ distribution of income is the before-tax-and-transfer payment distribution of income.

Chapter 16
Interest, Rent, and Profit

What This Chapter Is About

There are four broad categories of resources—land, labor, capital, and entrepreneurship. In an earlier chapter we discussed the payment to labor—the wage rate. In this chapter we discuss the payments to land, capital, and entrepreneurship.

Key Concepts in the Chapter

a. positive rate of time preference
b. nominal interest rate
c. real interest rate
d. present value
e. economic rent
f. pure economic rent

- A **positive rate of time preference** is a preference for earlier availability of goods over later availability.
- The **nominal interest rate** is the interest rate determined by the forces of supply and demand in the loanable funds market.
- The **real interest rate** is the nominal interest rate adjusted for expected inflation—that is, the nominal interest rate minus the expected inflation rate.
- **Present value** is the current worth of some future dollar amount of income or receipts.
- **Economic rent** is payment in excess of opportunity costs.
- **Pure economic rent** is a category of economic rent where the payment is to a factor that is in fixed supply, implying that it has zero opportunity costs.

Review Questions

1. Give an example to illustrate the difference between interest and the interest rate.

2. What does it mean if a person has a low positive rate of time preference?

3. Give an example of a roundabout method of production.

4. What do positive interest rates have to do with roundabout methods of production and positive rates of time preference?

5. Why do interest rates differ?

6. A capital good will cost a firm $5,000. The good will generate $1,200 each year for five years. After five years, the capital good must be scrapped and it has no scrap value. If the interest rate is 7 percent, should the firm buy the capital good? Explain your answer.

7. David Ricardo believed that land rent was price determined, not price determining. What did he mean?

8. Give an example to illustrate the difference between economic rent and pure economic rent.

9. What is the difference between an artificial rent and a real rent?

10. What might profit have to do with uncertainty? With innovation?

11. Profit and loss act as signals. Explain.

Problems

1. Fill in the blank spaces in the table.

Dollar amount received	Number of years before dollar amount is received	Interest rate (percent)	Present value
$1,000	2	5	
$10,000	3	6	
$100	2	7	

2. Fill in the blank spaces in the table.

Cost of capital good	Life of capital good	Income from capital good each year	Interest rate (percent)	Should the firm buy the capital good? (yes, no)
$4,000	3 years	$1,500	2	
$19,000	5 years	$4,000	5	
$20,000	6 years	$5,000	4	

3. Diagrammatically represent pure economic rent.

4. Diagrammatically represent economic rent.

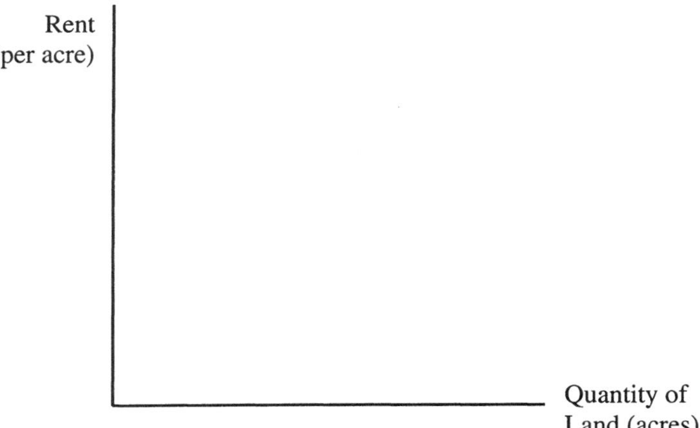

5. Fill in the blank spaces in the table.

Wage rate	Next best wage rate	Economic rent
$12	$11	
$10	$10	
$100	$66	

What Is the Question?

Identify the question for each of the answers that follow.

1. The production of capital goods that enhance productive capabilities and ultimately bring about increased consumption.

2. It is composed of the demand for consumption loans and the demand for investment loans.

3. If this is the case, then firms will borrow in the loanable funds market and invest in capital goods.

4. The interest rate determined by the forces of supply and demand in the loanable funds market.

5. They are equal when the expected inflation rate is zero.

6. The current worth of some future dollar amount of income receipts.

7. The supply curve is vertical in this case.

8. Consumers do this because they have a positive rate of time preference.

9. These turn away from losses.

What Is Wrong?

In each of the statements that follow, something is wrong. Identify what is wrong in the space provided.

1. Interest refers to the price paid by borrowers for loanable funds and to the return on cash.

2. Savers supply loanable funds because they have a negative rate of time preference.

3. A person with a high positive rate of time preference is more likely to be a saver than a person with a low positive rate of time preference.

4. David Ricardo argued that high land rents weren't an effect of high interest rates and high grain prices.

5. The present value of $4,000 in three years, if the interest rate is 5 percent, is $3,288.

6. A decreased threat of war would probably raise peoples' rate of time preference.

7. As the interest rate falls, present value falls.

8. Uncertainty exists when a potential occurrence is so unpredictable that the probability of it occurring is less than 1.

9. Economists emphasize accounting profit over economic profit because economic profit determines entry into and exit from an industry.

Multiple Choice

Circle the correct answer.

1. The supply of loanable funds most directly depends on
   a. people's investment activity.
   b. stock market activity.
   c. people's saving and newly created money.
   d. the profits and losses of firms.

2. Which of the following statements is true?
   a. The quantity supplied of loanable funds and the interest rate are inversely related.
   b. The supply curve of loanable funds is horizontal.
   c. One of the reasons the federal government demands loanable funds is that it needs to finance budget surpluses.
   d. Savers are people who consume less than their current income.
   e. none of the above

3. If consumers have a positive rate of time preference, this means they prefer
   a. earlier availability of goods to later availability.
   b. later availability of goods to earlier availability.
   c. goods to services, since services can be delivered more quickly.
   d. goods to services, since goods are more tangible.
   e. none of the above.

4. The people least likely to save are those people with a
   a. low rate of time preference, since they only slightly prefer present consumption to future consumption.
   b. low rate of time preference, since they greatly prefer present consumption to future consumption.
   c. high rate of time preference, since they greatly prefer present consumption to future consumption.
   d. efficient rate of time preference, since they do not prefer consuming luxury goods to necessities.
   e. roundabout rate of time preference, since they don't really care about consuming.

5. If the price for loanable funds is greater than the return on capital, then firms
   a. will borrow in the loanable funds market and invest in capital goods, and as this happens the quantity of capital decreases and its return rises.
   b. will borrow in the loanable funds market and invest in capital goods, and as this happens the quantity of capital increases and its return falls.
   c. do not borrow in the loanable funds market, and over time the capital stock will decrease and the return on capital will fall.
   d. do not borrow in the loanable funds market, and over time the capital stock will decrease and the return on capital will rise.

6. If a 5 percent inflation rate is expected by both the suppliers and demanders of loanable funds, then the
   a. nominal interest rate will rise, *ceteris paribus.*
   b. real interest rate will fall, *ceteris paribus.*
   c. real interest rate will rise.
   d. nominal interest rate will fall, *ceteris paribus.*

7. If the nominal interest rate is 10 percent and the expected inflation rate is 6 percent, the real interest rate equals
   a. 16 percent.
   b. 6 percent.
   c. 10 percent.
   d. 4 percent.
   e. none of the above

8. The present value of $10,000 two years in the futre, at a 5 percent interest rate, is approximately _________.
   a. $7,789
   b. $9,260
   c. $8,790
   d. $9,090

9. As interest rates decrease, present values _________, and firms will buy _________ capital goods.
   a. increase; fewer
   b. decrease; fewer
   c. increase; more
   d. decrease; more

10. A payment in excess of opportunity costs is called
    a. price.
    b. implicit price.
    c. economic rent.
    d. excess profits.
    e. none of the above

11. The economist David Ricardo argued that grain prices were ______ because land rents were ______.
    a. high; high
    b. low; high
    c. high; low
    d. low; low
    e. none of the above

12. Uncertainty
    a. is the result of a positive time preferentce.
    b. is the same thing as risk.
    c. exists when the probability of a given event can be estimated.
    d. is the result of a negative time preference.
    e. none of the above

13. Michael can work at job X earning $150,000 a year, or job Y earning $183,000 a year, or job Z earning $195,000 a year. If Michael chooses job Z, then economic rent equals
    a. $33,000.
    b. $45,000.
    c. $30,000.
    d. $12,000.
    e. none of the above

14. Entrepreneurship differs from the other factors of production in that
    a. the return to it is always negative.
    b. the return to it is always positive.
    c. it cannot be measured.
    d. the return to it is larger than the returns to the other factors of production.

15. A person buys A for $400 and sells it for $450. Which theory of profit is most consistent with this example?
    a. Profit is the return to the entrepreneur as innovator.
    b. Uncertainty is the source of profit.
    c. Profit is the return to being alert to arbitrage opportunities.
    d. a and b
    e. none of the above

True-False
Write "T" or "F" at the end of each statement.

16. The nominal interest rate is the real interest rate minus the expected inflation rate. ____

17. Present value refers to the future worth of some current dollar amount. ____

18. No factor besides land can receive pure economic rent. ____

19. Entrepreneurship is measured in terms of entins, such that 2 entins equal 1 enton. ____

20. The word interest refers to the price paid by borrowers for loanable funds and the return on capital in the production process. ____

Fill in the Blank
Write the correct word in the blank.

21. Investors (or firms) demand loanable funds so that they can invest in productive __________________ __________________ of production.

22. Over time, the price for loanable funds and the return on capital tend to __________________.

23. If the expected inflation rate is positive, the __________________ interest rate is greater than the __________________ interest rate.

24. The present value of $1,000 _______ year(s) from now is $925.92 at an 8 percent interest rate.

25. As present values __________________, firms will buy more capital goods, *ceteris paribus*.

Chapter 17
Market Failure: Externalities, Public Goods, and Asymmetric Information

What This Chapter Is About

Does the market sometimes fail to provide the optimal amount of a particular good? Some economists think so. This chapter is about market failure.

Key Concepts in the Chapter

a. market failure
b. externality
c. socially optimal (or efficient) output
d. Coase theorem
e. public good
f. free rider
g. asymmetric information

- **Market failure** refers to the situation in which the market does not provide the ideal or optimal amount of a particular good.
- **Externality** is a side effect of an action that affects the well-being of third parties.
- **Socially optimal output** (or efficient output) is the output level that takes into account and adjusts for all benefits and all costs. It occurs where MSB (marginal social benefits) equal MSC (marginal social costs).
- The **Coase theorem** states that in the case of trivial or zero transaction costs, the property rights assignment does not matter to the resource allocative outcome.
- A **public good** is a good, which if consumed by one person, does not reduce consumption by another person.
- A **free rider** is anyone who receives the benefits of a good without paying for it.
- **Asymmetric information** exists when either the buyer or the seller in a market exchange has some information that the other does not have.

Review Questions

1. Does the (competitive) market output always differ from the socially optimal output? Explain your answer.

2. What is market failure?

3. Do property rights assignments matter to the allocation of resources? Explain your answer.

4. What it is the objective of imposing a corrective tax? Does a corrective tax always work? Why or why not?

5. Is less pollution always preferred to the current amount of pollution? Explain your answer.

6. How does market environmentalism work?

7. What is the difference between a nonexcludable public good and an excludable public good?

8. Why doesn't the market produce nonexcludable public goods?

9. Explain how asymmetric information in a product market can lead to market failure.

10. Explain how asymmetric information in a factor market can lead to market failure.

11. How can adverse selection eliminate markets?

12. Give an example that illustrates moral hazard.

Problems

1. Using the data in the table, answer these two questions:

   a) What is the total cost of eliminating 6 units of pollution if a regulation is set mandating each firm to eliminate two units of pollution?

   b) What is the cost of eliminating 6 units of pollution if pollution permits are bought and sold for $650 each?

Cost of eliminating:	**Firm A**	**Firm B**	**Firm C**
1st unit of pollution	$100	$200	$1,000
2nd unit of pollution	$200	$400	$1,900
3rd unit of pollution	$300	$600	$2,300

2. Diagrammatically show how a corrective tax can go wrong (when trying to adjust for a negative externality).

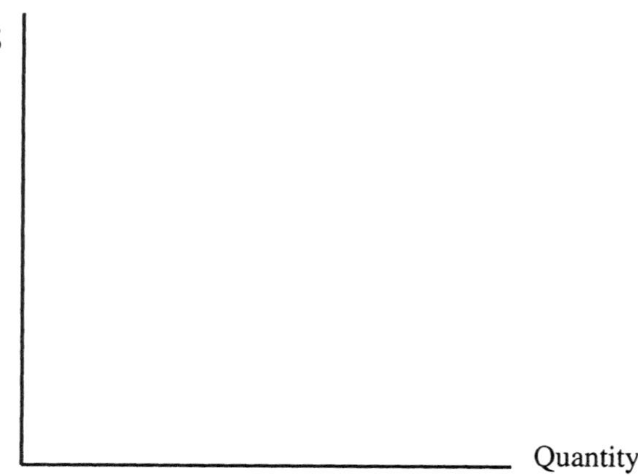

3. In the diagram that follows, the identified triangle identifies the market failure. Why?

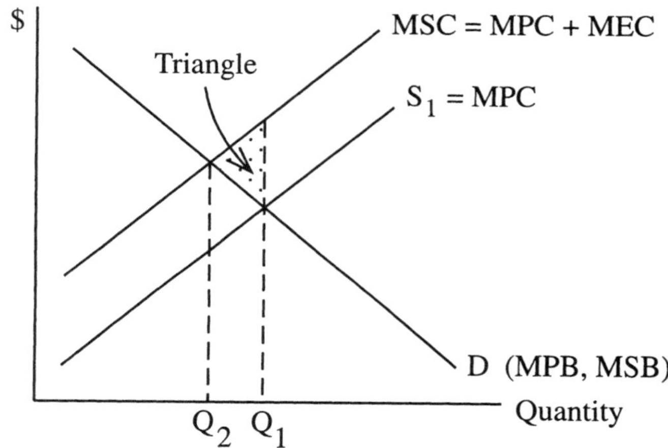

4. Under what condition will a corrective tax achieve the socially optimum output?

5. Diagrammatically explain how asymmetric information in a product market can lead to market failure?

$

Quantity

What Is the Question?

Identify the question for each of the answers that follow?

1. This exists when a person's or group's actions cause a cost to be felt by others.

2. MSC > MPC.

3. MSB > MPB.

4. In this case property rights assignments do not matter to the resource allocative outcome.

5. He stressed the reciprocal nature of externalities.

6. Consumption by one person reduces consumption by another person.

7. The person who makes it difficult, if not impossible, for the market to produce nonexcludable public goods.

8. This exists when either the buyer or the seller in a market exchange has some information that the other does not have.

9. This exists when the parties on one side of the market, who have information not known to others, self-select in a way that adversely affects the parties on the other side of the market.

What Is Wrong?

In each of the statements that follow, something is wrong. Identify what is wrong in the space provided.

1. The economist holds that less pollution is always better than the current amount of pollution because pollution is a bad.

2. A negative externality is a type of subsidy.

3. Given a positive externality, the marginal private benefit curve lies to the left of the demand curve, with the market output above the socially optimal output.

4. The side effect of an action that increases the well-being of others is called a neutral benefit.

5. If private property were established in the air, there would probably be more air pollution.

6. If a person who generates a negative externality incorporates into his private cost-benefit calculations the effects that this externality will have on third parties, the externality has been complementarized.

7. Generally, negative externalities result in too little of a good being produced.

8. If there are no externalities, then the socially optimum output occurs where MPB > MPC.

9. Marginal social costs equal marginal private costs plus internal costs.

Multiple Choice
Circle the correct answer.

1. Market failure is a situation in which
   a. prices are so low that producers will not produce goods.
   b. there are too many buyers, but not enough sellers.
   c. the market does not provide the ideal or optimal amount of a particular good.
   d. prices are so high that buyers won't buy the quantity of goods that sellers want to sell.

2. In which of the following situations could a negative externality potentially be involved?
   a. Patricia is sitting at home waiting for her friend to call. He never calls.
   b. Frank got caught in a rainstorm on his way to Miami.
   c. Fergie went to the beauty salon and got a new hairdo. She hates it.
   d. Xavier works late at night and tries to sleep late in the morning. Ever Tuesday and Thursday he is awakened at around 8:00 in the morning by his neighbor's television set. His neighbor is slightly deaf and turns the television up loud.
   e. none of the above

3. When a negative externality exists,
   a. social costs are greater than private costs.
   b. social costs equal private costs.
   c. external costs are greater than private costs.
   d. external costs are less than private costs.
   e. none of the above

4. When a positive externality exists,
   a. external benefits are greater than private benefits.
   b. external benefits are less than private benefits.
   c. social benefits are less than private benefits.
   d. social benefits equal private benefits.
   e. social benefits are greater than private benefits.

5. There are numerous ways of adjusting for externalities. One way is to persuade persons or groups that they ought to consider others when they act. Which of the following scenarios is consistent with this method of adjusting for (internalizing) externalities?
   a. The government stipulates how much pollution (over some period of time) a factory can emit into the air.
   b. Katrina is sitting at a restaurant when cigarette smoke drifts her way. She asks the manager to ask the person smoking if he would be considerate enough not to smoke. (The restaurant does not have designated smoking and nonsmoking areas.)
   c. Mark's next-door neighbor is having a loud party at 1:00 in the morning. Mark calls his neighbor up on the telephone and asks him to be more considerate.
   d. b and c
   e. a, b, and c

6. The Coase theorem states that
   a. private property rights evolve when the costs of defining property rights are less than the benefits.
   b. in the case of trivial or zero transaction costs, negative externalities are more likely to appear.
   c. when transaction costs are high, negative externalities are more common than positive externalities.
   d. in the case of trivial or zero transaction costs, the property rights assignment does not matter to the resource allocative outcome.

7. Which of the following statements is true?
   a. One way to adjust for negative externalities is for government to apply regulations to the activity that generates the externalities.
   b. A subsidy is used to adjust for a positive externality, a tax is used to adjust for a negative externality.
   c. Simply because taxes and subsidies are sometimes used to adjust for negative and positive externalities, respectively, it does not necessarily follow that the socially-optimal level of output will be reached.
   d. b and c
   e. a, b, and c

8. When a good is nonexcludable,
   a. it is impossible for individuals to obtain the benefits of the good without paying for it.
   b. it is possible for individuals to obtain the benefits of the good without paying for it.
   c. it is a government-provided good.
   d. the benefits of producing it outweigh the costs.
   e. none of the above

9. Most economists contend that the market will fail to produce nonexcludable public goods because of the
   a. rivalry problem.
   b. Coase problem.
   c. Demsetz problem.
   d. free-rider problem.

10. Much of the air is polluted. We would expect this natural resource to be less polluted if
    a. there were stiff fines for polluting the air.
    b. private property rights were established in the air.
    c. both a and b
    d. neither a nor b

True-False
Write "T" or "F" at the end of each statement.

11. National defense is a nonexcludable public good. ____

12. A public good is the same as a government-provided good. ____

13. A good is excludable if it is possible, or not prohibitively costly, to exclude someone from obtaining the benefits of the good once it has been produced. ____

14. Economists believe that there is an optimal amount of pollution, and that this probably isn't zero. ____

15. Coase discussed the reciprocal nature of externalities. ____

Fill in the Blank
Write the correct word in the blank.

16. ____________________ ____________________ is a situation in which the market does not provide the ideal or optimal amount of a particular good.

17. An externality is ____________________ if the person(s) or group that generated the externality incorporate into their own private cost-benefit calculations the external benefits of costs that third parties bear.

18. A good is ____________________ _______ ____________________ if its consumption by one person does not reduce its consumption by others.

19. ____________________ ____________________ occurs when one party to a transaction changes his or her behavior in a way that is hidden from, and costly to, the other party.

20. When either negative or positive externalities exist, the market output is different from the ____________________ ____________________ output.

Chapter 18
Public Choice:
Economic Theory Applied to Politics

What This Chapter Is About
This chapter uses economic tools to analyze decisions made in the public sector. Specifically, it looks at the behavior of voters, politicians, special-interest groups, and bureaucrats using the tools of economics.

Key Concepts in the Chapter

a. median voter model
b. rational ignorance

- The **median voter model** suggests that candidates in a two-person political race will move toward matching the preferences of the median voter.
- **Rational ignorance** is the state of not acquiring information because the costs of acquiring the information are greater than the benefits.

Review Questions

1. A politician running for office speaks in general terms. Is this consistent with the median voter model? Explain your answer.

2. A politician running for office labels herself "middle of the road," and she labels her opponent "extremist." Is this consistent with the median voter model? Explain your answer.

3. According to the median voter model, are politicians more likely to take polls to determine their position, or to first determine their position and then take polls? Explain your answer.

4. Why might a person who can vote choose not to vote?

5. A person may vote even though she knows that her single vote cannot affect the outcome of the election. Why would this person vote?

6. Give an example to illustrate why a person's vote in a presidential election may not matter to the outcome.

7. Jim, 24 years old, doesn't know the names of his U.S. senators. What does this have to do with rational ignorance?

8. Is everyone rationally ignorant of something? Explain your answer.

9. What are special-interest groups?

10. Why is a farmer more likely to be informed about agricultural policy than a member of the general public?

11. Even if members of the general public were well informed about special-interest legislation that would harm them, they might not lobby against it. Explain why.

12. What is rent? What is rent seeking?

13. Why is rent seeking socially wasteful?

Problems

1. A group of five persons is thinking of buying good X and splitting the cost. The group will use majority rule to decide whether good X will be purchased or not. In the table that follows, you will find the dollar value of the benefit and cost to each individual.

Person	Dollar value of the benefit to the individual	Dollar cost to the individual
A	$143	$100
B	$120	$100
C	$110	$100
D	$10	$100
E	$5	$100

Will the group buy good X? Is the purchase of the good an efficient purchase? Explain your answer.

What Is the Question?

Identify the question for each of the answers that follow.

1. The branch of economics that deals with the application of economic principles and tolls to public-sector decision making.

2. Candidates will speak in general terms; candidates will label their opponent in extreme terms; candidates will label themselves in moderate terms; candidates will take polls and if they are not doing well in their polls they will adjust their positions.

3. The state of not acquiring information because the costs of acquiring the information are greater than the benefits.

4. The exchange of votes to gain support for legislation.

5. In this case rent is usually called profit.

6. The expenditure of scarce resources to capture a pure transfer.

What Is Wrong?

In each of the statements that follow, something is wrong. Identify what is wrong in the space provided.

1. Legislation that concentrates the benefits on many and disperses the costs over a few is likely to pass, because the beneficiaries will have an incentive to lobby for it, whereas those who pay the bill will not lobby against it because each of them pays such a small part of the bill.

2. A public choice economist would likely state that people will not behave differently in different settings.

3. In a two-person race, the candidate on the right of the median voter is more likely to win the race than the candidate on the left of the median voter.

4. One of the predictions of the median voter model is that candidates will speak in specific terms instead of general terms because this is what the median voter wants.

5. Younger people are more likely to be rationally ignorant of various subjects than older people.

6. A government bureau maximizes profit and minimizes costs.

7. Farmers, lobbying for a legislative bill, are more likely to openly state, "We need this legislation because it will be good for us," instead of "We need this legislation for America's future."

Multiple Choice
Circle the correct answer.

1. Which of the following statements would a public choice theorist have some difficulty accepting as true?
   a. The only way to genuinely reform in this country is to elect really good and moral people to government.
   b. The people who work for a large government bureaucracy are fundamentally different people than those who work for a private firm.
   c. People respond to the costs and benefits of different institutional settings.
   d. a and b
   e. a, b, and c

2. Two policians, running for the same political office, move towards the middle of the political spectrum. This is behavior consistent with the
   a. median voter model.
   b. presidential middle theory.
   c. public choice rational ignorance theory of politics.
   d. candidate theory.
   e. none of the above

3. An economist is most likely to ask which of the following questions about a theory?
   a. If the theory is right, what should I expect to see in the real world?
   b. If the theory is right, then does it follow that the assumptions of the theory are right and can be used to explain different things?
   c. If the theory is right, then how simple is it?
   d. If the theory is right, can it be tested?

4. Public choice is a branch of
   a. political science that deals with the presidential elections and how they affect the economy.
   b. sociology that deals with human behavior in group settings.
   c. economics that deals with the theory of the firm.
   d. economics that deals with the application of economic principles and tools to public-sector decision making.
   e. none of the above

5. A public choice theorist would be most likely to say that government failure is a consequence of the
   a. ineptitude of bureaucrats.
   b. rational behavior of the participants of the political process.
   c. ignorance of voters.
   d. greed of special interest groups.
   e. b, c, and d

6. The model that predicts the candidate in the two-person race that comes closer to occupying the center of the voter distribution will win, is built on the assumption that people
   a. vote for the Democratic candidate if they are Democrats and they vote for the Republican candidate if they are Republicans.
   b. don't vote in close elections.
   c. vote for the candidate who comes closer to matching their own views.
   d. vote their pocketbooks.
   e. c and d

7. Which of the following statements is false?
   a. If the costs of voting are greater than the benefits of voting, a person will decide not to vote.
   b. The simply majority decision rule can generate inefficient results.
   c. Voting does not take into account the intensity of individuals' preferences.
   d. One cannot be uninformed on government and political matters and be considered rational, too.
   e. c and d

8. Rational ignorance refers to
   a. the honeymoon period that every president experiences soon after he is elected.
   b. the fact that some voters are not smart enough to be informed on some things.
   c. the state of not acquiring information because the costs of acquiring the information are greater than the benefits.
   d. political candidates criticizing each other based on something other than the facts.
   e. none of the above

9. The "average" member of the public is likely to know less about government agricultural policies than a farmer. The reason for this is:
   a. a farmer is smarter than the "average" member of the public.
   b. government agricultural policies are more likely to directly affect a farmer than the "average" member of the public, and so a farmer has a sharper incentive to be informed about them.
   c. a farmer is a member of a special interest group, and a member of a special interest group is more informed on all issues than the "average" member of the public.
   d. a and c
   e. none of the above

10. An elected representative may vote for a piece of special-interest legislation without fear of retaliation from the general public because
    a. many voters are rationally ignorant.
    b. people forgive quickly.
    c. all politicians do it, so in relative terms one politician is no worse for doing it than another.
    d. b and c
    e. none of the above

True-False

Write "T" or "F" after each statement.

11. James Buchanan is a public choice economist. ____

12. Public choice economists contend that people exhibit different behavior in the private sector than they do in the public sector. ____

13. The simple majority decision rule does not take into account the intensity of individuals' preferences. ____

14. Logrolling is the exchange of votes to gain support for legislation. ____

15. It is irrational not to vote in a presidential election. ____

Fill in the Blank

Write the correct word in the blank.

16. ____________________ ____________________ is said to exist when government enacts policies that produce inefficient and /or inequitable results as a consequence of the rational behavior of the participants in the political process.

17. Many potential voters will not vote because the ________________ of voting—in terms of time spent going to the polls and so on—outweigh the ____________________ of voting measured in terms of the probability of their single vote affecting the election outcome.

18. Candidates for political office will speak more in ____________________ terms than ____________________ terms.

19. Near the end of a political campaign, we would expect two candidates running for the same office to be __________________ to each other in terms of their policy positions than at the beginning of the campaign.

20. _________________ ____________________ won the Nobel Prize in Economics in 1986 for his work in public choice theory.

Chapter 19
International Trade

What This Chapter Is About
This chapter is about international trade—why people in different countries trade with each other, the effects of tariffs and quotas, and more.

Key Concepts in the Chapter
a. comparative advantage
b. consumers' surplus
c. producers' surplus

- **Comparative advantage** is the situation in which a country can produce a good at lower opportunity cost than another country.
- **Consumers' surplus** is the difference between the maximum buying price and the price paid.
- **Producers' surplus** is the difference between the price received (by the seller) and the minimum selling price.

Review Questions

1. Why do people in different countries trade with each other?

2. Why are countries better off specializing and trading (with each other) than not specializing and not trading?

3. How will a tariff affect (domestic) consumers' surplus?

4. How will a quota affect (domestic) producers' surplus?

5. Why might quotas be imposed even when the benefits of quotas (to the beneficiaries) are less than the costs of the quotas?

6. Outline the details of the infant-industry argument for trade restrictions.

7. What is the antidumping argument for trade restrictions?

8. Suppose a tariff or quota saves some domestic jobs. Would an economist say it is worth it? Explain your answer.

9. What is the role of the WTO?

10. There is a net loss from tariffs. What does this mean?

Problems

1. Fill in the blank spaces in the second table, based on the information in the first table.

Country A can produce these combinations of X and Y	**Country B can produce these combinations of X and Y**
120X, 0Y	60X, 0Y
80X, 60Y	40X, 20Y
40X, 120Y	20X, 40Y
0X, 180Y	0X, 60Y

Opportunity cost of one unit of X for Country A	**Opportunity cost of one unit of Y for Country A**	**Opportunity cost of one unit of X for Country B**	**Opportunity cost of one unit of Y for Country B**

2. Using the diagram that follows, identify the area of consumers' surplus.

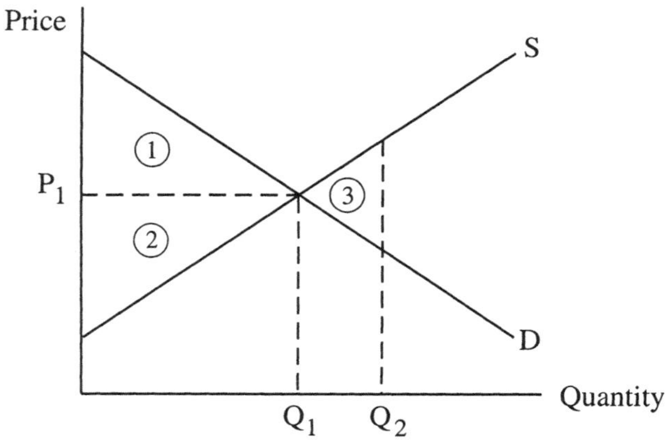

3. Using the diagram that follows, identify the area of producers' surplus.

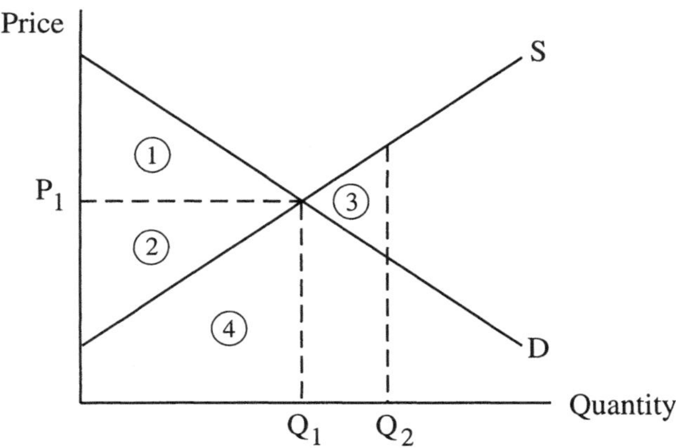

4. In the diagram (that follows), the world price is P_W. The price after a tariff has been imposed is P_T. Identify the change in consumers' surplus due to the tariff. Identify the change in producers' surplus due to the tariff.

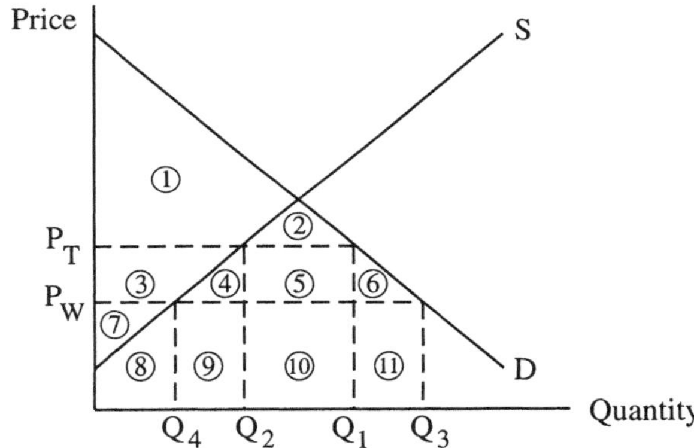

5. In the diagram (that follows), identify the gain due to the tariff. Next, identify the loss due to the tariff.

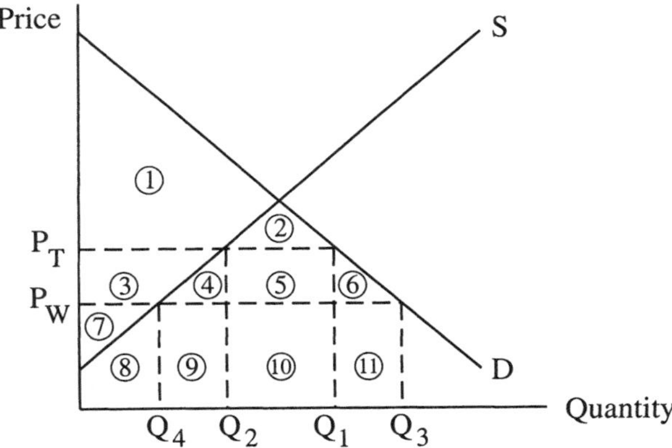

6. In the diagram (that follows), identify the net loss due to the tariff.

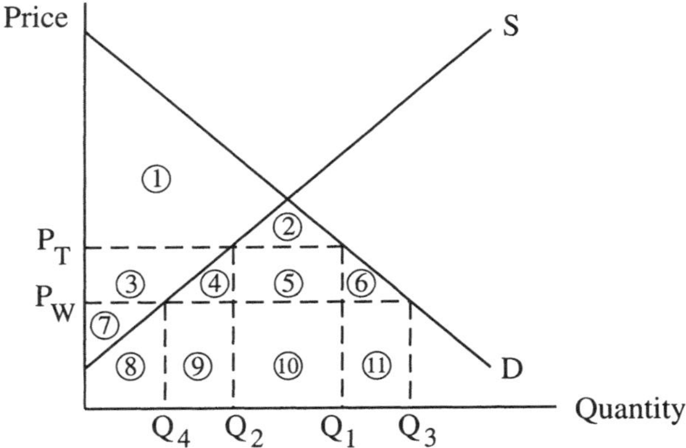

7. In the diagram (that follows), P_W is the world price and P_Q is the price after a quota has been imposed. Identify the increase in additional revenue received by importers due to the quota.

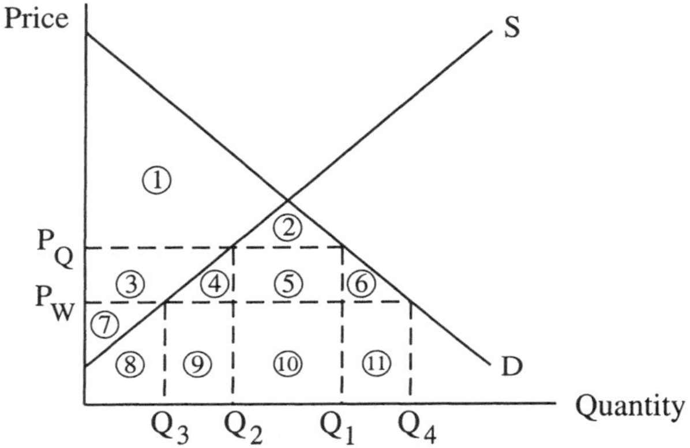

8. Using the diagram that follows, fill in the blank spaces in the table below.

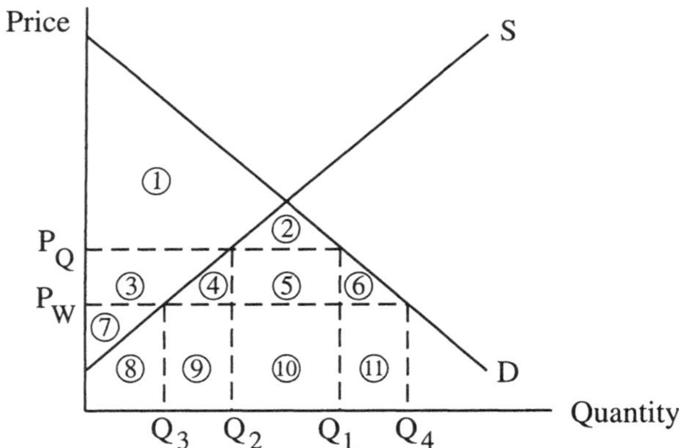

Price after quota	**Loss in consumers' surplus due to the quota**	**Gain in producers' surplus due to the quota**	**Increase in revenue received by importers due to the quota**	**Net loss due to the quota**
P_Q				

What is the Question?
Identify the questions for each of the answers that follow.

1. This will allow the country to consume beyond its production possibilities frontier (PPF).

2. As a result, imports decrease.

3. The sale of goods abroad at a price below their cost and below the price charged in the domestic market.

4. The situation in which a country can produce a good at lower opportunity cost than another country.

5. The gains are less than the losses plus the tariff revenues.

What Is Wrong?
In each of the statements that follow, something is missing. Identify what is wrong in the space provided.

1. A PPF for the world can be drawn when 1) countries do not specialize and trade and 2) when they do specialize and trade. The world PPF will be the same in both cases.

2. The national-defense argument states that certain goods are necessary to the national defense and therefore should be produced only by allies.

3. A quota raises more government revenue than a tariff.

4. Consumers' surplus and producers' surplus fall as a result of a tariff being imposed on imported goods.

5. What producers gain from a quota is greater than what consumers lose from a quota.

6. If the United States sells a good for less in France than it does in Brazil, then the United States is said to be dumping goods in France.

7. A voluntary export restraint is an agreement between two countries in which importing countries voluntarily agree to limit their imports of a good from another country.

8. A quota is a tax on the amount of a good that may be imported into a country.

Multiple Choice
Circle the correct answer.

EXHIBIT A

United States		Japan	
Good X	Good Y	Good X	Good Y
120	0	30	0
80	10	20	10
40	20	10	20
0	30	0	30

1. In Exhibit A, the opportunity cost of one unit of Y for the United States is ________, whereas the opportunity cost of one unit of Y for Japan is ________.
   a. 2X; 5X
   b. 10X; 2X
   c. 4X; 1X
   d. 6X; 5X
   e. none of the above

2. In Exhibit A, the United States is the lower opportunity cost producer of ________ and Japan is the lower opportunity cost producer of ________.
   a. good X; good Y
   b. both goods; neither good
   c. neither good; both goods.
   d. good Y; good X

3. Considering the data in Exhibit A, which of the following terms of trade would both countries agree to?
   a. 5.5X = 1Y
   b. 0.5X = 1Y
   c. 5X = 1Y
   d. 2X = 1Y

4. Jack paid $40 for good X and gained $10 consumers' surplus. What is the highest price Jack would have paid for the good?
   a. $50
   b. $30
   c. $60
   d. $65
   e. There is not enough information to answer the question.

5. Producers' surplus is the difference between the price ________ receive for a good and the ________ price for which they would have ________ the good.
   a. sellers; minimum; sold
   b. buyers; maximum; bought
   c. sellers; maximum; sold
   d. buyers; minimum; bought

6. The national defense argument for trade restriction contends that
   a. the president should have the authority to erect trade barriers in case of war or national emergency.
   b. free trade makes a country dependent on other countries and this weakens the national defense.
   c. a country should produce those goods necessary fro national defense purposes even if it doesn't have a comparative advantage in them.
   d. if your enemy erects trade restrictions, so should you.
   e. b and c

7. Dumping refers to
   a. buying goods at low prices in foreign countries and selling them at high prices in the United States.
   b. expensive goods being sold for low prices.
   c. government actions to remedy "unfair" trade practices.
   d. the sale of goods abroad at a price below their cost and below the price charged in the domestic market.

8. A tariff is a
   a. restriction on the number of people that can work in an export business.
   b. legal limit on the amount of a good that may be imported.
   c. business fee incurred to ship goods abroad.
   d. tax on imports.
   e. none of the above

9. Under a policy of prohibiting exports,
   a. domestic consumers have greater consumers' surplus than under a policy of permitting exports.
   b. domestic consumers have less consumers' surplus than under a policy of permitting exports.
   c. domestic producers have greater producers' surplus than under a policy of permitting exports.
   d. a and c
   e. b and c

10. Under a tariff policy,
    a. domestic consumers have greater consumers' surplus than under a policy of free trade.
    b. domestic consumers have less consumers' surplus than under a policy of free trade.
    c. domestic producers have greater producers' surplus than under a policy of free trade.
    d. a and c
    e. b and c

11. Company A is a new company that produces a good that is already produced in many foreign countries and sold in the United States. Most likely, the argument it will voice in its attempt to be protected from foreign competition is the
    a. antidumping argument.
    b. low-foreign-wages argument.
    c. job creating argument.
    d. infant industry argument.
    e. national defense argument.

12. Tariffs and quotas are
    a. beneficial for producers in a protected industry, but not beneficial for the workers in the industry.
    b. beneficial for producers in a protected industry, but not beneficial for consumers.
    c. beneficial for workers in a protected industry, but not beneficial for consumers.
    d. not beneficial for the workers in a protected industry or for consumers.
    e. b and c

13. A tariff is imposed on good X. The tariff will ________ the price of good X in the domestic market, ________ the number of units of good X imported into the domestic market, and ________ consumers' surplus.
    a. lower; raise; raise
    b. raise; lower; lower
    c. raise; lower; raise
    d. lower; raise; lower
    e. none of the above

14. Tariffs and quotas are often imposed when government is responsive to ________ interests, and the benefits of tariffs and quotas are often ________.
    a. consumer; dispersed
    b. consumer; concentrated
    c. producer; dispersed
    d. producer; concentrated

15. Which of the following is not an example of a trade restriction?
    a. tariff
    b. quota
    c. dumping
    d. a and b
    e. a, b, and c

True-False
Write "T" or "F" at the end of each statement.

16. Consumers' surplus is greater at higher prices than lower prices. ____

17. There is a net loss from tariffs. ____

18. Specialization and trade allow a country's inhabitants to consume at a level beyond its production possibilities frontier. ____

19. If the price received is $40 and producers' surplus is $10, then the minimum selling price is $30. ____

20. A quota is a legal limit on the amount of a good that may be imported. ____

Fill in the Blank
Write the correct word in the blank.

21. The ______________ argument states that domestic producers should not have to compete (on an unequal basis) with foreign producers that sell products below cost and below the prices they charge in their domestic markets.

22. As a result of a quota, the number of imported goods will ______________.

23. As a result of a tariff, consumers' surplus ______________.

24. The gains from a quota are ______________ than the losses from a quota.

25. The gains from free trade are ______________ than the losses from protected (non-free) trade.

Chapter 20
International Finance

What This Chapter Is About

The main subject of this chapter is exchange rates. What are exchange rates? How are exchange rates determined? What are the effects of changes in exchange rates? These questions and more are answered in this chapter.

Key Concepts in the Chapter

a. balance of payments
b. current account balance
c. capital account balance
d. merchandise trade balance
e. exchange rate
f. appreciation
g. depreciation
h. optimal currency area

- The **balance of payments** is a periodic statement of the money value of all transactions between residents of one country and residents of all other countries.
- The **current account balance** is the summary statistic for exports of goods and services, imports of goods and services, and net unilateral transfers abroad.
- The **capital account balance** is the summary statistic for the outflow of U.S. capital and the inflow of foreign capital. It is equal to the difference between the outflow of U.S. capital and the inflow of foreign capital.
- The **merchandise trade balance** is the difference between the value of merchandise exports and the value of merchandise imports.
- The **exchange rate** is the price of one currency in terms of another currency.
- **Appreciation** refers to an increase in the value of one currency relative to other currencies.
- **Depreciation** refers to a decrease in the value of one currency relative to other currencies.
- An **optimal currency area** is a geographic area in which exchange rates can be fixed or a common currency used without sacrificing domestic economic goals—such as low unemployment.

Review Questions

1. Give an example of a transaction that would be considered a debit item in the balance of payments.

2. Give an example of a transaction that would be considered a credit item in the balance of payments.

3. What is the difference between the current account balance and the merchandise trade balance?

4. What items compose the capital account?

5. What is the difference between a flexible and a fixed exchange rate system?

6. The demand for pounds is related to the supply of dollars. How so?

7. The supply of pounds is related to the demand for dollars. How so?

8. It took 106 yen to buy 1 dollar on Tuesday and 110 yen to buy 1 dollar on Wednesday. Has the dollar appreciated or depreciated from Tuesday to Wednesday? Explain your answer.

9. What factors can lead to a change in exchange rates?

10. Give an example of a currency that is overvalued.

11. What is the difference between a currency that is devalued and one that has depreciated?

Problems

Answer questions 1 through 5 based on the table that follows.

Item	**Dollar amount**
Merchandise exports	+ 400
Income from U.S. assets abroad	+ 36
Services (exports)	+ 80
Outflow of U.S. capital	– 33
Statistical discrepancy	– 20
Inflow of foreign capital	+ 50
Increase in U.S. official reserve assets	– 5
Decrease in foreign official assets in the U.S.	+ 4
Merchandise imports	– 410
Services (imports)	– 34
Net unilateral transfers abroad	– 18
Income from foreign assets in U.S.	– 50

1. What does the merchandise trade balance equal?

2. What does the current account balance equal?

3. What does the capital account balance equal?

4. What does the official reserve balance equal?

5. What does the balance of payments equal?

6. Suppose there are only two currencies in the world, pesos and dollars. Fill in the blank spaces in the table.

If the	**Then the**
demand for dollars rises in the foreign exchange market	
	supply of dollars falls on the foreign exchange market
	supply of pesos rises on the foreign exchange market

7. Fill in the blank spaces where a question mark appears in the table.

If	**Then**
$1 = 106 yen	1 yen = ?
$1 = 74 Kenyan shillings	1 shilling = ?
$1 = 1,500 Lebanese pounds	1 pound = ?

8. Fill in the blank spaces in the table.

The exchange rate is	**And the item costs**	**What does the item cost in dollars?**
$1 = 106 yen	18,000 yen	
$1 = £0.50	£ 34.00	
$1 = 9.44 pesos	89 pesos	

9. Fill in the blank spaces in the table.

The exchange rate changes from	**Has the dollar appreciated or depreciated?**
$2 = £1 to $2.50 = £1	
109 yen = $1 to 189 yen = $1	
10 pesos = $1 to 8 pesos = $1	

10. Fill in the blank spaces in the table.

If …	**The dollar will (appreciate, depreciate)**
the real interest rate in the U.S. rises relative to real interest rates in other countries	
income in foreign countries (that trade with the U.S.) rises relative to income in the United States	
the inflation rate in the U.S. rises and the inflation rate in all other countries falls	

11. Fill in the blank spaces in the table.

If the equilibrium exchange rate is $1 = £ 0.50 and the official exchange rate is	**Then the dollar is (overvalued, undervalued)**
$1 = £ 0.60	
$1 = £ 0.30	

What is the Question?

Identify the question for each of the answers that follow.

1. Any transaction that supplies the country's currency in the foreign exchange market.

2. Any transaction that creates a demand for the country's currency in the foreign exchange market.

3. The summary statistic for the exports of goods and services, imports of goods and services, and net unilateral transfers abroad.

4. The difference between the value of merchandise exports and the value of merchandise imports.

5. One-way money payments.

6. The price of one currency in terms of another currency.

7. It predicts that the exchange rates between any two currencies will adjust to reflect changes in the relative price levels of the two countries.

8. Raising the official price of a currency.

What Is Wrong?

In each of the statements that follow, something is wrong. Identify what is wrong in the space provided.

1. The balance of payments is the summary statistic for the current account balance, capital account balance, net unilateral transfers abroad, and statistical discrepancy.

2. The demand for dollars on the foreign exchange market is linked to the supply of dollars on the foreign exchange market. In short, if the demand for dollars rises, the supply of dollars rises, too.

3. There are two countries, A and B. The income of Country B rises and the income of Country A remains constant. As a result, the currency of Country B appreciates.

4. There are two countries, C and D. The price level in Country C rises 10 percent and the inflation rate in Country D is zero percent. As a result, the demand for Country C's goods rises, and the supply of its currency falls.

5. A change in real interest rates across countries cannot change the exchange rate.

6. If the equilibrium exchange rate is £1 = \$1.50, and the official exchange rate is £1 = \$1.60, then the dollar is overvalued and the pound is undervalued.

7. An international monetary fund right is a special international money created by the IMF.

Multiple Choice
Circle the correct answer.

1. An international transaction that supplies the nation's currency also creates a
   a. supply of foreign currency, and is recorded as a credit in the balance of payments.
   b. demand for foreign currency, and is recorded as a credit in the balance of payments.
   c. demand for foreign currency, and is recorded as a debit in the balance of payments.
   d. supply of the nation's currency, and is recorded as a debit in the balance of payments.

2. If the French buy American computers, they
   a. demand U.S. dollars and supply French francs.
   b. demand U.S. dollars and demand French francs.
   c. supply U.S. dollars and demand French francs.
   d. supply both U.S. dollars and French francs.

Exhibit A

Components of the Balance of Payments	($ billions)
Exports of goods and services	+ 330
Merchandise exports (including military sales)	+ 150
Export services	+ 40
Income from U.S. assets abroad	+ 140
Imports of goods and services	– 390
Merchandise imports (including military sales)	– 220
Import services	– 80
Income from foreign assets abroad	– 90
Net unilateral transfers abroad	– 21
Outflow of U.S. capital	– 46
Inflow of foreign capital	+ 60
Increase in U.S. official reserve assets	– 21
Increase in foreign official assets in U.S.	+ 23
Statistical discrepancy	+ 65

3. In Exhibit A, the merchandise trade balance equals ______ billion dollars.
   a. – 80
   b. + 100
   c. – 70
   d. + 60
   e. none of the above

4. In Exhibit A, the current account balance equals ______ billion dollars.
   a. – 111
   b. – 81
   c. – 60
   d. + 63
   e. none of the above

5. In Exhibit A, the capital account balance equals ______ billion dollars.
   a. + 15
   b. – 10
   c. + 14
   d. – 14
   e. none of the above

6. In Exhibit A, the official reserve balance equals ______ billion dollars.
   a. + 2
   b. − 1
   c. + 10
   d. + 17
   e. none of the above

7. The three major components of the current account are
   a. exports of goods and services, imports of goods and services, and statistical discrepancy.
   b. outflow of U.S. foreign capital, inflow of foreign capital, and statistical discrepancy.
   c. merchandise exports, merchandise imports, and net unilateral transfers abroad
   d. exports of goods and services, imports of goods and services, and inflow of foreign capital.
   e. none of the above

8. The lower the dollar price per yen, the ______ Japanese goods are for Americans and the ______ Japanese goods Americans will buy; thus ______ yen will be demanded.
   a. more expensive; more; fewer
   b. more expensive; fewer; fewer
   c. less expensive; more; more
   d. less expensive; more; fewer
   e. none of the above

9. An American computer is priced at $5,500. If the exchange rate between the U.S. dollar and the British pound is $1.70 = £1, approximately how many pounds will a British buyer pay for the computer?
   a. £3,235
   b. £3,052
   c. £2,543
   d. £6,599

10. If the dollar price per pound moves from $1.90 = £1 to $1.40 = £1, the pound is said to have ______ and the dollar to have ______.
    a. depreciated; appreciated
    b. appreciated; appreciated
    c. appreciated; depreciated
    d. depreciated; depreciated

11. The U.S. dollar has appreciated relative to the French franc if it takes
    a. fewer francs to buy a dollar.
    b. fewer dollars to buy a franc.
    c. more dollars to buy a franc.
    d. a and c
    e. none of the above

12. Suppose the current exchange rate between the dollar and British pound is $1.70 = 1 £. Furthermore, suppose the price level in the United States rises 25 percent at a time when the British price level is stable. According to the purchasing power parity theory, what will be the new equilibrium exchange rate?
    a. $2.72 = £1
    b. $1.55 = £1
    c. $1.86 = £1
    d. $2.13 = £1

13. The purchasing power parity theory predicts less nearly accurately in the _____ run, and when there is a ______ difference in inflation rates across countries.
    a. long; small
    b. short; large
    c. long; large
    d. short; small

14. Under a fixed exchange rate system, if the Mexican peso is overvalued then there exists
    a. a shortage of pesos.
    b. a surplus of pesos.
    c. the equilibrium level of pesos.
    d. there is not enough information to answer the question (we need to know the actual exchange rate)

15. One of the things a nation must do if it is on an international gold standard is
    a. link its money supply to its gold holdings.
    b. increase taxes.
    c. declare itself to be on a flexible exchange rate system.
    d. revalue its currency.
    e. none of the above

True-False

Write "T" or "F" after each statement.

16. From the 1870s to the 1930s, many nations tied their currencies to gold. ____

17. Under the Bretton Woods system, nations were expected to maintain fixed exchange rates (within a narrow range) by buying and selling their own currency for other currencies. ____

18. Any transaction that supplies the nation's currency is recorded as a debit in the balance of payments. ____

19. The current account balance is the summary statistic for exports of goods and services, imports of goods and services, and the statistical discrepancy. ____

20. Any transaction that supplies a foreign currency is recorded as a credit in the balance of payments. ____

Fill in the Blank

Write the correct word in the blank.

21. The ______________ ______________ ______________ is the difference between the value of merchandise exports and the value of merchandise imports.

22. The ______________ ______________ ______________ ______________ predicts that changes in the relative price levels of two countries will affect the exchange rate in such a way that one unit of nation's currency will continue to buy the same amount of foreign goods as it did before the change in the relative price levels.

23. When nations adopt the gold standard, they automatically ____________ their exchange rates.

24. A __________________ occurs when the official price of currency (under the fixed exchange rate system) is lowered.

25. Central banks play a much larger role under a ______________ exchange rate system than under a ______________ exchange rate system.

Answer Key

Chapter 1
Answers

Review Questions

1. Yes and no. This is only part of scarcity. Scarcity is the condition in which people have infinite wants *and* there are not enough resources (finite resources) to satisfy those wants.
2. A good gives a person utility or satisfaction; a bad gives a person disutility or dissatisfaction. People want goods and they don't want bads.
3. Josie likes to play music on Friday night. Music is a good on Friday night. Josie doesn't like to play music when she is studying for an exam. At that time, music is a bad.
4. The opportunity cost of your reading this study guide is whatever you would be doing if you weren't reading it. If you would be watching television, then watching television is the opportunity cost of your reading this study guide.
5. People are interested in only doing things when the benefits are greater than the costs. As the cost of smoking rises, it will be the case (for some people) that the benefits of smoking will no longer be greater than the costs, and therefore they will quit smoking.
6. marginal
7. Harriet considers what is relevant. Only the benefits of the next hour and the costs of the next hour are relevant to her. Costs and benefits in the past are not relevant. What does it matter what the costs and benefits have been? What matters is what they are expected to be. Marginal benefits and marginal costs deal with "additions," hence they deal with benefits and costs to come.
8. Answers will vary. Here is a sample answer. Someone takes a sleeping pill at night in order to get a restful sleep. Getting a restful sleep is the intended effect. The person does get a restful sleep, but also feels rather groggy for the first two hours she is up in the morning. Feeling groggy is an unintended effect.
9. Because scarcity exists—because our wants are greater than the resources available to satisfy them—we must decide (choose) which of our wants we will satisfy and which of our wants we won't satisfy. When we make choices, we necessarily incur an opportunity cost. After all, to choose to do X is to choose not to do Y. Y is the opportunity cost of doing X.
10. To think in terms of what would have been is to think in terms of opportunity cost. For example, you choose to go for a jog by the beach. What might have been had you not decided to jog by the beach? What would you have done instead? Whatever it was, it was the opportunity cost of your jogging by the beach.
11. A theory is an abstract representation of reality.
12. Probably so. People "build" theories (even casually) in order to answer questions that are not easily answered. In their pursuit of answers, they focus in on what they believe are key causal factors to explain what it is they want explained. Everyone does this, not only the economist, biologist, and psychologist. On some level, almost everyone builds theories or theorizes.
13. The seven steps are: (a) decide on what it is you want to explain; (b) identify the variables you think are important to explaining what you want to explain; (c) state the assumptions of a theory; (d) state the hypothesis; (e) test the theory by comparing its predictions against real-world events; (f) if the evidence supports the theory, take no further action; (g) if the evidence rejects the theory, then formulate a new theory or amend the old theory.
14. Because theories that have sounded wrong (in the past) have turned out to the right. The round-earth theory sounded wrong to many people long ago, but it predicts well. If human beings were to have complete information, and knew everything there is to know, then we might be able to judge theories by how they "sound" to us. Unfortunately, though, we do not have complete information and we make mistakes. We need to take a scientific approach to judging theories. Theories should be judged according to how well they explain and predict things.

15. An assumption is something someone believes is true but can't prove is true. Jim assumes that everyone works to be happy. He can't prove this, but he believes it is true.
16. Answers will vary. The following is an example in which association is causation: George steps on a nail and later his foot begins to hurt. George's stepping on a nail and his foot hurting are associated in time—one event comes closely before the other. Furthermore, it was stepping on the nail that caused George's foot to hurt. The following is an example in which association is not causation: It is sunny and warm today and Jennifer lost her wallet. The sunny, warm day is associated with Jennifer's losing her wallet in time, but the sunny, warm day didn't cause Jennifer to lose her wallet.
17. The right amount of time to study—or the efficient amount of time to study—is the amount of time at which the marginal benefits of studying equal the marginal costs.
18. Answers will vary.

Theory on a Television Show

1. Two things might have happened: (a) when George walked up to the woman, she would have treated him the way women always treat him; or (b) when George confronted the two rowdy men in the movie theater, they would have behaved toward him the way two men would always behave toward George if he confronted them. Generally, for Jerry's theory to be incorrect, George would have to go against his every instinct, and things would have to turn out the same way as they always do.
2. It is still early in your study of economics to know the answer, but it is worth taking an educated guess. The following are some of the things that economists build theories to explain: unemployment, economic growth, business cycles (the ups and downs of the economy), why firms produce the level of output that they produce, how firms price their goods, inflation, exchange rates, and much more.

Problems

1.

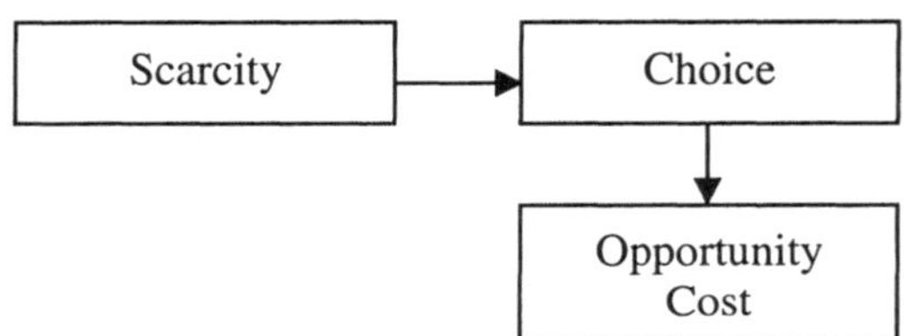

2.

Factor	Benefits of attending college	Costs of attending college	More likely to go to college? Yes or No
Jim thought he would earn $20 an hour if he didn't go to college, but learns that he will earn $35 an hour instead.		↑	No
His friends are going to college and he likes being around his friends.	↑		Yes
The salary gap between college graduates and high school graduates has widened.	↑		Yes
Jim learns something about himself: he doesn't like to study.		↑	No
The college he is thinking about attending just opened a satellite campus near Jim's home.		↓	Yes
The economy has taken a downturn and it looks like there are very few jobs for high school graduates right now.		↓	Yes

3.

Statement	The person is assuming that this does not change:
People who don't brush their teeth will get cavities.	People will not change the amount of fluoridated water they drink.
As people get older, they tend to put on weight because their metabolism slows down.	People will not change the amount they exercise.
If he studies more, he will get higher grades.	He won't change how focused he is when he studies.

4. a. microeconomics, b. macroeconomics, c. macroeconomics, d. macroeconomics, e. microeconomics, f. microeconomics, g. microeconomics

5. Answers will vary. In each case, you want to ask yourself what you would do if you chose not to do the activity specified. The following are some sample answers.

Activity	Opportunity Cost
Study one more hour each night	Watch television
Take a long trip to someplace you have always wanted to visit	Buy a new car
Sit in the back of the room in one of your classes	Sit in the middle of the room
Talk up more in class	Daydream
Get a regular medical checkup	Play tennis
Surf the Web more	Watch television

What Is Wrong?

1. People have finite wants and infinite resources.

   People have infinite wants and resources are finite. This is scarcity.

2. People prefer more bads to fewer bads.

   Since people receive disutility from bads, they want fewer bads. Alternatively, you could say that people prefer more goods to fewer goods.

3. Scarcity is an effect of competition.

   Competition is an effect of scarcity.

4. The lower the opportunity cost of playing tennis, the less likely a person will play tennis.

   The lower the opportunity cost of playing tennis, the more likely a person will play tennis. The higher the opportunity cost of playing tennis, the less likely a person will play tennis.

5. Abstract means to add more variables to the process of theorizing.

   When we abstract, we remove variables that we, as theorists, don't think explain the phenomena at hand.

6. Microeconomics is the branch of economics that deals with human behavior and choices as they relate to highly aggregate markets or the entire economy.

   Macroeconomics is the branch of economics that deals with human behavior and choices as they relate to highly aggregate markets or the entire economy.

7. Positive economics is to normative economics what opinion is to truth.

    Positive economics and truth are more closely aligned, as are normative economics and opinion.

8. Because there are rationing devices, there will always be scarcity.

    Because there is scarcity, there will always be rationing devices.

9. The four factors of production, or resources, are land, labor, capital, and profit.

    Profit is not a factor of production, it is a payment to a factor of production. The missing factor of production is entrepreneurship.

10. Karen doesn't like to study so no one likes to study. This is an example of the association is not causation issue.

    This is an example of the fallacy of composition.

Multiple Choice

1. c
2. b
3. a
4. b
5. c
6. c
7. d
8. a
9. b
10. a
11. a
12. c
13. a
14. c
15. c
16. d

True-False

17. T
18. F
19. T
20. F
21. F
22. F

Fill in the Blank

23. fallacy of composition
24. association is causation
25. ceteris paribus
26. Macroeconomics
27. fails to reject
28. marginal
29. capital
30. entrepreneur
31. Alfred Marshall

Chapter 2
Answers

Review Questions

1. *Ex ante* position. *Ex ante* means before the exchange.
2. \$3. Consumers' surplus is the difference between maximum buying price (\$10) and price paid (\$7).
3. Compare your consumers' surplus (CS) before and after the change. If your CS is higher after, you have been made better off; if it is lower, you have been made worse off; if it is unchanged, then you are neither better nor worse off.
4. It means consumers prefer low to high prices for what they buy.
5. The transaction costs of buying a hamburger are lower than selling a house. There are many things involved in selling a house—finding an agent to list the house, signing contracts, etc.
6. Jake buys a cigarette from George and then smokes the cigarette while sitting next to Tabitha. Tabitha is allergic to cigarette smoke.
7. 1X = 1.5Y; 1Y = 0.66X
8. Through specialization and trade people can consume more goods. But this doesn't answer why this happens. It happens because when people specialize, they produce those things that they can produce at a lower cost than other people. In other words, they are doing what they do best and then trading with others. If everyone does what he or she does best, you would naturally think that everyone has to be better off—at least as compared to the situation where no one does his or her best.
9. People trade to make themselves better off. The necessary condition: People have to value what they will trade for more than what they will trade with. For example, if Yvonne trades \$10 for a book, she values the book (which she doesn't currently have) more than the \$10 (which she currently does have).
10. We have to give up 10 units of X to produce the first 10 units of Y, but we have to give up 20 units of X to produce the second 10 units of Y.
11. It indicates constant costs.
12. It indicates increasing costs.
13. These are two points *on* its PPF, which means the two points are efficient. Efficiency implies the impossibility of gains in one area without losses in another. This is what a tradeoff is about: more of one thing, but less of something else.
14. An advance in technology; more resources.
15. Answers will vary. The example you come up with should make it possible to produce more goods with the same resources.
16. What goods will be produced? How will the goods be produced? For whom will the goods be produced?

Problems

1. \$140
2. \$15
3. 1 hat = \$30 or 1 hat = \$20. Any price lower than \$40 gives us the correct answer.
4. If the entrepreneur can lower Karen's transaction costs from \$60 to \$24 (a reduction of \$36), then Karen will make the trade. Karen will think this way: I pay \$370 to the seller, and \$5 to the entrepreneur, for a total of \$375. My maximum buying price is \$400, so I will receive \$25 consumers' surplus. But what about transaction costs? As long as my transaction costs are not more than, say, \$24, I will receive at least \$1 consumers' surplus and the exchange is worth it to me. The entrepreneur will have to lower Randy's transaction costs from \$60 to \$14 (a reduction of \$46). Randy will think this way: I receive \$370 from the buyer and I pay \$5 to the entrepreneur. This leaves me with \$365. My minimum selling price is \$350, so I receive \$15 consumers' surplus. But what about transaction costs? As long as my transaction costs are not higher than, say, \$14, I will receive \$1 producers' surplus and the exchange is worth it to me.

5.

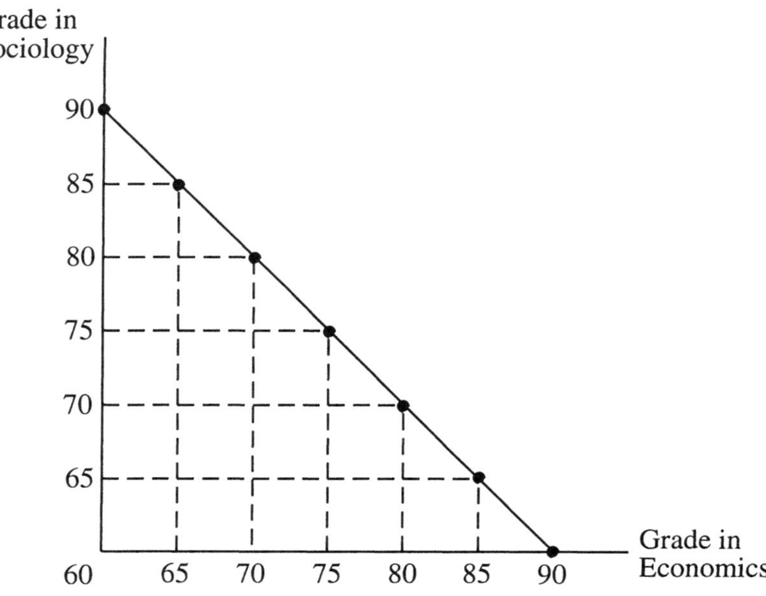

6. 5 fewer points in sociology.
7. Points A and D
8. Points B and C
9. Points E and F
10. Yes, point D could be efficient. The reason why is that there are tradeoffs moving from one efficient point to another. In other words, more of one good comes with less of another good.
11.

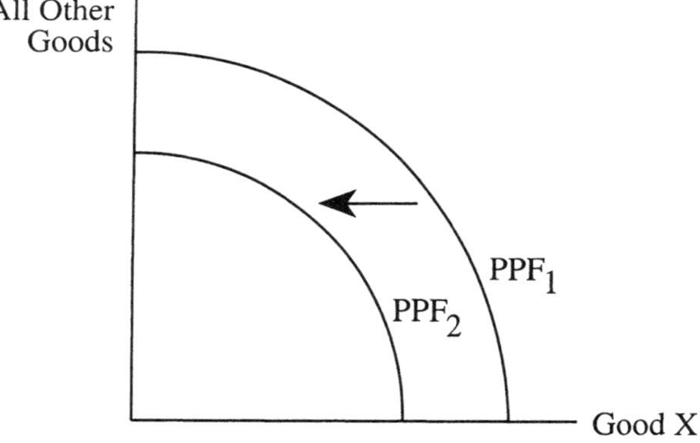

12.

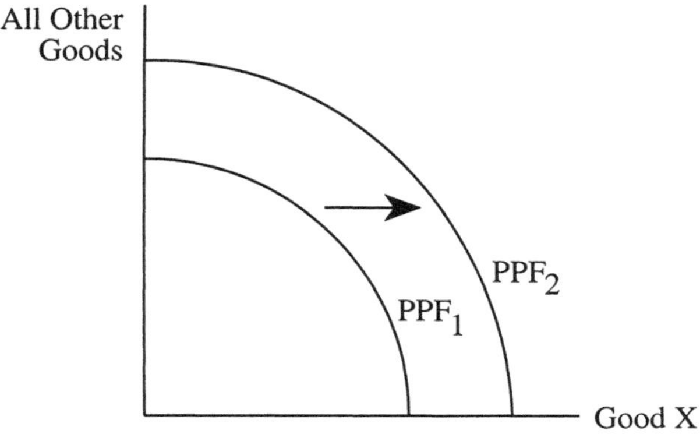

What Is Wrong?

1. If costs are increasing, the PPF is a straight (downward-sloping) line.

   If costs are increasing, the PPF is bowed outward. Alternatively you could say: If costs are constant, the PPF is a straight line.

2. Mary said that she received $40 consumers' surplus when she paid $50 for the good and only $30 consumers' surplus when she paid $45 for the good.

   Mary is wrong since the lower the price, the more consumers' surplus.

3. If Jones can produce either (a) 100 units of X and 100 units of Y or (b) 200 units of X and zero units of Y, then he has a comparative advantage in the production of Y.

   We don't know whether he has a comparative advantage in Y or not. To know this, we have to compare his costs to someone else's costs.

4. The following PPF represents a 2-for-1 opportunity cost of apples.

   It is a 1-for-1 opportunity cost of apples. For every apple produced, one orange is not produced. For every one orange produced, one apple is not produced.

5. There are probably more unemployed resources at point A than at point D.

   There are more unemployed resources at D, a point below the PPF.

6. Efficiency implies the possibility of gains in one area without losses in another area.

   Efficiency implies the impossibility of gains in one area without losses in another area. Alternatively, you could have written, Inefficiency implies the possibility of gains in one area without losses in another area.

7. If Georgina reads one more book, she will have to give up doing something else. This shows that Georgina is inefficient.

   When there is efficiency, there are tradeoffs. Georgina cannot do more of one thing without doing less of something else.

8. For a given quantity of output, a rise in price reduces producers' surplus and increases consumers' surplus.

   For a given quantity of output, a rise in price reduces consumers' surplus and increases producers' surplus. Alternatively, you could have written: For a given quantity of output, a fall in price reduces producers' surplus and increases consumers' surplus.

9. If Bobby can produce either (a) 100 units of good X and 50 units of good Y, or (b) 25 units of good X and 80 units of good Y, then the cost of 1 unit of good X is 1.5 units of good Y.

   The cost of 1 unit of good X is 0.4 units of good Y.

10. John says, "I bought this sweater yesterday and I think I got a bad deal." It follows that in the *ex ante* position John thought he would be better off with the sweater than with the money he paid for it, but in the *ex post* position he prefers the money to the sweater.

    This could be true, but it could be that John is not disheartened about the trade (of money for the sweater), but about the terms of exchange. He may simply have preferred to pay less for the sweater.

Multiple Choice

1. b
2. d
3. c
4. c
5. c
6. e
7. a
8. b
9. d
10. b
11. a
12. a
13. e
14. d
15. e

True-False

16. T
17. F
18. F
19. T
20. T

Fill in the Blank

21. What goods will be produced? How will the goods be produced? For whom will the goods be produced?
22. Inefficiency
23. Efficiency
24. 8

Chapter 3
Answers

Review Questions

1. Price and quantity demanded are inversely related, *ceteris paribus*.
2. Price and quantity demanded move in opposite directions: as price rises, quantity demanded falls, and as price falls, quantity demanded rises.
3. Amount of a good buyers are willing and able to buy at a particular price. For example, quantity demanded may be 100 units at $10 per unit.
4. Quantity demanded is a specific number—such as 100 units. Demand is a relationship between various prices and various quantities demanded.
5. income, preferences, prices of related goods (substitutes and complements), number of buyers, expectations of future price.
6. to the right
7. to the left
8. Amount of a good sellers are willing and able to produce at a particular price.
9. Quantity supplied is constant as price changes. Stated differently, quantity supplied is independent of (does not depend on) changes in price.
10. Price and quantity supplied are directly related.
11. prices of relevant resources, technology, number of sellers, expectations of future price, taxes and subsidies, government restrictions
12. to the right
13. to the left
14. Quantity of the good is on the horizontal axis, price is on the vertical axis.
15. The absolute price of a good is the money price of a good—such as $3,000 for a computer. The relative price of a good is the price of the good in terms of some other good. For example, if the absolute price of a computer is $3,000, and the absolute price of a TV set is $1,000, then the relative price of a computer (in terms of TV sets) is 3 TV sets.
16. Equilibrium price and quantity rise.
17. Equilibrium price falls and equilibrium quantity rises.
18. Equilibrium price and quantity rise.
19. Equilibrium price rises and equilibrium quantity falls.
20. Consumers' surplus falls. Consumers' surplus equals maximum buying price minus price paid, so if price paid rises, consumers' surplus must fall.

Problems

1.

Factor	**Demand**	**Supply**	**Equilibrium Price**	**Equilibrium Quantity**
Price of a substitute rises	↑		↑	↑
Price of a complement falls	↑		↑	↑
Income rises (normal good)	↑		↑	↑
Income falls (inferior good)	↑		↑	↑
Price of relevant resource rises		↓	↑	↓
Technology advances		↑	↓	↑
Quota		↓	↑	↓
Number of buyers rises	↑		↑	↑
Number of sellers rises		↑	↓	↑
Buyers expect higher price	↑		↑	↑
Sellers expect higher price		↓	↑	↓
Tax on production		↓	↑	↓
Preferences become more favorable with respect to the good	↑		↑	↑

2.

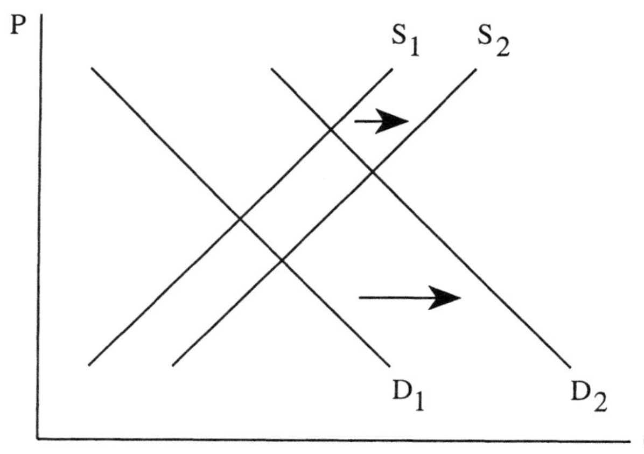

3.

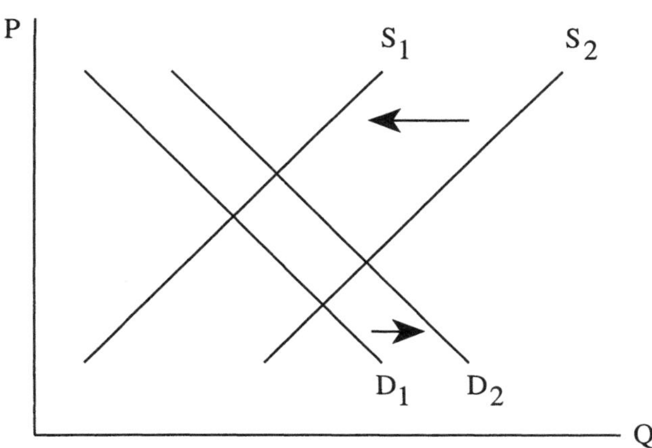

4. A + B + C + D
5. E + F + G + H
6. 140 – 50 = 90 units
7. 180 – 60 = 120 units
8.

Price	Quantity demanded by John	Quantity demanded by Mary	Quantity demanded (market demand)
$10	100	130	230
$12	80	120	200
$14	50	100	150

9. $6
10. Jack's first candy bar gives him more utility than the second; the second gives him more utility than the third; and so on.

What Is Wrong?

1. If the price of a good rises, the demand for the good will fall.

   If the price of a good rises, the quantity demand for the good will fall. (not demand)

2. Consumers' surplus is equal to the minimum selling price minus price paid.

   Consumers' surplus is equal to the maximum buying price minus price paid.

3. As income rises, demand for a normal good rises; as income falls, demand for an inferior good falls.

   ...as income falls, demand for an inferior good rises.

4. The supply curve for Picasso paintings is upward-sloping.

   The supply curve for Picasso paintings is vertical.

5. As price rises, supply rises; as price falls, supply falls.

   As price rises, quantity supplied rises; as price falls, quantity supplied falls.

6. Quantity demanded is greater than supply when there is a shortage.

   Quantity demanded is greater than quantity supplied when there is a shortage.

7. If supply rises, and demand is constant, equilibrium price rises and equilibrium quantity rises.

   If supply rises, and demand is constant, equilibrium price falls and equilibrium quantity rises.

8. The law of diminishing marginal utility states that as a consumer consumes additional units of a good, each successive unit gives him or her more utility than the previous unit.

   ...each successive unit gives him or her less utility than the previous unit.

9. According to the law of demand, as the price of a good rises, the quantity demanded of the good rises, *ceteris paribus.*

   According to the law of demand, as the price of a good rises, the quantity demanded of the good falls, ceteris paribus.

Multiple Choice

1. d
2. c
3. e
4. b
5. c
6. b
7. b
8. b
9. e
10. b
11. d
12. a
13. a
14. d
15. d

True-False

16. F
17. F
18. T
19. F
20. T

Fill in the Blank

21. falls; rises
22. market
23. inferior
24. increases
25. equals
26. tie-in

Chapter 4
Answers

Review Questions

1. Requirements for admission (scores on standardized tests, grade point averages) will rise. As student tuition remains constant in the face of rising demand, the gap between the student tuition and equilibrium tuition will increase. Or, the shortage of spaces at the university will increase. There will be "more work" for the nonprice rationing devices to do.
2. To get a lower price, (1) demand can fall, (2) demand can fall and supply can rise, (3) demand can rise by less than supply rises, or (4) supply can rise.
3. By price.
4. Answers will vary. Generally, you want to identify goods that have a used market. Cars were discussed in the text. Books are another good that have a used market. For example, there is a used textbook market.
5. If the university charges a below-equilibrium price for parking, there will be a shortage of parking spaces. Something will have to ration the available parking spots. It is more likely to be first-come-first-served (FCFS). What happens if you're not one of the first in line to park? You might end up being late to class.
6. Raise price, raise supply, lower demand. The freeway congestion is evidence of a shortage. There are three ways to get rid of a shortage. The first is to allow price to move up to its equilibrium level, where quantity demanded is equal to quantity supplied. The second is to raise supply enough so that there is no more shortage. The third is to lower demand enough so that there is no more shortage. Increasing supply, in the context of freeway congestion, means adding more freeways. Lowering demand means, perhaps, giving people an incentive to carpool to a greater degree.
7. Because if, at any point in time, gold prices weren't the same everywhere in the world, there would exist an opportunity to buy gold in one location at a low price and sell it in another location at a high price. This difference in gold prices would lead to a reallocation of gold supply and, eventually, the same price for gold everywhere.
8. Yes, patients will pay more for health care when they have the right to sue their provider than when they do not have the right to sue. That's because when patients have the right to sue, the costs to the provider of providing health care are higher, and thus the supply curve of health care is closer to the origin. This results in a higher price for health care.
9. The price (people pay) for good weather is one component of the overall price for housing in a good-weather city.
10. A tip exists if the equilibrium price for a seat is greater than the price charged for the seat. Hotel casinos in Las Vegas price some seats at less than equilibrium, so a tip naturally emerges; baseball team owners do not price their seats at less than equilibrium and so there is no need for a tip.

Problems

1. Suppose there is a downward-sloping demand for losing one's temper. If so, the higher the price to lose one's temper, the less one will lose one's temper. Yvonne's father charges her a higher price to lose her temper than Yvonne's mother charges her. Notice that people don't often lose their tempers with their bosses (the price you would have to pay is too high), but will lose their tempers with family members, etc.
2. Driving takes time. For example, it might take 20 minutes, going at 50 mph, to go from point X to point Y. The more valuable time is, the more a person will want to economize on time. How valuable time is may be a function of one's wage rate. The higher one's wage rate, the more valuable time is, and the more one will want to economize on time. The 68-year-old retired person may face a lower wage rate than t he 32-year-old working person and so time is less valuable to the older person than to the younger person. We would expect the 68-year-old to care less about whether or not he drives slowly because time is less valuable to him or her.

3. Answers will vary. Here is a sample answer. When students pay the equilibrium, professors know that the quantity demanded of spots at the university equals the quantity supplied. If they do something that students don't like, then the demand curve may fall (for education at the university) and, at the given tuition, quantity supplied will be greater than quantity demanded. In other words, there will be a surplus. Will the university get rid of some professors when this happens? Now consider the case when students pay below-equilibrium tuition. Professors know that there is a shortage of space at the university. If they do something that some of their students don't like, and the students leave the university, there are others to take their places (because of the shortage). We predict the following. *If* there is a difference between the way a professor wants to teach a class and the way students want it taught, the professor is more likely to respond to the preferences of the students in the first setting (where students pay equilibrium tuition) than in the second setting (where there is a shortage of students due to a below-equilibrium tuition being charged).
4. Answers will vary. This is a good question to think about.
5. After decriminalization, the demand for marijuana increases by the same amount as the supply of marijuana.
6. Both believe there will be a cutback in employment, so there is no disagreement as to direction (down). The argument is over the magnitude of the downward change.
7. It must be vertical. The supply curve of kidneys discussed in the text was upward-sloping, not vertical. An upward-sloping supply curve illustrates a direct relationship between price and quantity supplied.
8. If a candy bar sells for more in location X than Y, candy bars will be moved from Y to X in search of the higher price. In other words, the supply of candy bars will be reallocated in such a way that no candy bar (in any location) will sell for more or less than any other candy bar. It is not as easy to reallocate houses on land. In short, if a house sells for more in location X than Y, it is difficult (if not impossible) to pick up the house (attached to the land it is on) and move it from Y to X. Since the supply of houses on land cannot be reallocated as easily as candy bars, we would expect that housing prices may differ between locations whereas candy bar prices will not.
9. A car that does not sell does not mean "a bad car." It could simply mean a higher-than-equilibrium price. Jones's car may be a great car, for which the equilibrium price may be, say, $30,000. However, if Jones is charging $100,000 for the car, no one will buy it.
10. He or she forgets, overlooks, or ignores that professors in different fields do not all face the same market conditions. The demand for economists may be higher than the demand for sociologists, and if the supply of each is the same, the equilibrium wage for economists will be higher than the equilibrium wage for sociologists. Suppose we pay economists the same as sociologists, and that the salary we pay each is midway between the equilibrium wage of economists and the equilibrium wage of sociologists. What happens now? There will be a shortage of economists and a surplus of sociologists.

What May Have Been Overlooked?

1. The higher the demand for something, the greater the quantity demanded.

   This is true at a given price. However, a lower price and lower demand can generate a greater quantity demanded than a higher price and higher demand.

2. I think how I behave is independent of the setting that I am in. I act the same way no matter what the setting.

   The person has overlooked the fact that the price of acting a certain way may be different in different settings and that people usually respond to changes in price.

3. If there were no flea markets or garage sales (where people can buy old furniture), new furniture companies would sell more (new) furniture.

   This is the used-car-market example in disguise. The person sees one fact that affects the demand for new furniture, but not another. She sees the fact that if there were fewer buyers of old furniture, there would be more buyers of new furniture. What she doesn't see is that the demand for new furniture is higher if furniture (purchased) can be resold.

4. The rock bank has the best interest of its fans in mind. It knows it can charge $80 a ticket, but it charges only $20 a ticket so that its fans won't have to pay so much.

   What the rock band forgets is that people pay in money or in something else. If $80 is the equilibrium price, then $20 is a below-equilibrium price, at which there will be a shortage of tickets. How will the tickets be rationed? By a combination of first-come-first-served (FCFS). FCFS will no doubt lead to fans standing in long lines to get tickets, some of whom will end up not getting the tickets. Fans will pay by standing in line instead of more money.

5. If my university doesn't charge for student parking, then I am definitely better off than I would be if it did charge for student parking.

   Not necessarily. If there is some positive equilibrium price for parking, then a zero price will create a shortage of parking spots and some nonprice rationing device will come into play. It will probably be first-come-first-served (FCFS), which will cause students to have to pay for parking spots in time instead of money.

6. The tuition at Harvard is very high, so Harvard must be charging the equilibrium tuition to students. Still, Harvard uses such things as GPA, SAT and ACT scores for admission purposes. It must be wrong that these nonprice rationing devices (GPA, etc.) are used only by colleges and universities that charge below-equilibrium tuition.

   The demand for Harvard may be very high, such that even at the high tuition charged, there still is a shortage of spots at Harvard. In other words, Harvard can still charge a high tuition and the high tuition may still not be high enough to equal the equilibrium tuition.

7. If a good doesn't have a money price, it has no price at all.

   Price connotes sacrifice, or giving up something to get something. Someone offers you free tickets to a concert if you will drive to his house and pick up the tickets and later that week mow his lawn. No money has changed hands, but if you accept the deal you will have to pay a nonmoney price for the tickets.

Multiple Choice

1. e
2. b
3. b
4. b
5. c
6. c
7. b
8. e
9. b
10. e
11. e
12. a
13. b
14. b
15. d

True-False

16. T
17. T
18. T
19. F
20. T

Fill in the Blank

21. quantity demanded
22. higher
23. nonprice rationing
24. equilibrium; admission
25. John's; Bill

Chapter 5
Answers

Review Questions

1. Price elasticity of demand is equal to the percentage change in quantity demanded divided by the percentage change in price. It is a measure of the responsiveness in quantity demanded to a change in price.
2. The more substitutes for a good, the higher the price elasticity of demand. The fewer substitutes for a good, the lower the price elasticity of demand.
3. No. The more substitutes for a good, the higher the price elasticity of demand, but still the elasticity coefficient can be less than 1 (which makes demand for the good inelastic).
4. The more time that has passed (since a change in price), the higher price elasticity of demand.
5. The larger one's budget that goes for the purchase of a good, the higher price elasticity of demand.
6. Cross elasticity of demand measures the responsiveness in quantity demanded of one good given a change in the price of another good.
7. It means that the percentage change in quantity demanded of a good is less than the percentage change in income. For example, if income rises by 10 percent and quantity demanded for good A rises by 5 percent, then good A is income inelastic.
8. It is a measure of the responsiveness in quantity supplied to a change in price.

Problems

1.

Price and quantity demanded at point A	Price and quantity demanded at point B	Price elasticity of demand is equal to	Is demand (elastic, unit elastic, or inelastic)?
$10 100	$8 140	3.0	elastic
$8 200	$15 120	0.82	inelastic
$7 40	$10 33	0.54	inelastic

2.

Price elasticity of demand is	Change	Price elasticity of demand (rises, falls, remains unchanged)
0.34	more substitutes for the good	rises
1.99	more time passes since change in price	rises
2.20	smaller percentage of one's budget spent on the good	falls

3.

Demand is	Price (rises, falls)	Total revenue (rises, falls, remains unchanged)
elastic	falls	rises
inelastic	rises	rises
unit elastic	rises	remains unchanged
inelastic	falls	falls
elastic	rises	falls

4.

Price of good X (rises, falls)	Quantity demanded of good Y (rises, falls)	Cross elasticity of demand is	The two goods, X and Y, are (substitutes, complements)
rises by 10 percent	falls by 5 percent	0.5	complements
falls by 20 percent	rises by 4 percent	5	substitutes
rises by 8 percent	rises by 5 percent	0.625	complements

5.

Income (rises, falls)	Quantity demanded (rises, falls)	Income elasticity of demand is
rises by 20 percent	rises by 10 percent	0.5
falls by 10 percent	falls by 15 percent	1.5
rises by 5 percent	rises by 20 percent	4.0

6.

Price (rises, falls)	Quantity supplied (rises, falls)	Is supply (elastic, inelastic, unit elastic)?
rises 3 percent	rises 4 percent	elastic
rises 1 percent	rises 6 percent	elastic
falls 20 percent	falls 10 percent	inelastic

7.

Initial equilibrium price and quantity		New equilibrium price and quantity (after $1 tax has been placed on supplier)		Percentage of the tax paid by the seller in terms of a higher price	Percentage of the tax paid by the seller in terms of a lower price kept
$40	100	$40.44	90	44 percent	56 percent
$9	87	$9.57	80	57 percent	43 percent
$10	200	$10.76	150	76 percent	24 percent

8. $1 tax (per unit of production) is placed on the seller. With D_1, price rises more than with D_2.

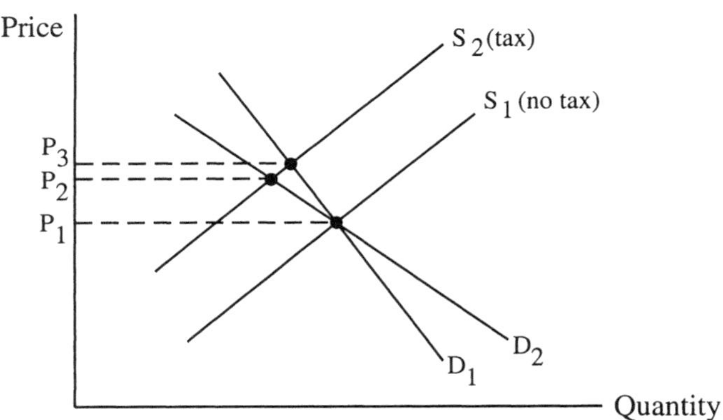

What Is the Question?

1. Measures the responsiveness of quantity demanded given a change in price.

   What is price elasticity of demand?

2. Price and total revenue are directly related.

   What is the relationship between price and total revenue if demand is inelastic?

3. Quantity demanded changes by 20 percent if price changes by 10 percent.

   What does price elasticity of demand equal to 2 mean?

4. There is no change in quantity demanded as price changes.

   What is the relationship between price and quantity demanded if demand is perfectly inelastic?

5. The number of substitutes, the percentage of one's budget spent on the good, time (since the change in price), and luxury vs. necessity.

   What are the four determinants of price elasticity of demand?

6. Price of one good rises and quantity demanded for another good rises.

   What does it mean if cross elasticity of demand is greater than zero and two goods are substitutes?

7. In either of these cases, the tax placed on the seller is fully paid by the buyer.

   What happens if demand is perfectly inelastic or supply is perfectly elastic?

What Is Wrong?

1. If price rises, and total revenue falls, then demand is inelastic.

   If price rises, and total revenue falls, then demand is elastic.

2. The elasticity coefficient is greater than 1 for a good that is income inelastic.

   The elasticity coefficient is greater than 1 for a good that is income elastic. Alternatively, you could write: The elasticity coefficient is less than 1 for a good that is income inelastic.

3. Cars have more substitutes than Ford cars.

   Cars have fewer substitutes than Ford cars.

4. As we move down a demand curve, price elasticity of demand rises.

   As we move down a demand curve, price elasticity of demand falls. Alternatively, you could write: As we move up a demand curve, price elasticity of demand rises.

5. For inelastic demand, quantity demanded changes proportionately more than price changes.

   For inelastic demand, quantity demanded changes proportionately less than price changes. Alternatively, you could write: For elastic demand, quantity demanded changes proportionately more than price changes.

6. A perfectly inelastic demand curve can be downward-sloping.

   A perfectly inelastic demand curve is vertical. Alternatively, you could write: An inelastic demand curve is downward-sloping.

7. The elasticity coefficient is greater than zero for goods that are complements.

   The elasticity coefficient is less than zero for goods that are complements. Alternatively, you could write: The elasticity coefficient is greater than zero for goods that are substitutes.

8. If demand is inelastic, buyers pay the full tax that is placed on sellers.

   If demand is perfectly inelastic, buyers pay the full tax that is placed on sellers.

9. If income elasticity of demand is 1.24, it means that for every 1 percent change in income there is a 1.24 percent change in price.

   If income elasticity of demand is 1.24, it means that for every 1 percent change in income there is a 1.24 percent change in quantity demanded.

10. Price elasticity of supply measures the responsiveness of quantity supplied to changes in income.

    Price elasticity of supply measures the responsiveness of quantity supplied to changes in price.

Multiple Choice

1. a
2. c
3. b
4. e
5. c
6. d
7. a
8. a
9. b
10. d
11. c
12. a
13. d
14. a
15. b

True-False

16. T
17. T
18. F
19. F
20. F

Fill in the Blank

21. elasticity coefficient, elastic
22. inelastic
23. increases
24. lower
25. elastic

Chapter 6
Answers

Review Questions

1. John eats the first apple and receives 10 utils of utility. He eats the second apple and receives 8 utils of utility. The total utility he receives from eating two apples is 18 utils. The marginal utility of the first apple is 10 utils; the marginal utility of the second apple is 8 utils.
2. Yvonne gets more utility from walking the first mile than the second mile and more utility from the second mile than the third mile.
3. If a person makes an interpersonal utility comparison, he states that one person receives more utility from doing X than another person receives from doing X. For example, John watches April and Rebecca, two young children, playing in the sandbox. John says that April gets more utility from playing in the sandbox than Rebecca. John is making an interpersonal utility comparison. How does John know how much utility each of the two children receive? The answer is, he doesn't.
4. Diamonds, which are not necessary for life, sell for a higher price than water, which is necessary for life. Water, which has more use value than diamonds, sells for less than diamonds.
5. Goods that have high total utility (a reflection of high use value) may have lower marginal utility than goods that have relatively low total utility. Price is a reflection of marginal utility, not total utility.
6. It says that a person receives more utility per unit of money (say, $1) buying A than B. When the consumer has not equated MU-P ratios, he will rearrange his purchases until he has equated MU-P ratios and is in consumer equilibrium.
7. They buy more of some goods and less of other goods until the MU-P ratio of all the goods they purchase is the same.
8. Price falls from $10 to $8 and, as a result, quantity demanded rises from 100 to 150. Because of the price fall, real income rises. Because of the higher real income, the person buys 20 more units of the good. It follows that 30 of the additional units of the good were purchased because relative price fell. This change in quantity demanded due to a change in relative price (and nothing else) is referred to as the substitution effect.
9. Price falls from $10 to $8 and, as a result, quantity demanded rises from 100 to 150. Because of the price fall, real income rises. Because of the higher real income, the person buys 20 more units of the good. It follows that 20 of the additional units of the good were purchased because price fell causing real income to rise. This change in quantity demanded due to a change in income (brought about by a change in price) is referred to as the income effect.
10. It is the additional cost of producing and selling an additional unit of a good.
11. Zizzo and Oswald set up a series of experiments in which four groups of people were given equal sums of money and asked to gamble with their new money. At the end of each act of gambling, two of the four persons in each group had more money, and two had less. Each of the four persons was then given the opportunity to pay some money to reduce the take of the others in the group. Sixty-two percent of the participants did just this: they made themselves worse off in order to make someone else worse off. The explanation for this type of behavior is that individuals are concerned with relative rank and status more than with absolute well-being.
12. A person who compartmentalizes values things of equal value differently in different settings. Example: Smith earns $1,000 by working hard at a job and $1,000 at the roulette table in Las Vegas. Does he treat the two $1,000 amounts the same? If not, then he is compartmentalizing. If he would be more likely to spend the $1,000 winnings than the hard-earned $1,000, then he is compartmentalizing.

Problems

1.

Unit	Total utility (utils)	Marginal utility (utils)
1st	100	100
2nd	146	46
3rd	174	28

2. 3 units of X and 2 units of Y.

3.

Price falls by	Change in quantity demanded	Additional units consumer would buy due to higher real income	Additional units purchased due to the substitution effect
$2	133	60	73
$4	187	85	102
$3	222	125	97

4.

Units of good X	Total cost	Marginal cost
1	$40	$40
2	$89	$49
3	$149	$60

5.

Number of hours playing baseball	Total benefits (in utils)	Marginal benefits (in utils)
1	100	100
2	178	78
3	210	32

What Is the Question?

1. The additional utility gained from consuming an additional unit of good X.

   What is marginal utility?

2. Marginal utility turns negative.

   What happens to marginal utility when total utility declines?

3. The consumer will buy more of good X and less of good Y.

   If $MU_X/P_X > MU_Y/P_Y$ what will the consumer do?

4. That portion of the change in the quantity demanded of a good that is attributable to a change in its relative price.

   What is the substitution effect?

5. The change in total cost divided by the change in quantity of output.

   What is marginal cost equal to?

6. It slopes downward (left to right) because of the law of diminishing marginal utility.

   What is the shape of the marginal utility or marginal benefit curve?

7. Ownership makes things more valuable.

   What is the endowment effect?

What Is Wrong?

1. If total utility is falling, then marginal utility is greater than zero.

   If total utility is falling, then marginal utility is negative.

2. A millionaire gets less utility from an additional $100 than a poor person receives from an additional $100.

   We don't know if this is true or not. A millionaire may get less utility, more utility, or the same amount of utility from an additional $100 as a poor person receives.

3. The income effect refers to that portion of the change in the quantity demanded of a good that is attributable to a change in its relative price.

   The substitution effect refers to that portion of the change in the quantity demanded of a good that is attributable to a change in its relative price. Alternatively, you could write, The income effect refers to that portion of the change in the quantity demanded of a good that is attributable to a change in real income (brought about by a change in price).

4. If total cost rises, marginal cost must rise, too.

   Marginal cost doesn't have to rise as total cost rises. For example, if total cost is $100 for one unit of a good and $180 for two units of the good, marginal cost goes from $100 to $80. In other words, marginal cost is falling as total cost is rising.

5. If total benefits rise, then marginal benefits must rise, too.

   Marginal benefits don't have to rise as total benefits rise. For example, if total benefit is 100 utils for one unit of a good and 180 utilis for two units of the good, marginal benefit goes from 100 to 80. In other words, marginal benefit is falling as total benefit is rising.

6. If the marginal utility-price ratio for good A is greater than the marginal utility-price ratio for good B, then a consumer will buy more of both good A and B.

   If the marginal utility-price ratio for good A is greater than the marginal utility-price ratio for good B, then a consumer will buy more of good A. The person may reallocate dollars from the purchase of B to A.

Multiple Choice

1. c
2. b
3. d
4. b
5. e
6. b
7. c
8. c
9. b
10. b
11. d
12. d
13. a
14. a
15. a

True-False

16. T
17. T
18. T
19. T
20. F

Fill in the Blank

21. diamond-water paradox
22. (consumer) equilibrium
23. income effect
24. marginal utility
25. higher (or greater)

Chapter 7
Answers

Review Questions

1. Firm X produces desks. Due to an increased demand for desks, the price of desks rises. Firm X responds to the higher price of desks by producing more desks.
2. The manager of a firm (that produces doors) tells the employees to paint the doors a different color than they have been painting the doors.
3. The sum of what individuals can produce as a team is greater than the sum of what the individuals can produce working alone.
4. The benefits and costs of shirking. This chapter focused on the costs of shirking and stated that the lower the costs of shirking (to the individual), the more likely the individual will shirk.
5. A person who takes the profits or incurs the losses of the firm.
6. Potential shirkers may be less likely to shirk if they are currently earning above-market wages. That's because there would be a cost to their shirking. Namely, if they are caught shirking, and lose their jobs, they then will be faced with earning market wages instead of above-market wages.
7. Outside the firm, supply and demand are determining prices, to which the firm responds. For example, as the price of the good the firm produces rises, the firm may decide to produce more units of the good. Inside the firm, employees are trading some of their independence for a monitor who will make sure they don't shirk. Why do the employees want to make sure they don't shirk? Because shirking reduces the benefits they expect to receive by joining the firm.
8. Satisficing behavior is directed at meeting some profit target. Maximizing profit is directed at obtaining the most profit possible.
9. Unlimited liability is a legal term that signifies that the personal assets of the owners of a firm may be used to settle the debts of the firm.
10. There are three disadvantages: (1) partners face unlimited liability; (2) decision making can be complex and frustrating; (3) withdrawal or death of a partner can end the partnership or cause its restructuring.
11. There are two disadvantages: (1) profit is taxed twice; (2) problems may arise due to separation of ownership from control.
12. A person who has unlimited liability can be sued by creditors for the debts incurred by the firm; a person who has limited liability cannot be.
13. Net worth is equal to assets minus liabilities.
14. The person who buys the bond is making a loan to the firm; the person who buys shares of stock is buying an ownership right in the firm. In short, the bond buyer is a lender, the stock buyer is an owner.
15. There are no residual claimants in a nonprofit firm. There are residual claimants in a business firm.

Problems

1.

Type of firm	**Example**
Proprietorship	hair salon
Partnership	advertising agency
Corporation	Dell Computer Corporation

2.

Advantages of proprietorships	Disadvantages of proprietorships
1. Easy to form and to dissolve.	1. Proprietor faces unlimited liability.
2. All decision-making power resides with the sole proprietor.	2. Limited ability to raise funds for business expansion.
3. Profit is taxed only once.	3. Usually ends with death of proprietor.

3.

Assets ($ millions)	Liabilities ($ millions)	Net worth ($ millions)
10	7	3
100	65	35
198	77	121

4.

Face value of bond	Coupon rate	Annual coupon payments
$10,000	5.0 percent	$500
$20,000	7.5 percent	$1,500
$10,000	6.5 percent	$650

What Is the Question?
Identify the question for each of the answers that follow.

1. These economists suggest that firms are formed when benefits can be obtained from individuals working as a team.

   Who are Alchian and Demsetz?

2. The process in which managers direct employees to perform certain tasks.

   What is managerial coordination?

3. This rises as the cost of shirking falls.

   What happens to the amount of shirking as the cost of shirking falls?

4. This is the person in a business firm who coordinates team production and reduces shirking.

   Who is the monitor?

5. Persons who share in the profits of a business firm.

   Who are residual claimants?

6. Richard Cyert, James March, and Herbert Simon.

   Who are the economists that argue that firms seek only to achieve some satisfactory target profit level?

7. This type of business firm generated the largest percentage of total business receipts.

   What is a corporation?

8. One advantage is that they are easy to form and to dissolve.

   What is one advantage of a sole proprietorship?

9. One disadvantage is that profits are taxed twice.

   What is one disadvantage of a corporation?

10. It is also known as equity.

    What is net worth also known as?

11. Assets minus liabilities.

    What is net worth equal to?

What Is Wrong?

1. Alchian and Demsetz argue that firms are formed when there are benefits to forming firms.

   Not exactly. There may be benefits to forming a firm, but that is not enough. Alchian and Demsetz argue that firms are formed (by individuals) when the sum of what individuals can produce in a firm is greater than the sum of what individuals can produce working alone.

2. Five people form a firm and decide to equally split the proceeds of what they produce and sell. The individual costs of shirking are lower in this setting than in a setting where ten people form a firm and decide to equally split the proceeds of what they produce and sell.

   For a given level of profit, the individual costs of shirking are higher in this setting (five-person firm) than in a setting where ten people form a firm and decide to equally split the proceeds of what they produce and sell.

3. Economists who advance the efficiency wage theory argue that paying employees above-market wage rates will cause them to shirk more than if they were simply paid market wage rates.

   Economists who advance the efficiency wage theory argue that paying employees above-market wage rates will cause them to shirk less than if they were simply paid market wage rates.

4. Partnerships are the most common form of business organization in the United States.

   Proprietorships are the most common form of business organization in the United States.

5. Assets plus liabilities equal net worth.

   Assets minus liabilities equal net worth.

6. Total liabilities plus net worth equal accounts payable.

   Total liabilities plus net worth equal assets.

7. When a person buys a share of stock issued by a firm, the person effectively grants a loan to the firm.

    When a person buys a share of stock issued by a firm, the person becomes an owner of the firm. Alternatively, you could write: When a person buys a bond issued by a firm, the person effectively grants a loan to the firm.

8. There are fewer residual claimants in a business firm than in a nonprofit firm.

    There are no residual claimants in a nonprofit firm.

9. In private and public nonprofit firms, taxpayers pay the costs of the firm.

    In public nonprofit firms, taxpayers pay the costs of the firm. In private nonprofit firms, private citizens pay the costs.

Multiple Choice
1. c
2. d
3. b
4. c
5. b
6. b
7. c
8. c
9. c
10. e
11. e
12. a
13. a
14. d
15. a

True-False
16. T
17. T
18. T
19. T
20. T

Fill in the Blank
21. Unlimited liability
22. corporation
23. residual claimants
24. limited partnership
25. Limited liability

Chapter 8
Answers

Review Questions

1. A producer of a good pays $100 to buy some inputs necessary to produce the good.
2. An accountant who works for a firm, and earns $70,000 a year, quits her job to start her own accounting business. The forfeited $70,000 salary is an implicit cost of her new accounting business.
3. Economic profit is smaller than accounting profit because when calculating economic profit both explicit and implicit costs are subtracted from total revenue. When calculating accounting profit only explicit costs are subtracted from total revenue.
4. It is covering all its opportunity costs; stated differently, it is covering both its explicit costs and implicit costs.
5. Examples will vary here. Your example should be consistent with the definition of sunk cost. A sunk cost is a cost incurred in the past, that cannot be undone, and cannot be recovered.
6. James buys a pair of shoes that cannot be resold or returned to the store from which he purchased the shoes. The shoes are a sunk cost. The shoes hurt his feet but he decides to wear them anyway because he wants to get his money's worth out of the shoes. Really, he wants to recover the cost of the shoes somehow. He is trying to undo a sunk cost. He is worse off doing this than simply ignoring the sunk cost and choosing not to wear the shoes. When he wears the shoes, he increases the probability that he will have problems with his feet and have to visit a podiatrist. If he doesn't wear the shoes, he doesn't have this problem. He has lost the money he spent to buy the shoes in either case, so why not lose the money and have comfortable feet than lose the money and have uncomfortable feet.
7. The factory a producer rents.
8. The labor a producer hires.
9. Average total cost is total cost divided by output. Marginal cost is the change in total cost divided by the change in output. Marginal cost considers all "changes," average total cost does not.
10. With the addition of the sixth unit of a variable input, output rises from 100 to 120 units. With the addition of the seventh unit of a variable input, output rises from 120 to 135. The marginal physical product falls from 20 to 15. To see a more extensive example, see Exhibit 4 in the text chapter.
11. As diminishing marginal returns set in (and marginal physical product is declining), marginal cost begins to rise.
12. Marginal productivity is the change in output divided by the change in the variable input. Average productivity is output divided by the number of units of the variable input used to produce the output.
13. As diminishing marginal returns set in, marginal cost rises. At some point as marginal cost rises, it will rise above average total cost. When this happens, average total cost will rise.
14. The temperature in San Diego has been 70 degrees each day for the seven days. The average temperature for the week is 70 degrees. Then, the temperature falls to 60 degrees one day. Since the temperature on the additional day (the marginal day) is less than the average temperature, the average temperature will fall. The new average for the last seven days is 68 degrees.
15. It is a curve that shows the lowest unit cost at which the firm can produce any given level of output.
16. It means that its output increases by a greater percentage than the increase in its inputs, causing unit costs to fall.
17. A tax may affect fixed costs but not variable costs. Also, a tax may affect variable costs but not fixed costs. To illustrate, suppose a firm has to pay a lump-sum tax, no matter how much it produces. This tax will raise the firm's fixed costs. If a firm has to pay a tax per unit of output it produces, then this tax affects its variable costs.
18. The AFC curve continually declines (over output) because AFC = TFC/Q. TFC is constant, so that as Q rises, AFC must decline. The more Q rises, the smaller AFC becomes.

Problems

1. Fill in the blanks in the table.

Explicit costs	Implicit costs	Total revenue	Economic profit	Accounting profit
$40,000	$40,000	$100,000	$20,000	$60,000
$150,000	$30,000	$230,000	$50,000	$80,000
$30,000	$40,000	$300,000	$230,000	$270,000

2. Fill in the blank spaces in the table.

Variable cost	Fixed cost	Units of output produced	Average variable cost	Average fixed cost
$500	$1,000	100	$5.00	$10.00
$400	$500	200	$2.00	$2.50
$1,000	$200	400	$2.50	$0.50

3. Fill in the blank spaces in the table.

Variable cost	Fixed cost	Units of output produced	Average total cost
$500	$200	100	$7.00
$300	$400	50	$14.00
$400	$1,000	75	$18.67

4. Fill in the blank spaces in the table.

Average total cost is	Marginal cost is	Average total cost is (rising, fall, remaining unchanged)
$40	$45	rising
$30	$20	falling
$20	$37	rising

5. Fill in the blank spaces in the table.

Variable input (units)	Fixed input (units)	Quantity of output	Marginal physical product of variable input
0	1	0	0
1	1	20	20
2	1	45	25

6. Fill in the blank spaces in the table.

Marginal physical product (units)	Variable cost	Marginal cost
20	$400	$20
18	$360	$20
33	$660	$20

7. TFC does not change as output changes (rises or falls).

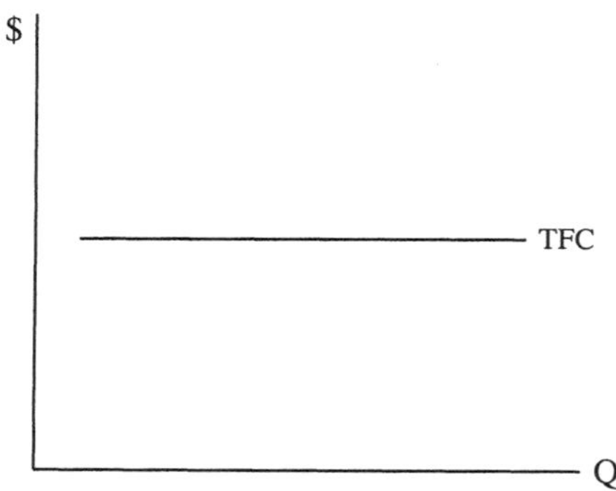

8. AFC is TFC/Q. TFC does not change as Q rises, so AFC must continually decline.

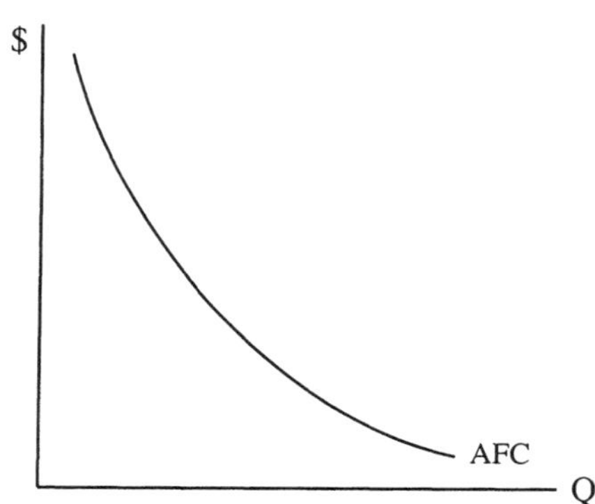

9. The MC curve must cut the ATC curve at its low point.

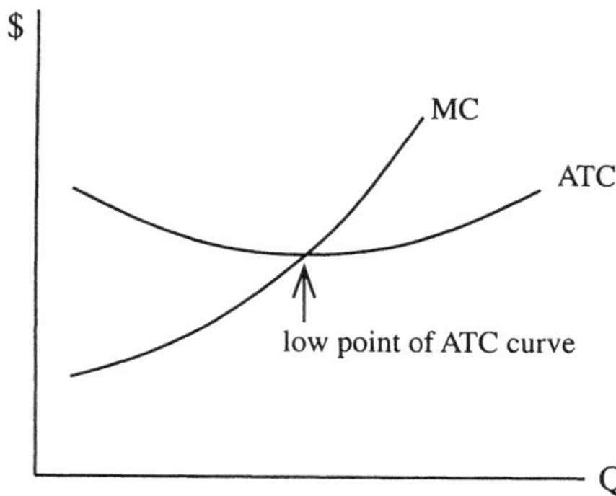

10. When the firm experiences increasing marginal returns, MC is falling; when it experiences constant marginal returns, MC is stable and neither rising nor falling; and when it experiences diminishing marginal returns, MC is rising.

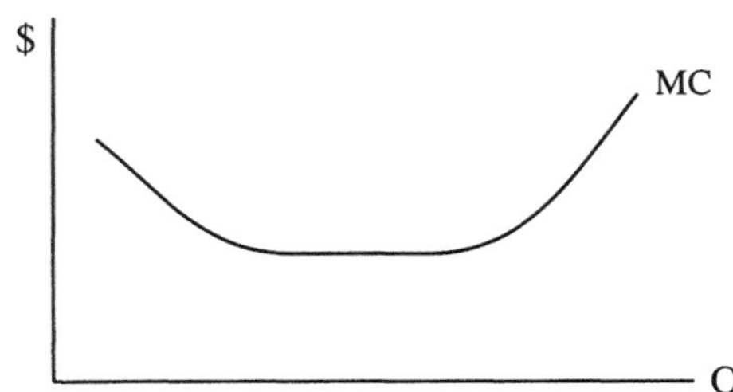

What Is the Question?

1. A cost that is incurred when an actual monetary payment is made.

   What is an explicit cost?

2. It is a cost that cannot be recovered.

   What is a sunk cost?

3. When marginal physical product is rising, this cost is declining.

   What is marginal cost?

4. These costs do not vary with output.

   What are fixed costs?

5. Total cost divided by output.

   What is average total cost or unit cost?

6. When this cost is above average total cost, average total cost is rising.

   What is marginal cost?

7. As output increases, the difference between average variable cost and this cost becomes smaller.

   What is average total cost?

8. The lowest output level at which average total costs are minimized.

   What is the minimum efficient scale?

9. This exists when inputs are increased by some percentage and output increases by a smaller percentage, causing unit costs to rise.

   What are diseconomies of scale?

What Is Wrong?

1. Economic profit is the difference between total revenue and explicit costs.

   Economic profit is the difference between total revenue and the sum of explicit and implicit costs. Alternatively, you could write: Accounting profit is the difference between total revenue and explicit costs.

2. When a firm earns zero economic profit it has not covered its total opportunity costs.

   When a firm earns zero economic profit it has covered its total opportunity costs. Alternatively, you could write: When a firm earns less than zero economic profit it has not covered its total opportunity costs.

3. The difference between the ATC curve and the AVC curve gets larger as output rises.

   The difference between the ATC and the AVC curves gets smaller as output rises.

4. Marginal physical product is equal to output divided by units of the variable input.

   Marginal physical product is equal to the change in output divided by a change in the units of the variable input. Alternatively, you could write: Average physical product is equal to output divided by units of the variable input.

5. When marginal physical product falls, marginal cost falls, too.

   When marginal physical product falls, marginal cost rises. Alternatively, you could write: When marginal physical product rises, marginal cost falls.

6.

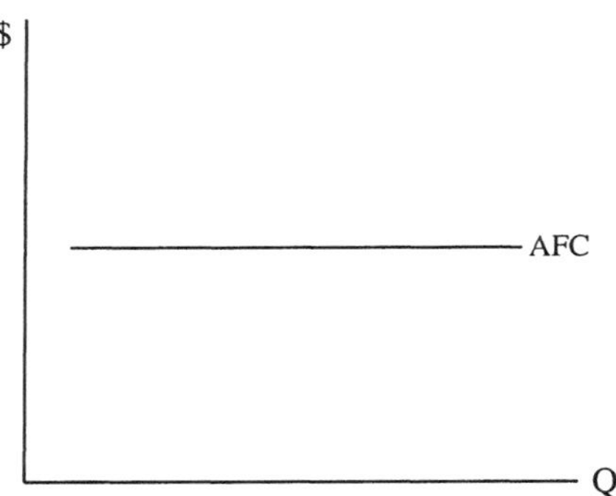

AFC curve is not supposed to be horizontal. It declines as output rises.

7.

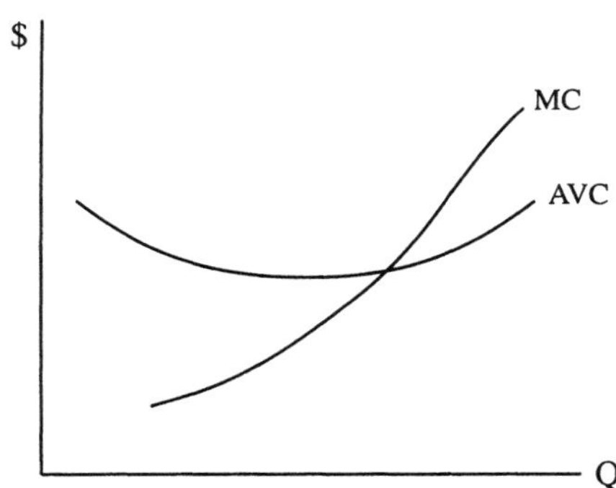

MC cuts AVC at wrong point. MC is supposed to cut AVC at the low point of AVC.

8.

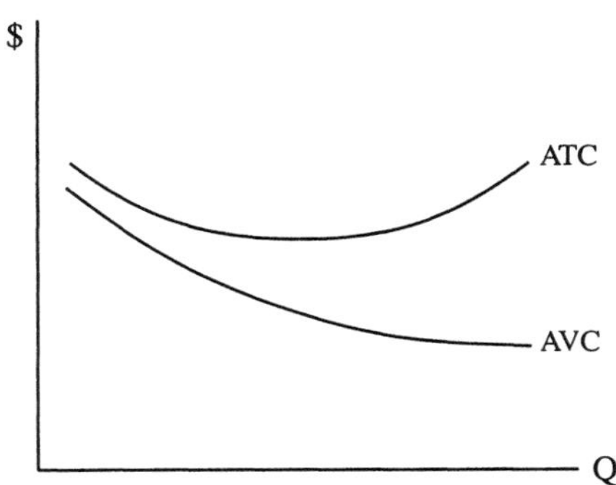

AVC is supposed to be closer to ATC as output rises.

9.

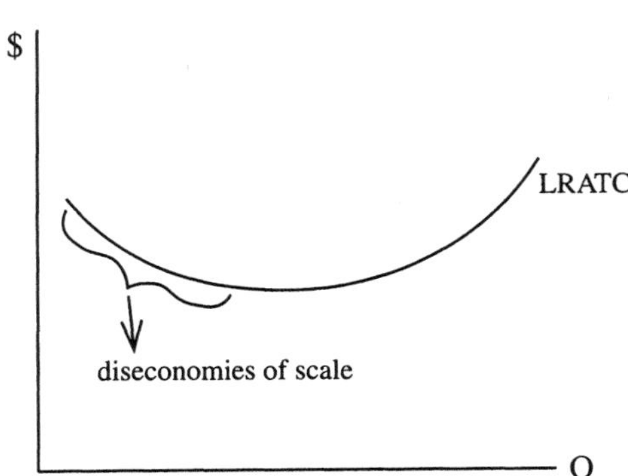

Diseconomies of scale is misrepresented. The area shown represents what happens to LRATC if economies of scale exist, not diseconomies of scale.

Multiple Choice

1. c
2. d
3. b
4. c
5. c
6. d
7. d
8. a
9. a
10. a
11. b
12. c
13. a
14. a
15. c

True-False

16. T
17. T
18. T
19. F
20. T

Fill in the Blank

21. long-run average total cost (LRATC)
22. minimum efficient scale
23. rise; diseconomies of scale
24. falls
25. marginal physical product

Chapter 9
Answers

Review Questions

1. There are many sellers and many buyers, none of which are large in relation to total sales or purchases. Each firm produces and sells a homogeneous product. Buyers and sellers have all relevant information about prices, product quality, sources of supply, and so forth. Firms have easy entry and exit.
2. It means that the seller does not have the ability to control the price of the product it sells; it takes (or sells its good at) the price determined in the market.
3. Plotting price against quantity derives a demand curve. Plotting marginal revenue against quantity derives a marginal revenue curve. Since, for a perfectly competitive firm, price equals marginal revenue, the two curves are the same.
4. To be resource-allocative efficient, price equals marginal cost at the quantity of output the firm produces. A firm will try to maximize profits by producing the quantity of output at which MR = MC. Since, for a perfectly competitive firm, MR = P, it follows that when a firm maximizes profit, it also meets the resource-allocative condition, P = MC.
5. Suppose MR declines and MC rises. Also suppose that the quantity at which MR = MC is 120 units. It follows then that for any quantity less than 120, MR > MC. Why then stop producing where the biggest difference between MR and MC appears? To do this would be to ignore the net benefit derived anytime MR is greater than MC. Take a look at Exhibit 3 in your text chapter. If the firm stops producing at 50 units, where the largest difference between MR and MC appears, it forfeits all net benefits derived by producing the next 75 units of the good.
6. It considers how much it loses if it shuts down and compares this to how much it loses (or earns) if it doesn't shut down. Essentially, this means it compares the price at which it sells the good to its average variable cost. If price is greater than average variable cost, it continues to produce in the short run. If price is less than average variable cost, it shuts down in the short run.
7. No. The firm earns profit only if, at the quantity of output at which MR = MC, price is greater than average total cost.
8. The firm will not produce if price is below AVC, so that portion of the MC curve that is below the AVC curve is not relevant to production.
9. The market supply curve is the horizontal summation of the individual firms' supply curves. For example, if there are two firms in the industry, A and B, and Firm A supplies 10 units at a $10 price, and Firm B supplies 20 units at a $10 price, then one point on the market supply curve represents $10 and 30 units.
10. The market supply curve is upward sloping. This is because the individual firm's supply curve is upward sloping. The firm's supply curve is upward sloping because its supply curve is that portion of its MC curve above its AVC curve, and this portion of its MC curve is upward sloping. But why do MC curves slope up at all? In the last chapter we learned that MC rises when marginal physical product declines (or, in other words, when diminishing marginal returns set in).
11. Here are the three conditions: P = MC, P = SRATC, and LRATC = SRATC.
12. If price is above short-run average total cost, the firm is earning positive economic profits and there is an inconsistency with one of the long-run equilibrium conditions (specifically, P = SRATC).
13. If SRATC is greater than LRATC, then the firm is not producing its output at the lowest possible cost, which is one of the conditions of long-run equilibrium (specifically SRATC = LRATC).
14. A constant-cost industry is one in which average total costs do not change as industry output increases or decreases, and when firms enter or exit the industry, respectively.
15. The firms in the market will increase output and new firms will enter the market. In time, price will fall and the profits will be no longer. In the long run, there will be only normal profits (zero economic profit) in the market.

16. No, because it sells a homogeneous good and to advertise its product is to advertise its competitors' products, too. While a firm may not advertise, the industry may advertise. The industry advertises in the hopes of increasing the market demand for the goods that the sellers produce and sell.
17. It means that the firm is not producing its output at the lowest per unit costs possible.

Problems

1.

Price	Quantity	Total revenue	Marginal revenue
$10	1	$10	$10
$10	2	$20	$10
$10	3	$30	$10

2.

Price	Quantity	Total revenue
$40	100	$4,000
$40	50	$2,000
$40	80	$3,200

3.

Price	Quantity	Marginal revenue
$15	1	$15
$15	2	$15
$15	3	$15

4.

Price	Quantity	Average variable cost	Average total cost	Total variable cost	Will the firm (continue to produce, shut down)
$10	100	$7	$9	$700	continue to produce
$15	50	$13	$16	$650	continue to produce
$23	1,000	$24	$26	$2,400	shut down

5.

Price	Quantity	Average variable cost	Average total cost	Average fixed cost	Total cost
$10	100	$4	$6	$2	$600
$40	2,000	$45	$46	$1	$92,000
$25	198	$21	$23	$2	$4,554

6.

Price	Marginal cost	ATC	Is the perfectly competitive firm earning profits? (yes, no)	Is the perfectly competitive firm in long-run equilibrium? (yes, no)
$40	$40	$30	yes	no
$30	$30	$35	no	no
$25	$25	$23	yes	no

7.

Price	Quantity	ATC	AVC	Profit (+) or Loss (–)
$33	1,234	$31	$30	+ $2,468
$55	2,436	$25	$20	+ $73,080
$100	1,000	$110	$99	– $10,000

What Is the Question?

1. A seller that does not have the ability to control the price of the product it sells.

   What is a price taker?

2. The firm sells its good at market equilibrium price.

   At what (per unit) price does the perfectly competitive firm sell its good?

3. When price is below average variable cost.

   When does the firm shut down in the short run?

4. That portion of its MC curve above its AVC curve.

   What portion of the firm's MC curve is its supply curve?

5. The horizontal summation of the individual firms' supply curves.

   What is the market supply curve equal to?

6. There is no incentive for firms to enter or exit the industry, there is no incentive for firms to produce more or less output, and there is no incentive for firms to change plant size.

   What are the conditions that specify long-run competitive equilibrium?

7. P = SRATC, P = MC, and SRATC = LRATC.

   What are the conditions that specify long-run competitive equilibrium?

8. The long-run supply curve is upward sloping.

   What does the long-run supply curve look like for an increasing-cost industry?

9. The long-run supply curve is downward-sloping.

   What does the long-run supply curve look like for a decreasing-cost industry?

10. P = MC.

    What condition specifies resource allocative efficiency?

11. The firm produces its output at the lowest possible per unit cost.

    If a firm is productive efficient, what condition holds?

What Is Wrong?

1. Firms in a perfectly competitive market have easy entry into the market and costly exit from the market.

    Firms in a perfectly competitive market have easy entry into the market and easy exit from the market.

2. In long-run competitive equilibrium, the average or representative firm may earn positive economic profit.

    In long-run competitive equilibrium, the average or representative firm earns zero economic profit (or normal profit).

3. Price is greater than marginal revenue for a perfectly competitive firm.

    Price is equal to marginal revenue for a perfectly competitive firm.

4. A perfectly competitive firm will shut down in the short run if its price is below average total cost.

    A perfectly competitive firm will shut down in the short run if its price is below average variable cost. Alternatively, you could write: A perfectly competitive firm will not necessarily shut down if its price is below average total cost.

5. If a firm produces the quantity of output at which MR = MC, it is guaranteed to earn profits.

    If a firm produces the quantity of output at which MR = MC, it is not guaranteed to earn profits. It only earns profits if price is greater than average total cost.

6. The market supply curve is the vertical summation of the individual firms' supply curves.

    The market supply curve is the horizontal summation of the individual firms' supply curves.

7. If SRATC = LRATC for a firm, there is no incentive for the firm to enter or exit the industry.

    If SRATC = LRATC for a firm, there is no incentive for a firm to change plant size. Alternatively, you could write: If P = SRATC, there is no incentive for the firm to enter or exit the industry.

8. The long-run supply curve is downward-sloping for an increasing-cost industry.

    The long-run supply curve is downward-sloping for a decreasing-cost industry. Alternatively, you could write: The long-run supply curve is upward-sloping for an increasing-cost industry.

9. When average fixed cost is positive, average total cost is usually, but not always, greater than average variable cost.

    When average fixed cost is positive, average total cost is always greater than average variable cost.

10. A firm that produces its output at the lowest possible per-unit cost is said to exhibit resource allocative efficiency.

    A firm that produces its output at the lowest possible per-unit cost is said to exhibit productive efficiency.

Multiple Choice

1. d
2. a
3. a
4. e
5. e
6. d
7. a
8. d
9. c
10. d
11. d
12. a
13. b
14. c
15. a

True-False

16. F
17. F
18. F
19. T
20. T

Fill in the Blank

21. resource allocative efficiency
22. zero
23. MR = MC
24. short-run supply
25. more

Chapter 10
Answers

Review Questions

1. There is one seller; the single seller sells a product for which there are no close substitutes; there are extremely high barriers to entry.
2. A natural monopoly is a firm for which economies of scale are so pronounced that it will end up being the only firm that will survive in the industry.
3. A price searcher is a seller that can, to some degree, control the price of the product it sells. A monopolist fits this description. A monopoly can sell different quantities at different prices. It can raise price and still sell some of its output; it can lower price and sell more of its output. Contrast this with a perfectly competitive firm (which is a price taker). If the perfectly competitive firm raises price above market equilibrium, it sells nothing.
4. It produces the quantity of output at which MR = MC.
5. Look at Exhibit 6 in your text chapter. The perfectly competitive seller produces and sells the quantity at which the demand curve intersects the marginal cost curve, or Q_{PC}. The monopoly seller produces and sells the quantity at which the marginal revenue curve intersects the marginal cost curve, or Q_M. The perfectly competitive seller charges P_{PC} and the monopoly seller charges P_M.
6. It is rational for the individual to seek monopoly rents if the expected benefits of the rents are greater than the costs of obtaining the rents. However, from society's perspective, resources are wasted because resources that could be used to produce goods and services are instead used to bring about transfers.
7. Perfect price discrimination occurs when the seller charges the highest price each consumer would be willing to pay for the product rather than go without. Second-degree price discrimination occurs when the seller charges a uniform price per unit for one specific quantity, a lower price for an additional quantity, and so on. Third-degree price discrimination occurs when the seller charges different prices in different markets or charges a different price to different segments of the buying population.
8. The seller must exercise some control over price (it must be a price searcher); the seller must be able to distinguish among buyers who would be willing to pay different prices; it must be impossible or too costly for one buyer to resell the good to other buyers.
9. Yes. A perfectly price-discriminating monopolist charges the highest price for each unit of the good it sells. This means its price is always equal to marginal revenue. In short, its demand curve and marginal revenue curve are the same (as is the case for the perfectly competitive firm, which is resource allocative efficient). The perfectly price-discriminating monopolist will produce the quantity of output at which MR = MC, and since P = MR, then P = MC. P = MC is the condition that must be satisfied before a seller is resource allocative efficient.

Problems

1.

Price	Quantity	Total revenue	Marginal revenue
$10	1	$10	$10
$9	2	$18	$8
$8	3	$24	$6

2. Consumers' surplus under perfect competition = P_1AB
   Consumers' surplus under monopoly = P_2AC

3. The triangle is CBD.

4. It produces the quantity at which MR = MC (which is Q_1 in the exhibit) and charges the highest (per unit) price consistent with this quantity (which is P_1 in the exhibit).

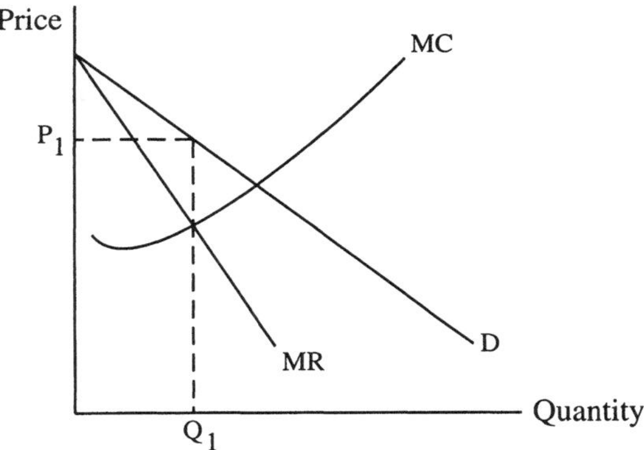

5.

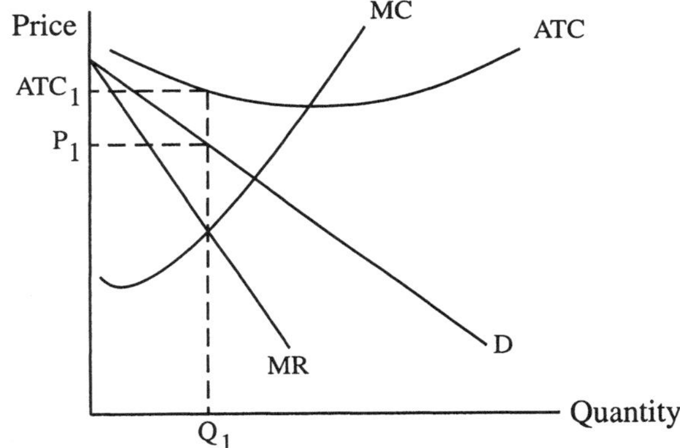

What Is the Question?

1. A right granted to a firm by government that permits the firm to provide a particular good or service and excludes all others from doing the same.

   What is a public franchise?

2. An exclusive right to sell something.

   What was the original meaning of the word monopoly?

3. Price is greater than marginal revenue.

   What is the relationship between price and marginal revenue for the monopolist?

4. Actions of individuals and groups who spend resources to influence public policy in the hope of redistributing (transferring) income to themselves from others.

   What is rent seeking?

5. This occurs when the seller charges a uniform price per unit for one specific quantity, a lower price for an additional quantity, and so on.

   What is second-degree price discrimination?

6. The increase in costs and organizational slack in a monopoly resulting from the lack of competitive pressure to push costs down to their lowest possible level.

   What is X-inefficiency?

7. Total revenue is greater if the monopolist can do this.

   What happens to total revenue for the monopolist if it can go from being a single-price monopolist to a price-discriminating monopolist?

8. If it does this, the monopolist will be resource allocative efficient.

   What will happen if a single-price monopolist becomes a perfectly price-discriminating monopolist?

What Is Wrong?

1. The single-price monopolist exhibits resource allocative efficiency.

   The single-price monopolist does not exhibit resource allocative efficiency. Alternatively, you could write: The perfectly price-discriminating monopolist exhibits resource allocative efficiency. Or, from the last chapter: The perfectly competitive firm exhibits resource allocative efficiency.

2. One of the assumptions in theory of monopoly is that the single seller sells a product for which there are no perfect substitutes.

   One of the assumptions in theory of monopoly is that the single seller sells a product for which there are no close substitutes.

3. For the monopolist, price is equal to marginal revenue.

   For the monopolist, price is greater than marginal revenue.

4. If fixed costs exist, then a firm that maximizes revenue automatically maximizes profit, too.

   If fixed costs exist, then a firm that maximizes revenue does not automatically maximize profit.

5. The monopoly seller produces the quantity of output at which MR = P and charges the highest price per unit for this quantity.

   The monopoly seller produces the quantity of output at which MC = MR and charges the highest price per unit for this quantity.

6. A monopoly seller cannot incur losses, since it is the single seller of a good.

   A monopoly seller can incur losses; it will incur losses if the highest price at which it can sell its output is less than its ATC.

7. Perfect price discrimination occurs when the seller charges a uniform price per unit for one specific quantity, a lower price for an additional quantity, and so on.

   Second-degree price discrimination occurs when the seller charges a uniform price per unit for one specific quantity, a lower price for an additional quantity, and so on. Alternatively, you could write: Perfect price discrimination occurs when the seller charges the highest price each consumer would be willing to pay for the product rather than go without it.

8. A monopoly seller can charge any price it wants for the good it produces and sells.

   A monopoly seller cannot charge any price it wants for the good it produces and sells; it is limited by the height of the demand curve it faces.

Multiple Choice

1. c
2. b
3. c
4. d
5. d
6. e
7. c
8. d
9. a
10. a
11. e
12. a
13. c
14. d
15. d

True-False

16. F
17. T
18. F
19. T
20. F

Fill in the Blank

21. Natural monopoly
22. Price searcher
23. arbitrage
24. X-inefficiency
25. Gordon Tullock

Chapter 11
Answers

Review Questions

1. There are many buyers and sellers, each firm produces and sells a slightly differentiated product, there is easy entry and exit.
2. A perfectly competitive firm and a monopolistic competitive firm face many rivals.
3. A monopolistic competitive firm and a monopoly firm face a downward-sloping demand curve and each is a price searcher.
4. The quantity at which MR = MC.
5. No. To be resource allocative efficient, a firm must produce the quantity of output at which P = MC. For the quantity of output the monopolistic competitive firm faces, P > MC.
6. Essentially because it faces a downward-sloping demand curve.
7. There are few sellers and many buyers, firms produce and sell either homogeneous or differentiated products, there are significant barriers to entry.
8. The percentage of industry sales accounted for by the four largest firms.
9. The essence is that individually rational behavior leads to an outcome that is less-than-best for all parties concerned.
10. To act as if there is only one seller so that monopoly profits can be captured.
11. If a firm cheats, and other firms do not cheat, it earns higher profits.
12. There is easy entry into the market and costless exit from the market, new firms entering the market can produce the product at the same cost as current firms, firms exiting the market can easily dispose of their fixed assets by selling them elsewhere.
13. Initially, the U.S. and Soviet Union are competing in an arms race. Each then realizes it can be better if both countries stop the race. They enter into a cooperative agreement to stop the arms race, but once the agreement has been made, each country realizes it can be made better off if it continues to build up its arms while the other country holds to the agreement. In the end, each country adopts the "strategy" of building up its arms and hoping the other does not. In the end, both countries are back in the arms race. In short, the two countries are in a prisoner's dilemma setting.

Problems

1.

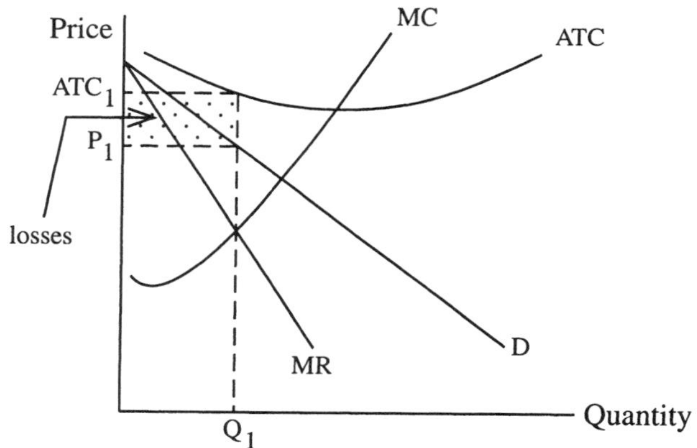

2.

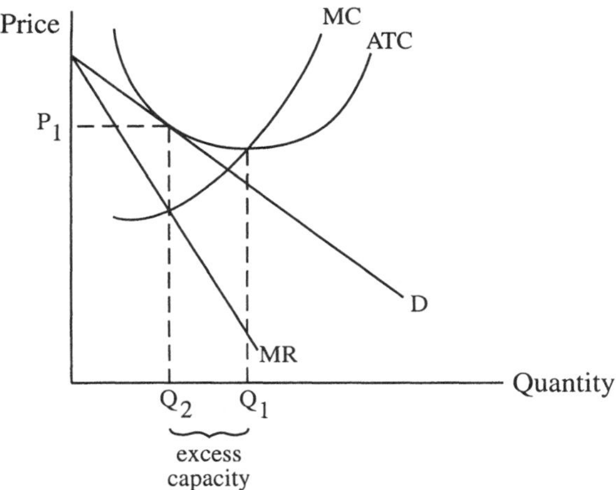

3. P_1CDB; P_1EFA
4. The top four firms in the industry have 12 percent, 10 percent, 8 percent, and 3 percent of industry sales, respectively. The four-firm concentration ratio is 33 percent.
5. The problem of forming the cartel, the problem of formulating policy, the problem of entry into the industry, and the problem of cheating.

What Is the Question?

1. States that a monopolistic competitor in equilibrium produces an output smaller than the one that would minimize its costs of production.

   What does the excess capacity theorem state?

2. It does not produce at the lowest point on its ATC curve because the demand curve it faces is downward-sloping.

   Why doesn't a monopolistic competitive firm produce at the lowest point on its ATC curve?

3. There are significant barriers to entry in this market structure.

   What is oligopoly?

4. Individually rational behavior leads to a jointly inefficient outcome.

   What is a prisoner's dilemma (game)?

5. The key behavioral assumption is that oligopolists in an industry act as if there is only one firm in the industry.

   What is the key behavioral assumption of cartel theory?

6. This is a way out of the prisoner's dilemma for two firms trying to form a cartel.

   What role does the enforcer play in a prisoner's dilemma (game)?

7. If a single firm lowers price, other firms will do likewise, but if a single firm raises price, other firms will not follow suit.

    What is the key behavioral assumption of the kinked demand curve theory?

8. The theory fails to explain how the original price comes about.

    What is a criticism of the kinked demand curve theory?

9. One firm determines price and the all other firms take this price as given.

    What is the key behavioral assumption of the price leadership theory?

10. There is easy entry into the market and costless exit from the market, new firms entering the market can produce the product at the same cost as current firms, and firms exiting the market can easily dispose of their fixed assets by selling them elsewhere.

    What are the conditions that characterize a contestable market?

What Is Wrong?

1. The monopolistic competitor is a price taker and the oligopolist is a price searcher.

    Both the monopolistic competitor and the oligopolist are price searchers.

2. For the monopolistic competitor, price lies below marginal revenue.

    For the monopolistic competitor, price lies above marginal revenue.

3. When profits are normal, the monopolistic competitor exhibits resource allocative efficiency.

    It doesn't matter whether profits are normal are not, the monopolistic competitor does not exhibit resource allocative efficiency.

4. The cartel theory assumes that firms in an oligopolistic industry act in a manner consistent with there being only a few firms in the industry.

    The cartel theory assumes that firms in an oligopolistic industry act in a manner consistent with there being only one firm in the industry.

5. The kinked demand curve theory assumes that if a single firm raises price, other firms will do likewise, but if a single firm lowers price, other firms will not follow.

    The kinked demand curve theory assumes that if a single firm raises price, other firms will not follow, but if a single firm lowers price, other firms will do likewise.

6. The price leadership theory assumes that the dominant firm in the industry determines price and all other firms sell below this price.

    The price leadership theory assumes that the dominant firm in the industry determines price and all other firms will sell at this price.

7. Both monopolistic competitive firms and oligopolistic firms produce the quantity of output at which price equals marginal revenue.

   Both monopolistic competitive firms and oligopolistic firms produce the quantity of output at which marginal cost equals marginal revenue.

8. A contestable market is one in which there is easy entry into the market and costless exit from the market, new firms entering the market can produce the product at the same costs as current firms, and firms exiting the market only have to suffer the loses of their fixed assets.

   A contestable market is one in which there is easy entry into the market and costless exit from the market, new firms entering the market can produce the product at the same costs as current firms, and firms exiting the market can easily dispose of their fixed assets (less depreciation).

Multiple Choice

1. d
2. a
3. d
4. a
5. c
6. b
7. b
8. c
9. c
10. d
11. b
12. b
13. b
14. a
15. b

True-False

16. F
17. T
18. T
19. T
20. F

Fill in the Blank

21. George Stigler
22. cartel
23. cheat
24. excess capacity theorem
25. hit-and-run

Chapter 12
Answers

Review Questions

1. Selling to a retailer on the condition that the retailer will not carry any rivals' products.
2. The more broadly the market is defined, the more substitutes that exist for the good that a firm produces, and the less likely the antitrust authorities will identify the firm as a monopolist.
3. Suppose there are four firms in an industry and each firm has 25 percent of the market. The Herfindahl index is the sum of each firm's market share squared, or $25^2 + 25^2 + 25^2 + 25^2$.
4. A vertical merger is between two firms in the same industry, but at different stages of production. For example, a car manufacturer could merge with a tire manufacturer. A horizontal merger is between two firms in the same industry that sell the same good. For example, two companies that sell office-supply products could merge.
5. price discrimination
6. The higher switching costs are, the greater the permanency of the network monopoly.
7. The complaint charged that Microsoft possessed monopoly power in the market for personal computing operating systems and was using that monopoly power to gain dominance in the Internet browser market.
8. An agency initially regulates an industry but, in time, the industry ends up controlling the agency.
9. If a firm is guaranteed a profit rate, then it has no incentive to keep its costs down.
10. Economists believe that there are both costs and benefits to regulation and that regulation, should only be undertaken if the benefits are greater than the costs.

Problems

1.

Provision of the antitrust act	**Name of the Act**
Every person who shall monopolize, or attempt to monopolize, or combine or conspire with any other person or persons to monopolize any part of the trade or commerce...shall be guilty of a misdemeanor.	Sherman Act
Prohibits suppliers from offering special discounts to large chain stores unless they also offer the discounts to everyone else.	Robinson-Patman Act
Empowers the Federal Trade Commission to deal with false and deceptive acts or practices.	Wheeler-Lea Act
Declares illegal unfair methods of competition in commerce.	Federal Trade Commission Act
Declares illegal exclusive dealing and tying contracts.	Clayton Act

2.

Number of firms in the industry	**Market shares of the firms, in order from top to bottom**	**Herfindahl index**
6	20, 20, 20, 20, 10, 10	1,800
10	20, 10, 10, 10, 10, 10, 10, 10, 5, 5	1,150
10	10, 10, 10, 10, 10, 10, 10, 10, 10, 10	1,000

3.

Proposed merger	What type of merger? (horizontal, vertical, conglomerate)
Between two firms, each of which produces and sells tires.	horizontal
Between two firms, one of which produces and sells houses and the other which produces and sells wood.	vertical
Between two firms, one of which produces and sells books and one of which produces and sells bottled water.	conglomerate

4. P_1
5. P_2
6. If the firm charges P_1 it will incur losses. Losses are identified.

What Is the Question?

1. This antitrust act made interlocking directorates illegal.

   What is the Clayton Act?

2. One advantage is that it provides information about the dispersion of firm size in an industry.

   What is one advantage of the Herfindahl index over the four- or eight-firm concentration ratio?

3. This is descriptive of the situation where a particular product or technology becomes settled upon as the standard and is difficult or impossible to dislodge as the standard.

   What is the lock-in effect?

4. This is the time period between when a natural monopoly's costs change and when the regulatory agency adjusts prices of the natural monopoly.

   What is regulatory lag?

5. Holds that regulators are seeking to do, and will do through regulation, what is in their best interest.

   What is the essence of the public choice theory of regulation?

6. One criticism is that it does not explain which specific acts constitute "restraint of trade."

   What is one criticism of the Sherman Act?

7. This theory holds that regulators are seeking to do, and will do through regulation, what is in the best interest of the public or society at larger.

   What is the public interest theory of regulation?

What Is Wrong?

1. The size of the market is irrelevant to whether a firm is a monopolist or not.

   No, the size of the market matters. The more broadly the market is defined (and therefore the larger the market is), the less likely a firm will be considered a monopolist.

2. A conglomerate merger is a merger between companies in the same market.

   A horizontal merger is a merger between companies in the same market. Alternatively, you could write: A conglomerate merger is a merger between companies in different markets (or industries).

3. For a network good, its value increases as the expected number of units bought decreases.

   For a network good, its value increases as the expected number of units sold increases.

4. The lock-in effect reduces switching costs.

   The lock-in effect increases switching costs.

5. The more broadly a market is defined, the more likely a firm will be considered a monopolist.

   The more broadly a market is defined, the less likely a firm will be considered a monopolist.

6. George Stigler and Claire Friedland studied both unregulated and regulated electric utilities and found a small difference in the rates charged by them.

   George Stigler and Claire Friedland studied both unregulated and regulated electric utilities and found no difference in the rates charged by them.

7. The federal government looks more closely at proposed vertical mergers than horizontal mergers.

   The federal government looks more closely at proposed horizontal mergers than vertical mergers.

8. A profit-maximizing natural monopoly will produce the quantity of output at which MR = MC and charge the price that equals its ATC.

   A profit-maximizing natural monopoly will produce the quantity of output at which MR = MC and charge the highest (per unit) price possible.

9. The capture theory of regulation holds that no matter what the motive for the initial regulation and the establishment of the regulatory agency, eventually the bureaucrats that run the agency will control the industry.

   The capture theory of regulation holds that no matter what the motive for the initial regulation and the establishment of the regulatory agency, eventually the regulated industry will control the regulators.

Multiple Choice

1. a
2. b
3. b
4. d
5. a
6. c
7. b
8. d
9. d
10. d
11. b
12. a
13. b
14. a
15. d

True-False

16. T
17. F
18. F
19. T
20. T

Fill in the Blank

21. public interest theory of regulation
22. Federal Trade Commission Act
23. natural monopoly
24. market
25. size; market power

Chapter 13
Answers

Review Questions

1. There is a demand for restaurant meals. If the demand for restaurant meals increases, the demand for restaurant workers will increase. The demand for restaurant workers is a derived demand—it depends on changes in the demand for restaurant meals.
2. The factor demand curve is the MRP curve. MRP is equal to MR x MPP. At some point, MPP will decline, which will make MRP decline, which will cause the factor demand curve to be downward sloping.
3. When P = MR.
4. It should buy the quantity at which MRP = MFC. As long as MRP > MFC, the benefits of purchasing another factor unit are greater than the costs, that is, there is a net benefit of purchasing another factor unit.
5. The least-cost rule states that the MPP-to-factor price ratio is the same for all factors. If the ratio is higher for factor X than Y, then it is cheaper to buy less of Y and more of X. Why? Because there is a greater change in output for a $1 expenditure on X than Y. That is essentially what a higher MPP-to-factor price ratio says.
6. Elasticity of demand for the product that labor produces, ratio of labor costs to total costs, and number of substitute factors.
7. No, the income effect may arise, but simply be outweighed by the substitution effect.
8. Product demand and supply (and therefore product price and marginal revenue), and the MPP of labor. See relevant exhibit in the text chapter.
9. Wage rates in other markets, nonpecuniary aspects of the job, number of persons who can do the job, training costs, and moving costs.
10. It may be too costly for an employer to generate full information on a potential employee, and therefore the employer may make a decision to hire (not to hire) based on less than full information. Had the employer known more, the decision might have been different.

Problems

1.

Quantity of factor Z	Quantity of output	Product price	Total revenue	Marginal revenue product
1	30	$40	$1,200	$1,200
2	50	$40	$2,000	$800
3	60	$40	$2,400	$400

2.

Quantity of factor Z	Price of factor Z	Total cost	Marginal factor cost
1	$10	$10	$10
2	$10	$20	$10
3	$10	$30	$10

3.

MPP of factor X (units)	Price of factor X	MPP of factor Y (units)	Price of factor Y	Should the firm buy more of factor X or factor Y?
30	$2	40	$1.25	Y
50	$4	100	$5.00	Y
100	$30	100	$40.00	X

4.

Change	Does this affect the demand for labor (yes, no)?	Does this affect the supply of labor (yes, no)?	Effect on wage (up, down, no change)
product supply falls	yes	no	up
product demand rises	yes	no	yes
training costs rise	no	yes	up
positive change in the nonpecuniary aspects of the job	no	yes	down

5.

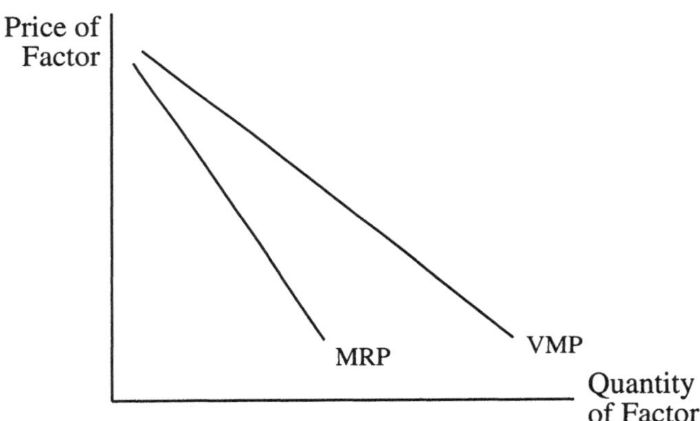

6.

What Is the Question?

1. The additional revenue generated by employing an additional factor unit.

   What is marginal revenue product?

2. It is also the factor demand curve.

   What is the MRP curve?

3. It slopes downward because the MPP of the factor eventually declines.

   Why does the factor demand curve (or MRP curve) slope downward?

4. It will buy the number of factor units for which MRP = MFC.

   What quantity of factor units will the firm purchase?

5. The firm will buy more of factor X and less of factor Y.

   What will the firm do if the MPP-to-price ratio for factor X is greater than the MPP-to-price ratio for factor Y?

6. It is equal to the MPP of the factor divided by the cost of the factor.

   What does output produced per $1 of cost equal?

7. The percentage change in the quantity demanded of labor divided by the percentage change in the wage rate.

   What does elasticity of demand for labor equal?

8. It is upward sloping because the substitution effect outweighs the income effect.

   Why is the supply of labor curve upward sloping?

9. One of the reasons is that jobs have different nonpecuniary qualities.

   Why are supply conditions in different labor markets different?

10. States that firms in competitive or perfect product and factor markets pay factors their marginal revenue products.

    What does the marginal productivity theory state?

What Is Wrong?

1. If price equals marginal revenue, then VMP is greater than MRP.

   If price equals marginal revenue, then VMP equals MRP.

2. The factor demand curve usually lies above the MRP curve.

   The factor demand curve is the MRP curve.

3. The firm will purchase the quantity of a factor at which the difference between the MRP and MFC of the factor are maximized.

   The firm will purchase the quantity of a factor at which MRP = MFC.

4. An increase in MPP will shift the factor demand curve to the left.

   An increase in MPP will shift the factor demand curve to the right. Alternatively, you could write, A decrease in MPP will shift the factor demand curve to the left.

5. If the demand for the product that labor produces is highly elastic, a small percentage increase in price will decrease quantity demanded of the product by a relatively small percentage.

   If the demand for the product that labor produces is highly elastic, a small percentage increase in price will decrease quantity demanded of the product by a relatively large percentage.

6. The more substitutes for labor, the lower the elasticity of demand for labor; the fewer substitutes for labor, the higher the elasticity of demand for labor.

   The more substitutes for labor, the higher the elasticity of demand for labor; the fewer substitutes for labor, the lower the elasticity of demand for labor.

7. Screening is the process used by employers to increase the probability of choosing good employees (to promote) from within the firm.

   Screening is the process used by employers to increase the probability of choosing good employees—from within or outside the firm.

8. A firm minimizes costs by buying factors in the combination at which the MPP-to-price ratio for the expensive factors is greater than the MPP-to-price ratio for the less expensive factors.

   A firm minimizes costs by buying factors in the combination at which the MPP-to-price ratio for all factors is the same.

9. The supply curve is upward-sloping for a factor price taker.

   The supply curve is horizontal for a factor price taker.

10. The higher the labor cost-total cost ratio, the lower the elasticity of demand for labor.

    The higher the labor cost-total cost ratio, the higher the elasticity of demand for labor. Alternatively, you could write: The lower the labor cost-total cost ratio, the lower the elasticity of demand for labor.

Multiple Choice

1. a
2. d
3. a
4. a
5. b
6. e
7. c
8. d
9. d
10. c
11. b
12. a
13. a
14. d
15. a

True-False

16. T
17. T
18. T
19. F
20. F

Fill in the Blank

21. Value marginal product (VMP)
22. screening
23. quantity demanded of labor; wage rate
24. MRP = MFC
25. derived

Chapter 14
Answers

Review Questions

1. Employ all members of the union, maximize the total wage bill, and maximize the income of a limited number of union members.
2. Since the demand curve for union labor is downward-sloping, as the wage rate rises, the number of union workers employed falls.
3. It would need to reduce the availability of substitute products or reduce the availability of substitute factors.
4. By increasing the demand for the product it produces, by increasing the price of substitute factors, and by increasing the marginal physical product (productivity) of members.
5. In a closed shop, a person must join the union before he or she can be hired. With a union shop, one can be hired without being a member of the union. However, the worker must join the union within a certain time of becoming employed.
6. Because it is the only (or single) buyer of a factor, just as a monopolist is the only (or single) seller of a good.
7. For a monopsonist, MFC is greater than the wage rate.
8. Suppose labor is homogeneous and mobile. If there is an increase in the wage rate in the union sector (brought about by collective bargaining), there will be fewer people working in the union sector. Some of the people no longer working in the union sector will supply their labor services in the nonunion sector and the wage rate (in that sector) will fall.
9. That labor unions have a negative impact on productivity and efficiency through unnecessary staffing requirements, strikes, and more.
10. The quantity at which MRP = MFC.

Problems

1.

Description	Type of union
A union whose membership is made up of individuals who practice the same craft or trade.	craft (trade) union
A union whose membership is made up of individuals who work for the local, state, or federal government.	public employee union
A union whose membership is made up of individuals who work in the same firm or industry but do not all practice the same craft or trade.	industrial union

2.

Action	Effect on elasticity of demand for union labor (rises, falls, remains unchanged)
reduced availability of substitute products	falls
reduced availability of substitute factors	falls

3.

Action	Effect on demand for union labor (rises, falls, remains unchanged)
MPP of union labor falls	falls
product demand rises	rises
substitute factor prices fall	falls

4.

Action	Does it affect the demand for union labor, or the supply of union labor?
MPP of union labor rises	demand for union labor
substitute factor prices rise	demand for union labor
introduction of union shop	supply of union labor

5. Labor union changes supply curve from SS to S^*S.

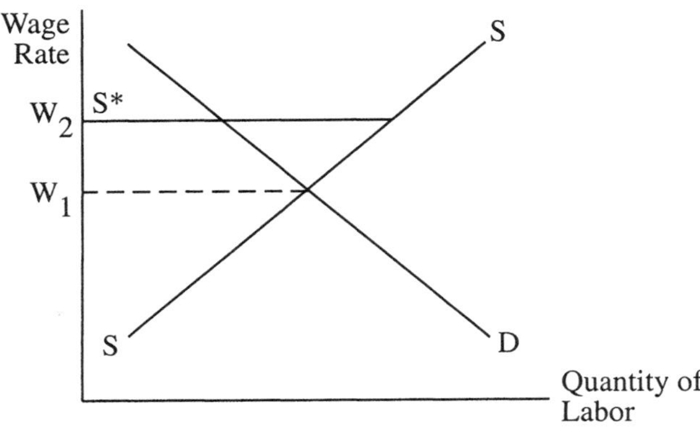

6.

Number of workers	Wage rate	Total labor cost	Marginal factor cost
1	$10.00	$10.00	$10.00
2	$10.10	$20.20	$10.20
3	$10.20	$30.60	$10.40
4	$10.30	$41.20	$10.60
5	$10.40	$52.00	$10.80

What Is the Question?

1. An organization whose members belong to a particular profession.

   What is an employee association?

2. The labor union will want this wage rate to prevail if its objective is to maximize the total wage bill.

   What is the wage rate that corresponds to the unit elastic point on the demand for union labor curve?

3. The wage-employment tradeoff decreases.

   What happens as the demand for labor becomes more inelastic (or less elastic)?

4. The purpose is to convince management that the supply curve is what the union says it is.

   What is the purpose of a strike?

5. MFC is greater than the wage rate.

    What is the relationship between MFC and the wage rate for a monopsonist?

6. An organization in which an employee must belong to the union before he or she can be hired.

    What is a closed shop?

7. Increasing product demand, increasing substitute factor prices, and increasing marginal physical product.

    What will lead to an increase in the demand for union labor?

8. The change in total labor cost divided by the change in the number of workers.

    What is marginal factor cost equal to?

What Is Wrong?

1. If the objective of the labor union is to maximize the total wage bill, it will want the wage rate that corresponds to the inelastic portion of the labor demand curve.

    If the objective of the labor union is to maximize the total wage bill, it will want the wage rate that corresponds to the unit elastic point on the labor demand curve.

2. The more substitutes for union labor, the lower the elasticity of demand for union labor.

    The more substitutes for union labor, the higher the elasticity of demand for union labor. Alternatively, you could write: The fewer substitutes for union labor, the lower the elasticity of demand for union labor.

3. The National Working Rights Act allowed states to pass right-to-work laws.

    The Taft-Hartley Act allowed states to pass right-to-work laws.

4. The MFC curve lies below the supply of labor curve for a monopsonist.

    The MFC lies above the supply of labor curve for a monopsonist.

5. The percentage of the national income that goes to labor has been rising over the past 30 years.

    The percentage of the national income that goes to labor has been fairly constant over time.

6. If labor is homogeneous and mobile, an increase in the wage rate in the union sector will bring about an increase in the wage rate in the nonunion sector.

    If labor is homogeneous and mobile, an increase in the wage rate in the union sector will bring about a decrease in the wage rate in the nonunion sector.

7. An industrial union is a union whose membership is made up of individuals who practice the same craft or trade.

    A craft or trade is a union whose membership is made up of individuals who practice the same craft or trade. Alternatively, you could write: An industrial union is a union whose membership is made up of individuals who work in the same firm or industry but do not all practice the same craft or trade.

Multiple Choice

1. b
2. a
3. d
4. b
5. d
6. b
7. a
8. c
9. b
10. e
11. a
12. c
13. d
14. b
15. a

True-False

16. T
17. F
18. T
19. T
20. T

Fill in the Blank

21. right-to-work
22. monopsony
23. unit elastic
24. strike
25. MRP = MFC

Chapter 15
Answers

Review Questions

1. The *ex ante* distribution has not been adjusted for taxes and transfer payments, the *ex post* distribution has been.
2. Labor income, asset income, transfer payments, taxes.
3. The income share of different quintiles is identified. Then cumulative quintile (households) is plotted against cumulative income share. For example, suppose the lowest fifth (of households) has an income share of 10 percent and the second fifth (of households) has an income share of 15 percent. One point on the Lorenz curve identifies 20 percent of households against a 10 percent income share. A second point on the Lorenz curve identifies 40 percent of households against a 25 percent income share. For more details, see the relevant exhibit in the text chapter.
4. By comparing Gini coefficients, we cannot identify the percentage of income earned by a particular income group. For example, even though Country A may have a lower Gini coefficient than Country B, we don't know if the lowest fifth of households in Country A do, or do not, earn more income than the lowest fifth of households in Country B.
5. Innate abilities and attributes, work and leisure, education and other training, risk taking, luck, and wage discrimination.
6. The income distribution that should exist is the income distribution that people would agree to behind the veil of ignorance, where they do not know their position in the income distribution.
7. A person is said to be in absolute poverty if he or she earns an income below a certain dollar amount. A person is said to be in relative poverty if he or she is one of the lowest income earners. For example, if 95 percent of individuals earn more than Smith, Smith might be said to be falling into relative poverty. In short, absolute dollar amounts are relevant to absolute poverty and percentages are relevant to relative poverty.
8. People tend to earn more in middle age than in their youth. A very youthful population, therefore, might skew the income distribution toward greater inequality.
9. It argues that people should be paid their marginal revenue products.
10. It holds that the reduction or elimination of poverty is a public good and therefore everyone will take a free ride on someone else's efforts at trying to eliminate poverty. In this setting, very little poverty will be reduced or eliminated. It follows, then, that government is justified in taxing all persons to pay for the welfare assistance of some.

Problems

1.

Quintile	Percentage of total income, 2000
Lowest fifth	3.6
Second fifth	8.9
Third fifth	14.9
Fourth fifth	23.0
Highest fifth	49.6

2.

Quintile	Income share (percent)	Cumulative percentage of income	Cumulative percentage of households
Lowest fifth	10	10	20
Second fifth	12	22	40
Third fifth	22	44	60
Fourth fifth	25	69	80
Highest fifth	31	100	100

3.

Group	Percent of group in poverty, 2000
Total population	11.3
White	6.9
African-American	19.1
Hispanic	18.5
Under 18 years of age	16.2
18-24 years old	14.4
65 years old and older	10.2

4.

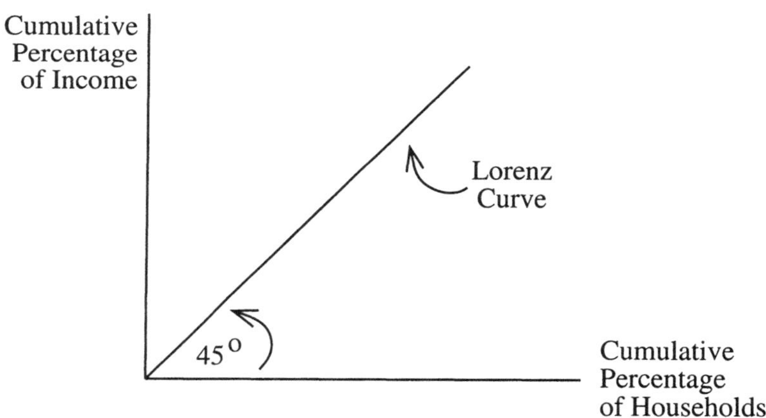

5.

Quintile	Income share
Lowest fifth	10 percent
Second fifth	20 percent
Third fifth	21 percent
Fourth fifth	22 percent
Highest fifth	27 percent

What Is the Question?

1. Payments to persons that are not made in return for goods and services currently supplied.

   What are transfer payments?

2. Labor income plus asset income plus transfer payments minus taxes.

   What does an individual's income equal?

3. This exists when individuals of equal ability and productivity are paid different wage rates.

   What is wage discrimination?

4. It is determined in factor markets.

   Where is the income distribution determined?

5. The Gini coefficient is 1.

   What is the Gini coefficient if there is complete income inequality?

6. The income level below which people are considered to be living in poverty.

   What is the poverty income threshold or poverty line?

7. An example is that everyone who earns less than $5,000 is living in poverty.

   What is absolute poverty?

8. An example is that the bottom one-tenth of income earners are living in poverty.

   What is relative poverty?

9. It holds that individuals currently not receiving welfare think they might one day need welfare assistance and thus are willing to take out a form of insurance for themselves by supporting welfare programs.

   What is the social insurance justification of welfare assistance?

What Is Wrong?

1. The income distribution in the United States in 2000 was more nearly equal than it was in 1967.

   The income distribution in the United States in 2000 was more nearly unequal (or less equal) than it was in 1967.

2. The government can change the distribution of income through taxes, but not through transfer payments.

   The government can change the distribution of income through taxes and transfer payments.

3. The Lorenz curve is a measurement of the degree of inequality in the distribution of income.

   The Gini coefficient is a measurement of the degree of inequality in the distribution of income. Alternatively, you could write: The Lorenz curve is the graphical representation of the income distribution.

4. The Rawlsian normative standard of the income distribution holds that there should be complete income equality.

   The absolute income equality standard holds that there should be complete income equality. Alternatively, you could write, The Rawlsian normative standard holds that the income distribution should be what is decided behind the veil of ignorance.

5. Asset income is equal to the wage rate an individual receives multiplied by the number of hours he or she works.

   Labor income is equal to the wage rate an individual receives multiplied by the number of hours he or she works. Alternatively, you could write: Asset income consists of such things as the return to saving, the return to capital investment, and the return to land.

6. In general, human capital refers to the increases in productivity brought about by humans when they use physical capital goods.

   In general, human capital refers to the labor productivity brought about through education, developing one's skills, and so on.

7. The Gini coefficient is zero (0) if there is an unequal income distribution.

   The Gini coefficient is zero if there is an absolutely equal income distribution. Alternatively, you could write: The Gini coefficient is between 0 and 1 if there is an unequal income distribution.

Multiple Choice
1. a
2. b
3. b
4. e
5. a
6. e
7. b
8. d
9. d
10. c

True-False

11. T
12. T
13. T
14. T
15. T

Fill in the Blank

16. Transfer payments
17. Gini coefficient
18. Wage discrimination
19. One (1)
20. *ex ante*

Chapter 16
Answers

Review Questions

1. A person borrows $100 and repays $120. Twenty dollars ($20) is interest; 20 percent is the interest rate, or the interest/principal ratio.
2. It means the person slightly prefers earlier to later availability of goods.
3. Instead of digging holes by hand, a person takes out time to produce a shovel to use to dig the holes.
4. People would not pay positive interest rates if they didn't have a positive rate of time preference or roundabout methods of production weren't productive.
5. Interest rates differ because loans are not the same with respect to all factors, such as risk, term of the loan, and cost of making the loan.
6. The present value of the income stream is $4,920, which is less than the cost of the capital good. The firm should not buy the capital good for $5,000.
7. He meant that it was because prices were high that land rent was high, not the other way around.
8. Suppose opportunity cost is $10 and the wage rate is $12. Economic rent is $2. Now suppose opportunity cost is $0 and the wage rate is $12. Pure economic rent is $12. Pure economic rent exists when opportunity costs are zero. Whenever opportunity costs are positive, we are dealing with economic rent instead of pure economic rent.
9. A rent is real if it has not been artificially brought about some way. Artificial rent is economic rent that is artificially contrived (usually by government).
10. One theory of profit states that profit would not exist if uncertainty did not exist. One theory of profit states that profit is the return to innovation.
11. Profit and loss are signals to resources. Resources flow toward profits and away from losses.

Problems

1.

Dollar amount received	Number of years before dollar amount is received	Interest rate (percent)	Present value
$1,000	2	5	$907.03
$10,000	3	6	$8,396.31
$100	2	7	$87.34

2.

Cost of capital good	Life of capital good	Income from capital good each year	Interest rate (percent)	Should the firm buy the capital good? (yes, no)
$4,000	3 years	$1,500	2	yes
$19,000	5 years	$4,000	5	yes
$20,000	6 years	$5,000	4	yes

3.

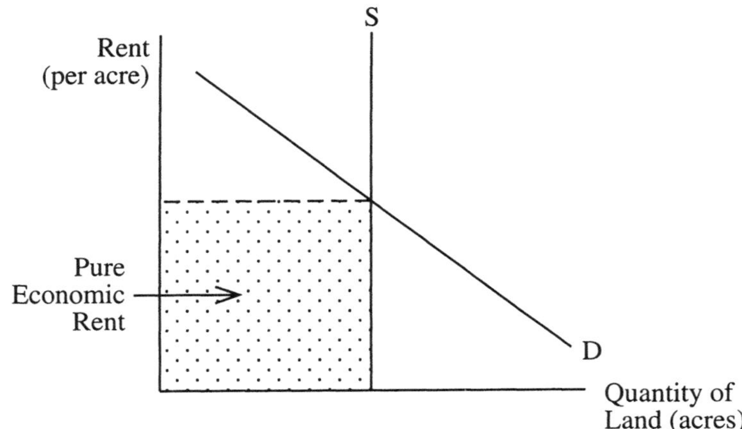

4.

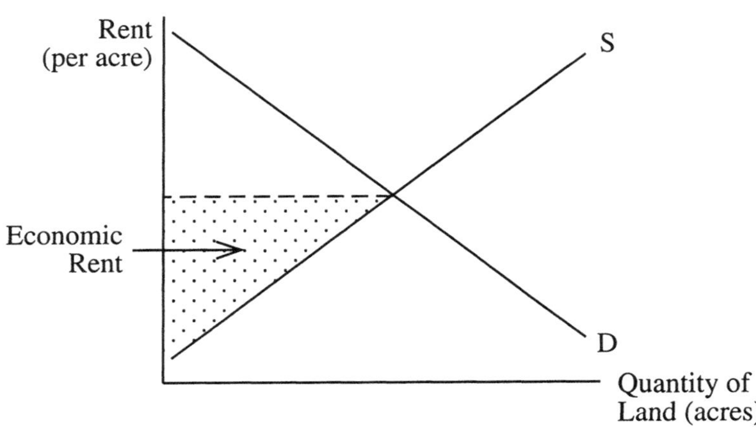

5.

Wage rate	Next best wage rate	Economic rent
$12	$11	$1
$10	$10	$0
$100	$66	$34

What Is the Question?

1. The production of capital goods that enhance productive capabilities and ultimately bring about increased consumption.

   What is the roundabout method of production?

2. It is composed of the demand for consumption loans and the demand for investment loans.

   What are the components of the demand for loans?

3. If this is the case, then firms will borrow in the loanable funds market and invest in capital goods.

   What will firms do if the return on capital is greater than the price for loanable funds?

4. The interest rate determined by the forces of supply and demand in the loanable funds market.

   What is the nominal interest rate?

5. They are equal when the expected inflation rate is zero.

   When are the nominal and real interest rates equal?

6. The current worth of some future dollar amount of income receipts.

   What is present value?

7. The supply curve is vertical in this case.

   What does the supply curve look like if there is pure economic rent?

8. Consumers do this because they have a positive rate of time preference.

   Why do consumers borrow funds?

9. These turn away from losses.

   What are resources?

What Is Wrong?

1. Interest refers to the price paid by borrowers for loanable funds and to the return on cash.

   Interest refers to the price paid by borrowers for loanable funds and to the return on capital.

2. Savers supply loanable funds because they have a negative rate of time preference.

   Savers do not have a negative rate of time preference, they have a positive time preference. They may have a lower rate of time preference than borrowers, though.

3. A person with a high positive rate of time preference is more likely to be a saver than a person with a low positive rate of time preference.

   A person with a low positive rate of time preference is more likely to be a saver than a person with a high positive rate of time preference.

4. David Ricardo argued that high land rents weren't an effect of high interest rates and high grain prices.

   David Ricardo argued that high land rents were an effect of high grain prices.

5. The present value of $4,000 in three years, if the interest rate is 5 percent, is $3,288.

   The present value of $4,000 in three years, if the interest rate is 5 percent, is $3,455.65

6. A decreased threat of war would probably raise peoples' rate of time preference.

   A decreased threat of war would probably lower peoples' rate of time preference. Alternatively, you could write: An increased threat of war would probably raise peoples' rate of time preference.

7. As the interest rate falls, present value falls.

   As the interest rate falls, present value rises. Alternatively, you could write: As the interest rate rises, present value falls.

8. Uncertainty exists when a potential occurrence is so unpredictable that the probability of it occurring is less than 1.

   Uncertainty exists when a potential occurrence is so unpredictable that a probability cannot be estimated.

9. Economists emphasize accounting profit over economic profit because economic profit determines entry into and exit from an industry.

   Economists emphasize economic profit over accounting profit because economic profit determines entry into and exit from an industry.

Multiple Choice

1. c
2. d
3. a
4. c
5. d
6. a
7. d
8. d
9. c
10. c
11. e
12. e
13. d
14. c
15. c

True-False

16. F
17. F
18. F
19. F
20. T

Fill in the Blank

21. roundabout methods
22. equality
23. nominal, real
24. one
25. increase

Chapter 17
Answers

Review Questions

1. No, when there are no externalities (positive or negative), the (competitive) market output and the socially optimal output are the same.
2. Market failure is the situation that exists when the market does not produce the optimal amount of a good.
3. They matter if there are positive transaction costs but not if transaction costs are trivial or zero.
4. The objective is to move from the market output to the socially optimal output. A corrective tax does not always work because sometimes the tax is more or less than the external cost.
5. No, since there are costs and benefits to eliminating pollution.
6. Government issues pollution permits and allows them to be bought and sold. In the end, the entities that can eliminate pollution at the lowest cost will end up eliminating pollution.
7. Both a nonexcludable and excludable public good are nonrivalrous in consumption, but a nonexclucable public good cannot be denied to a person while an excludable public good can be.
8. Because of the existence of free riders, who will be able to consume the good without paying for it. In short, because of free riders, no seller of a nonexcludable public good would be able to extract payment from people who benefit from the good.
9. With symmetric information the demand for a good may be lower than it would be with asymmetric information. It follows then that the market output is larger with asymmetric information than with symmetric information.
10. With symmetric information the supply of a factor may be less than it would be with asymmetric information. It follows then that more factor units will be employed with asymmetric information than with symmetric information.
11. Consider it in the used car market. The owners of "lemons" offer their cars for sale because they know, and only they know, that the average price they are being offered for their below-average car is a good deal. Through adverse selection, the supply of lemons rises on the market and the supply of good used cars falls. There is now a new average price that is less than it was earlier. Only people with below average cars think the average price is a good price. The people with above-average used cars drop out of the market. In time, the process continues and more and more owners of above-average cars drop out of the market. In the end there is no longer a market for good used cars but only for lemons.
12. Jones buys a health insurance policy. Afterward, she doesn't watch her health as much as she would have otherwise, but the seller of the health insurance policy does not know this.

Problems

1. a) $3,800; b) $1,800
2. The tax moves the output from Q_1 to Q_3 instead of from Q_1 to Q_2.

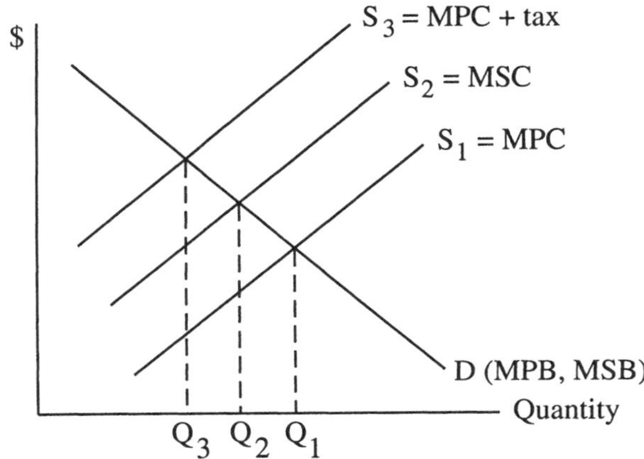

3. Because there are net costs of moving from the socially optimal output (Q_2) to the market output (Q_1). In other words, the costs of moving from Q_2 to Q_1 are greater than the benefits by the amount of the triangle.
4. When the tax equals marginal external cost.
5. With asymmetric information the demand curve is D_1, and with symmetric information it is D_2. If the outcome really would be Q_1 with asymmetric information and Q_2 with symmetric information, then the difference between Q_1 and Q_2 represents a market failure.

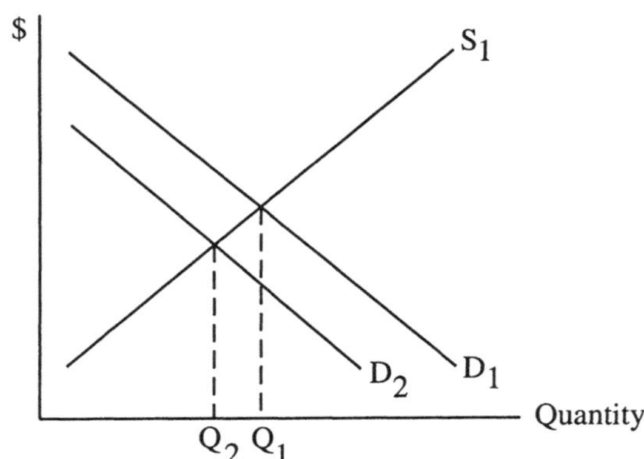

What Is the Question?

1. This exists when a person's or group's actions cause a cost to be felt by others.

   What is a negative externality?

2. MSC > MPC.

   What is the relationship between MSC and MPC when a negative externality exists?

3. MSB > MPB.

   What is the relationship between MSB and MPB when a positive externality exists?

4. In this case property rights assignments do not matter to the resource allocative outcome.

   Do property rights assignments matter to the resource allocative outcome when transaction costs are zero?

5. He stressed the reciprocal nature of externalities.

   Who is Ronald Coase?

6. Consumption by one person reduces consumption by another person.

   What does it mean if there is rivalry in consumption?

7. The person who makes it difficult, if not impossible, for the market to produce nonexcludable public goods.

   Who is the free rider?

8. This exists when either the buyer or the seller in a market exchange has some information that the other does not have.

    What is asymmetric information?

9. This exists when the parties on one side of the market, who have information not known to others, self-select in a way that adversely affects the parties on the other side of the market.

    What is adverse selection?

What Is Wrong?

1. The economist holds that less pollution is always better than the current amount of pollution because pollution is a bad.

    The economist does not hold that less pollution is always better than the current amount of pollution. The economist knows that the costs of eliminating some units of pollution may be greater than the benefits derived.

2. A negative externality is a type of subsidy.

    A negative externality is an adverse side-effect of an individual's or group's actions.

3. Given a positive externality, the marginal private benefit curve lies to the left of the demand curve, with the market output above the socially optimal output.

    Given a positive externality, the marginal social benefit curve lies to the right of the demand curve, with the market output below the socially optimal output.

4. The side effect of an action that increases the well-being of others is called a neutral benefit.

    The side effect of an action that increases the well-being of others is called a positive externality.

5. If private property were established in the air, there would probably be more air pollution.

    If private property were established in the air, there would probably be less air pollution.

6. If a person who generates a negative externality incorporates into his private cost-benefit calculations the effects that this externality will have on third parties, the externality has been complementarized.

    If a person who generates a negative externality incorporates into his private cost-benefit calculations the effects that this externality will have on third parties, the externality has been internalized.

7. Generally, negative externalities result in too little of a good being produced.

    Generally, negative externalities result in too much of a good being produced.

8. If there are no externalities, then the socially optimum output occurs where MPB > MPC.

    If there are no externalities, then the socially optimum output occurs where MPB = MPC.

9. Marginal social costs equal marginal private costs plus internal costs.

Marginal social costs equal marginal private costs plus marginal external costs.

Multiple Choice
1. c
2. d
3. a
4. e
5. d
6. d
7. d
8. b
9. d
10. c

True-False
11. T
12. F
13. T
14. T
15. T

Fill in the Blank
16. Market failure
17. internalized
18. nonrivalrous in consumption
19. Moral hazard
20. socially optimal

Chapter 18
Answers

Review Questions

1. Yes. To speak in specific terms is more likely to get a person labeled as being "to the right" or "to the left." Candidates do not want to be seen as "to the right" or "to the left," but instead "in the middle."
2. Yes. See answer to number 1.
3. They are more likely to take polls to determine their position. It is harder to move from an off-center position to a center position than it is to locate at the center position from the beginning.
4. The general answer is: because the costs of voting outweigh the benefits. Specifically, the reason the benefits may be so low (relative to the costs) is because the person only perceives benefits to voting if he believes his vote can affect the outcome. Since this isn't likely in a large-numbers election (where there are many eligible voters), there are no benefits to voting and therefore the person chooses not to vote.
5. There are some benefits she gets from voting that are unrelated to her vote's impact on the outcome of the election.
6. No matter who you voted for in the last presidential election, the outcome would have been the same.
7. It may have everything to do with rational ignorance. Jim may not know the names of his U.S. senators because he perceives the benefits of acquiring this information as less than the costs.
8. Probably so. It is unlikely that anyone finds the benefits of learning all those things there are to learn greater than the costs of learning all those things there are to learn. People usually prioritize and therefore find some things worth learning and other things not worth learning.
9. Subsets of the population who hold intense preferences with respect to some issue, action, or policy.
10. Because agricultural policy will have a bigger monetary effect on the farmer than on the member of the general public.
11. Because the costs of doing anything might be greater than the benefits. Suppose a piece of legislation will take $2 away from Joe. To lobby against the legislation, Joe might have to pay $40. Is it worth Joe paying $40 to save $2? No. Joe may decide to do nothing.
12. Rent is a payment in excess of opportunity cost. Rent seeking is the expenditure of scarce resources to bring about a pure transfer.
13. Because resources that are used to bring about a pure transfer could, instead, be used to produce goods.

Problems

1. The group will buy good X because this is the preference of a simple majority of the group. The purchase of good X is inefficient because the total benefits ($388) are less than the total cost ($500).

What Is the Question?

1. The branch of economics that deals with the application of economic principles and tolls to public-sector decision making.

    What is public choice?

2. Candidates will speak in general terms; candidates will label their opponent in extreme terms; candidates will label themselves in moderate terms; candidates will take polls and if they are not doing well in their polls they will adjust their positions.

    What are the predictions of the median voter model?

3. The state of not acquiring information because the costs of acquiring the information are greater than the benefits.

    What is rational ignorance?

4. The exchange of votes to gain support for legislation.

   What is logrolling?

5. In this case rent is usually called profit.

   When rent is the result of entrepreneurial activity designed to either satisfy a new demand or rearrange resources in an increasingly valuable way, what is it called?

6. The expenditure of scarce resources to capture a pure transfer.

   What is rent seeking?

What Is Wrong?

1. Legislation that concentrates the benefits on many and disperses the costs over a few is likely to pass, because the beneficiaries will have an incentive to lobby for it, whereas those who pay the bill will not lobby against it because each of them pays such a small part of the bill.

   Legislation that concentrates the benefits on few and disperses the costs over many is likely to pass, because the beneficiaries will have an incentive to lobby for it, whereas those who pay the bill will not lobby against it because each of them pays such a small part of the bill.

2. A public choice economist would likely state that people will not behave differently in different settings.

   A public choice economist believes that people do behave differently in different settings if costs and benefits are different in different settings.

3. In a two-person race, the candidate on the right of the median voter is more likely to win the race than the candidate on the left of the median voter.

   In a two-person race, the candidate closer to the median voter is more likely to win.

4. One of the predictions of the median voter model is that candidates will speak in specific terms instead of general terms because this is what the median voter wants.

   One of the predictions of the median voter model is that candidates will speak in general instead of specific terms.

5. Younger people are more likely to be rationally ignorant of various subjects than older people.

   There is no evidence that younger people are more likely to be rationally ignorant than older people. Rational ignorance appears to be independent of age.

6. A government bureau maximizes profit and minimizes costs.

   A government bureau does not attempt to maximize profit.

7. Farmers, lobbying for a legislative bill, are more likely to openly state, "We need this legislation because it will be good for us," instead of "We need this legislation for America's future."

   It's just the opposite. Farmers are more likely to say "We need this legislation for America's future." That is, they are more likely to utter the public-interest words than the special-interest words.

Multiple Choice
1. d
2. a
3. a
4. d
5. b
6. c
7. d
8. c
9. b
10. a

True-False

11. T
12. F
13. T
14. T
15. F

Fill in the Blank

16. Government failure
17. costs, benefits
18. general; specific
19. closer
20. James Buchanan

Chapter 19
Answers

Review Questions

1. People in different countries trade with each other for the same reason that people within a country trade with each other—to make themselves better off.
2. Through specialization, countries (as a group) can end up producing more than if they don't specialize. Since they can produce more through specialization, the possibility certainly exists that they can consume more, too. This is accomplished by their trading with each other.
3. A tariff will lower consumers' surplus.
4. A tariff will raise producers' surplus.
5. The benefits of the tariff may be concentrated over relatively few producers and the costs of the tariff may be dispersed over relatively many consumers. As a result, the average producer may receive more in gains than the average consumer loses, although consumers (as a group) lose more than producers (as a group) gain. This means the average producer has a sharper incentive to lobby for the tariff than the average consumer has to lobby against it.
6. Industries that are new (infants) in one country may have a hard time competing against their counterparts in other countries that have been around for awhile (and therefore are adults). The infant industries may need some assistance (protection) until they grow up and mature and are ready to compete on an equal basis.
7. A country is said to be dumping goods if it sells a good for less than its cost and below the price charged in the domestic market. Some people argue that this is unfair to domestic industries and therefore they should be protected from this action.
8. No, not necessarily. An economist might ask: What was the price to save the domestic job? If consumers have to pay $60,000 (in higher prices) to save every $40,000 job, it isn't worth saving those jobs.
9. The WTO's objective is to help trade flow "smoothly, freely, fairly, and predictably." It does this by administering trade agreements, assisting developing countries in trade-policy issues, and cooperating with other international organizations.
10. It means that the gains to the winners (or beneficiaries) of tariffs are less than the costs (or losses) to the losers.

Problems

1.

Opportunity cost of one unit of X for Country A	Opportunity cost of one unit of Y for Country A	Opportunity cost of one unit of X for Country B	Opportunity cost of one unit of Y for Country B
1.5Y	0.67X	1Y	1X

2. Area 1
3. Area 2
4. Change in consumers' surplus is the loss of areas 3, 4, 5, 6. Change in producers' surplus is the gain of area 3.
5. Gain from the tariff is area 3 (for producers) and area 5 (for government). Loss is the areas 3, 4, 5, and 6 (for consumers).
6. Net loss is the areas 4 and 6.
7. Area 5

8.

Price after quota	Loss in consumers' surplus due to the quota	Gain in producers' surplus due to the quota	Increase in revenue received by importers due to the quota	Net loss due to the quota
P_Q	Areas 3, 4, 5, 6	Area 3	Area 5	Areas 4 and 6

What Is the Question?

1. This will allow the country to consume beyond its production possibilities frontier (PPF).

   What will specialization and trade do for a country (in terms of its consumption)?

2. As a result, imports decrease.

   What will happen to imports as a tariff or quota is imposed.

3. The sale of goods abroad at a price below their cost and below the price charged in the domestic market.

   What is dumping?

4. The situation in which a country can produce a good at lower opportunity cost than another country.

   What does comparative advantage refer to?

5. The gains are less than the losses plus the tariff revenues.

   What is the net effect of a tariff?

What Is Wrong?

1. A PPF for the world can be drawn when 1) countries do not specialize and trade and 2) when they do specialize and trade. The world PPF will be the same in both cases.

   The world PPF will be further to the right when countries specialize and trade than when they do not.

2. The national-defense argument states that certain goods are necessary to the national defense and therefore should be produced only by allies.

   The national-defense argument states that certain goods are necessary to the national defense and therefore should be produced only by the domestic country.

3. A quota raises more government revenue than a tariff.

   A quota doesn't raise tariff revenue.

4. Consumers' surplus and producers' surplus fall as a result of a tariff being imposed on imported goods.

   Only consumers' surplus falls as a result of a tariff. Producers' surplus rises.

5. What producers gain from a quota is greater than what consumers lose from a quota.

   What producers gain from a quota is less than what consumers lose from a quota.

6. If the United States sells a good for less in France than it does in Brazil, then the United States is said to be dumping goods in France.

   The United States may not be dumping goods in this situation. Dumping requires the United States to sell goods for less than cost and less than the price charged in the domestic economy.

7. A voluntary export restraint is an agreement between two countries in which importing countries voluntarily agree to limit their imports of a good from another country.

   A voluntary export restraint is an agreement between two countries in which the exporting country voluntarily agrees to limit its exports of a good to another country.

8. A quota is a tax on the amount of a good that may be imported into a country.

   A tariff is a tax on the amount of a good that may be imported into a country.

Multiple Choice

1. c
2. a
3. d
4. a
5. a
6. c
7. d
8. d
9. a
10. e
11. d
12. e
13. b
14. d
15. c

True-False

16. F
17. T
18. T
19. T
20. T

Fill in the Blank

21. antidumping
22. fall
23. falls
24. less
25. more (greater)

Chapter 20
Answers

Review Questions

1. A person in the United States wants to buy a British good. The American has to supply dollars in the foreign exchange market in order to buy pounds.
2. A German wants to buy a U.S. good. The German has to supply marks (in the foreign exchange market) in order to demand dollars.
3. The current account balance takes into account more items than the merchandise trade balance. The merchandise trade balance looks at the difference between merchandise exports and merchandise imports. The merchandise account balance takes into account exports of goods and services (one component of which is merchandise exports), imports of goods and services (one component of which is merchandise imports) and net unilateral transfers abroad.
4. Outflow of U.S. capital and inflow of foreign capital.
5. With a flexible exchange rate system, the demand for and supply of currencies determine equilibrium exchange rates. It is no different than supply and demand determining the price of corn, television sets, or houses. In this case supply and demand simply determine the price of one currency in terms of another currency. With a fixed exchange rate system, governments determine the exchange rate. Under a fixed exchange rate system, exchange rates are determined by government edict, not market forces.
6. If a person in the United States wants to buy a British good, he must pay for the British good with pounds. Thus he will have a demand for pounds. How will he get these pounds? He will have to supply dollars in order to demand pounds in order to buy the British good.
7. If a person in the UK wants to buy a U.S. good, he must pay for good with dollars. Thus he will have a demand for dollars. How will he get these dollars? He will have to supply pounds in order to demand dollars in order to buy the U.S. good.
8. The dollar has appreciated. When it takes less of currency X to buy currency Y, currency X is said to have appreciated. It took $0.0094 to buy one yen on Tuesday, and $0.0090 to buy one yen on Wednesday.
9. A difference in income growth rates (among countries), a difference in relative inflation rates (among countries), and changes in real interest rates (among countries).
10. Suppose the equilibrium exchange rate is $1 = 106 yen and the official exchange rate is $1 = 150 yen. The dollar is overvalued.
11. Devaluation is an act of government; depreciation is an act of markets.

Problems
1. – $10
2. + $4
3. + $17
4. – $1
5. $ 0
6.

If the	Then the
demand for dollars rises in the foreign exchange market	supply of pesos rises on the foreign exchange market
demand for pesos falls on the foreign exchange market	supply of dollars falls on the foreign exchange market
demand for dollars rises in the foreign exchange market	supply of pesos rises on the foreign exchange market

7.

If	Then
$1 = 106 yen	1 yen = $0.0094
$1 = 74 Kenyan shillings	1 shilling = $0.135
$1 = 1,500 Lebanese pounds	1 pound = $0.000667

8.

The exchange rate is	And the item costs	What does the item cost in dollars?
$1 = 106 yen	18,000 yen	$169.81
$1 = £0.50	£ 34	$68
$1 = 9.44 pesos	89 pesos	$9.43

9.

The exchange rate changes from	Has the dollar appreciated or depreciated?
$2 = £1 to $2.50 = £1	depreciated
109 yen = $1 to 189 yen = $1	appreciated
10 pesos = $1 to 8 pesos = $1	depreciated

10.

If …	The dollar will (appreciate, depreciate)
the real interest rate in the U.S. rises relative to real interest rates in other countries	appreciate
income in foreign countries (that trade with the U.S.) rises relative to income in the United States	appreciate
the inflation rate in the U.S. rises and the inflation rate in all other countries falls	depreciate

11.

If the equilibrium exchange rate is $1 = £ 0.50 and the official exchange rate is	Then the dollar is (overvalued, undervalued)
$1 = £ 0.60	overvalued
$1 = £ 0.30	undervalued

What is the Question?

1. Any transaction that supplies the country's currency in the foreign exchange market.

    What is a debit?

2. Any transaction that creates a demand for the country's currency in the foreign exchange market.

    What is a credit?

3. The summary statistic for the exports of goods and services, imports of goods and services, and net unilateral transfers abroad.

   What is the current account balance?

4. The difference between the value of merchandise exports and the value of merchandise imports.

   What is the merchandise trade balance?

5. One-way money payments.

   What are unilateral transfers?

6. The price of one currency in terms of another currency.

   What is the exchange rate?

7. It predicts that the exchange rates between any two currencies will adjust to reflect changes in the relative price levels of the two countries.

   What does the purchasing power parity theory predict?

8. Raising the official price of a currency.

   What is revaluation?

What Is Wrong?

1. The balance of payments is the summary statistic for the current account balance, capital account balance, net unilateral transfers abroad, and statistical discrepancy.

   The balance of payments is the summary statistic for the current account balance, capital account balance, official reserve balance, and statistical discrepancy.

2. The demand for dollars on the foreign exchange market is linked to the supply of dollars on the foreign exchange market. In short, if the demand for dollars rises, the supply of dollars rises, too.

   The demand for dollars on the foreign exchange market is linked to the supply of other currencies on the foreign exchange market. In short, if the demand for dollars rises, the supply of other currencies rise, too.

3. There are two countries, A and B. The income of Country B rises and the income of Country A remains constant. As a result, the currency of Country B appreciates.

   There are two countries, A and B. The income of Country B rises and the income of Country A remains constant. As a result, the currency of Country B depreciates.

4. There are two countries, C and D. The price level in Country C rises 10 percent and the inflation rate in Country D is zero percent. As a result, the demand for Country C's goods rises and the supply of its currency falls.

   There are two countries, C and D. The price level in Country C rises 10 percent and the inflation rate in Country D is zero percent. As a result, the demand for Country C's goods falls and the supply of other countries' currencies fall. Alternatively, you could write: As a result, the demand for Country C's goods falls and the demand for its currency falls.

5. A change in real interest rates across countries cannot change the exchange rate.

   A change in real interest rates across countries can change the exchange rate.

6. If the equilibrium exchange rate is £1 = $1.50, and the official exchange rate is £1 = $1.60, then the dollar is overvalued and the pound is undervalued.

   If the equilibrium exchange rate is £1 = $1.50, and the official exchange rate is £1 = $1.60, then the dollar is undervalued and the pound is overvalued.

7. A international monetary fund right is a special international money crated by the IMF.

   A special drawing right is an international money crated by the IMF.

Multiple Choice
1. c
2. a
3. c
4. b
5. c
6. a
7. e
8. c
9. a
10. a
11. b
12. d
13. d
14. b
15. a

True-False
16. T
17. T
18. T
19. F
20. T

Fill in the Blank
21. merchandise trade balance
22. purchasing power parity theory
23. fix
24. devaluation
25. fixed; flexible